B·A·R Maid

zenescope

WWW.ZENESCOPE.COM
FACEBOOK.COM/ZENESCOPE

VOLUME ONE

CREATED BY
CLAYBURN MOORE

STORY
JOE BRUSHA
CLAYBURN MOORE

WRITER
PAT SHAND

ART DIRECTOR
ANTHONY SPAY

TRADE DESIGN
CHRISTOPHER COTE
STEPHEN SCHAFFER

EDITOR
PAT SHAND

THIS VOLUME REPRINTS THE COMIC
SERIES B.A.R. MAID #1-5 PUBLISHED
BY ZENESCOPE ENTERTAINMENT.

FIRST EDITION, JUNE 2014
ISBN: 978-1-939683-57-1

WWW.ZENESCOPE.COM
FACEBOOK.COM/ZENESCOPE

ZENESCOPE ENTERTAINMENT, INC.
Joe Brusha • President & Chief Creative Officer
Ralph Tedesco • Editor-in-Chief
Jennifer Bermel • Director of Licensing & Business Development
Anthony Spay • Art Director
Christopher Cote • Senior Designer & Production Manager
Dave Franchini • Direct Market Sales & Customer Service

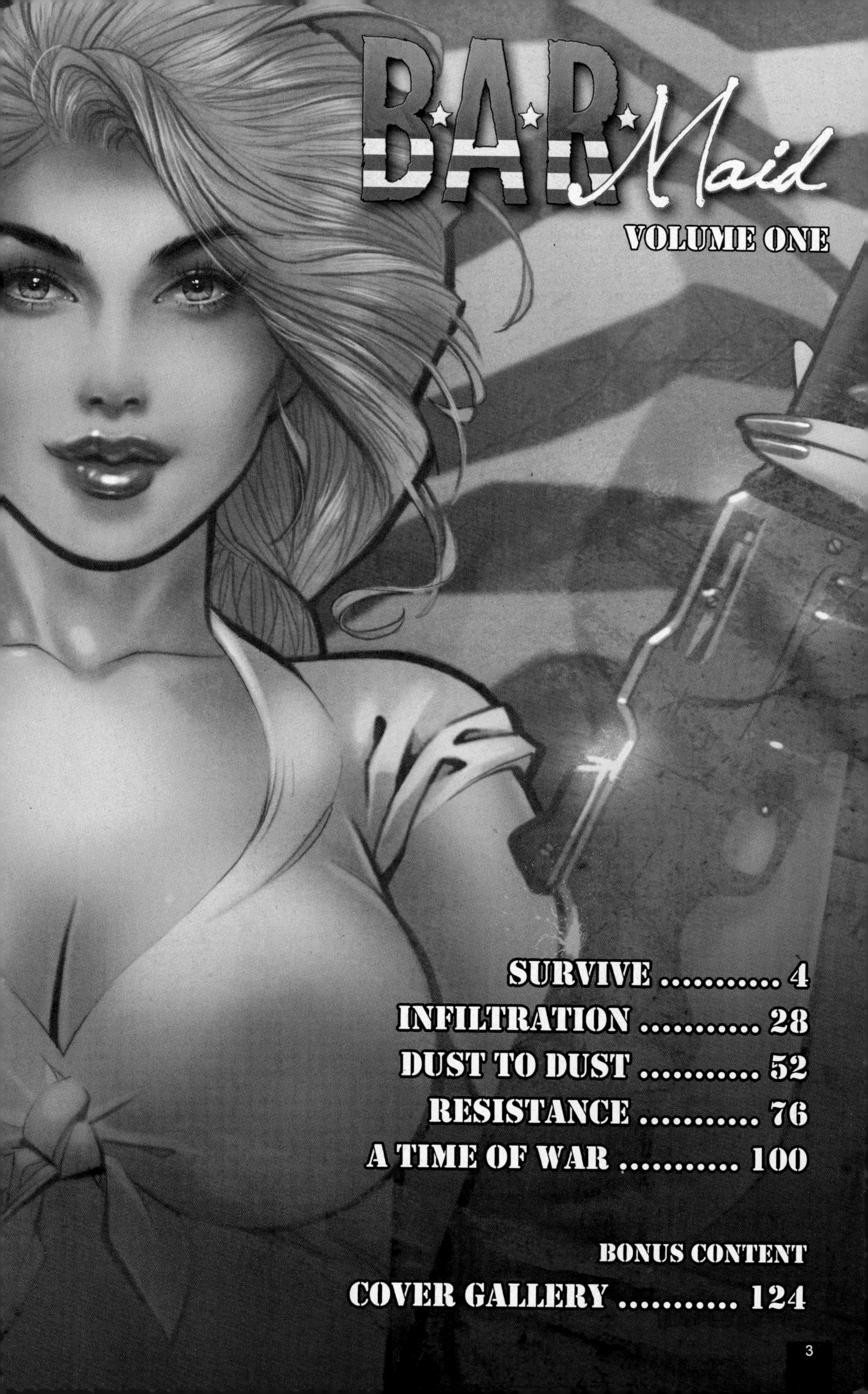

B.A.R. Maid

VOLUME ONE

BONUS CONTENT

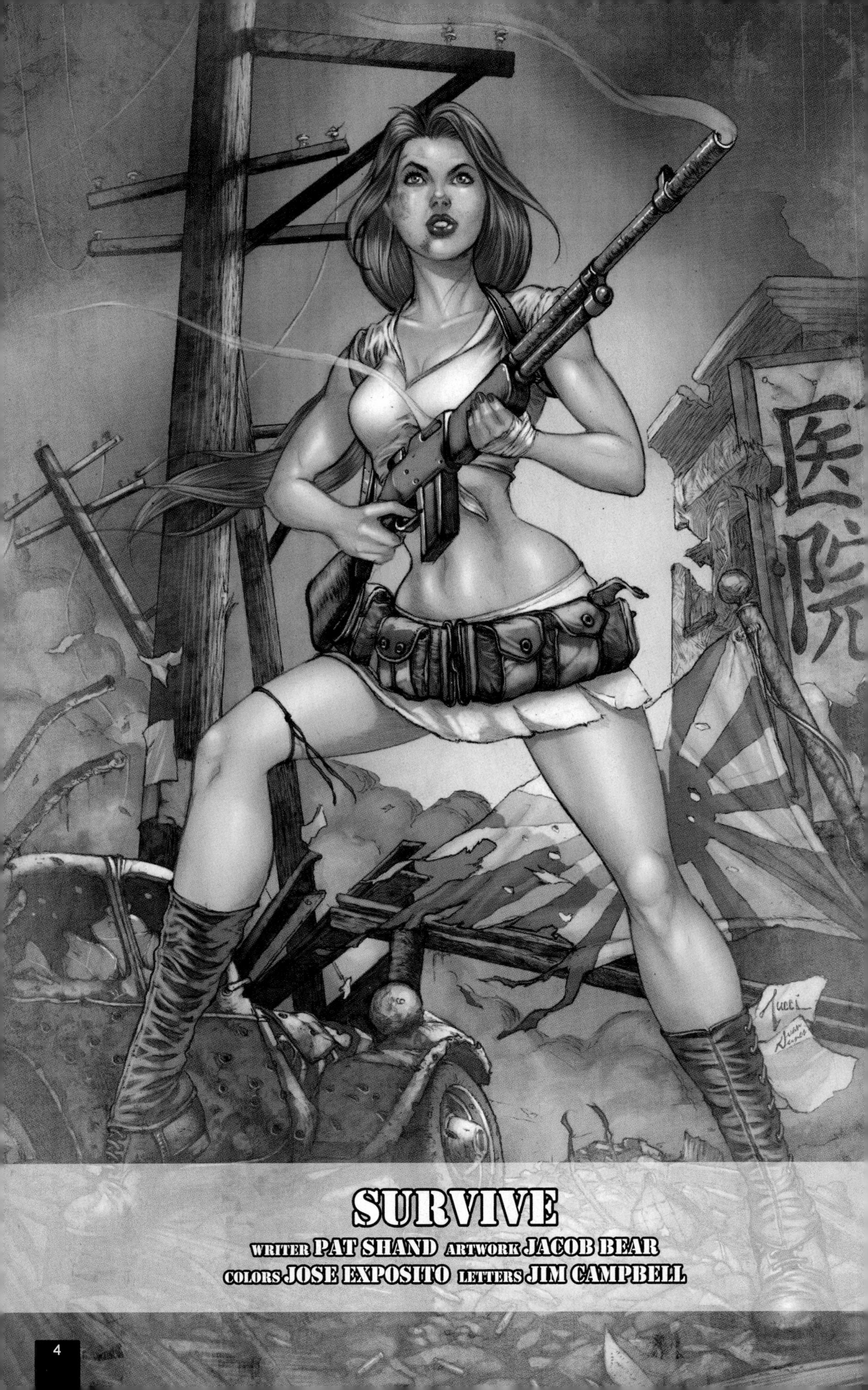
医院

SURVIVE

WRITER **PAT SHAND** ARTWORK **JACOB BEAR**
COLORS **JOSE EXPOSITO** LETTERS **JIM CAMPBELL**

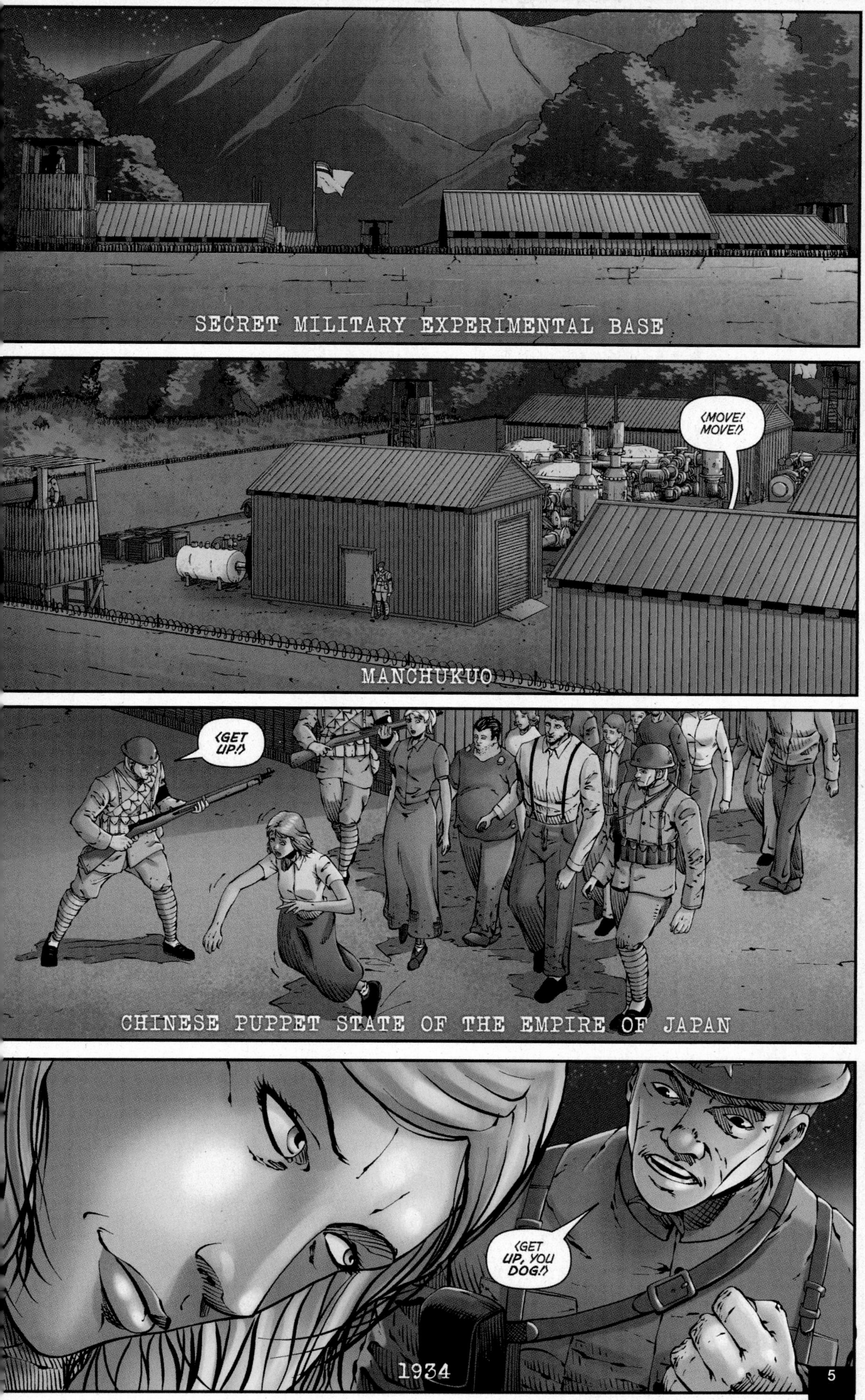
SECRET MILITARY EXPERIMENTAL BASE
‹MOVE! MOVE!›
MANCHUKUO
‹GET UP!›
CHINESE PUPPET STATE OF THE EMPIRE OF JAPAN
‹GET UP, YOU DOG!›
1934

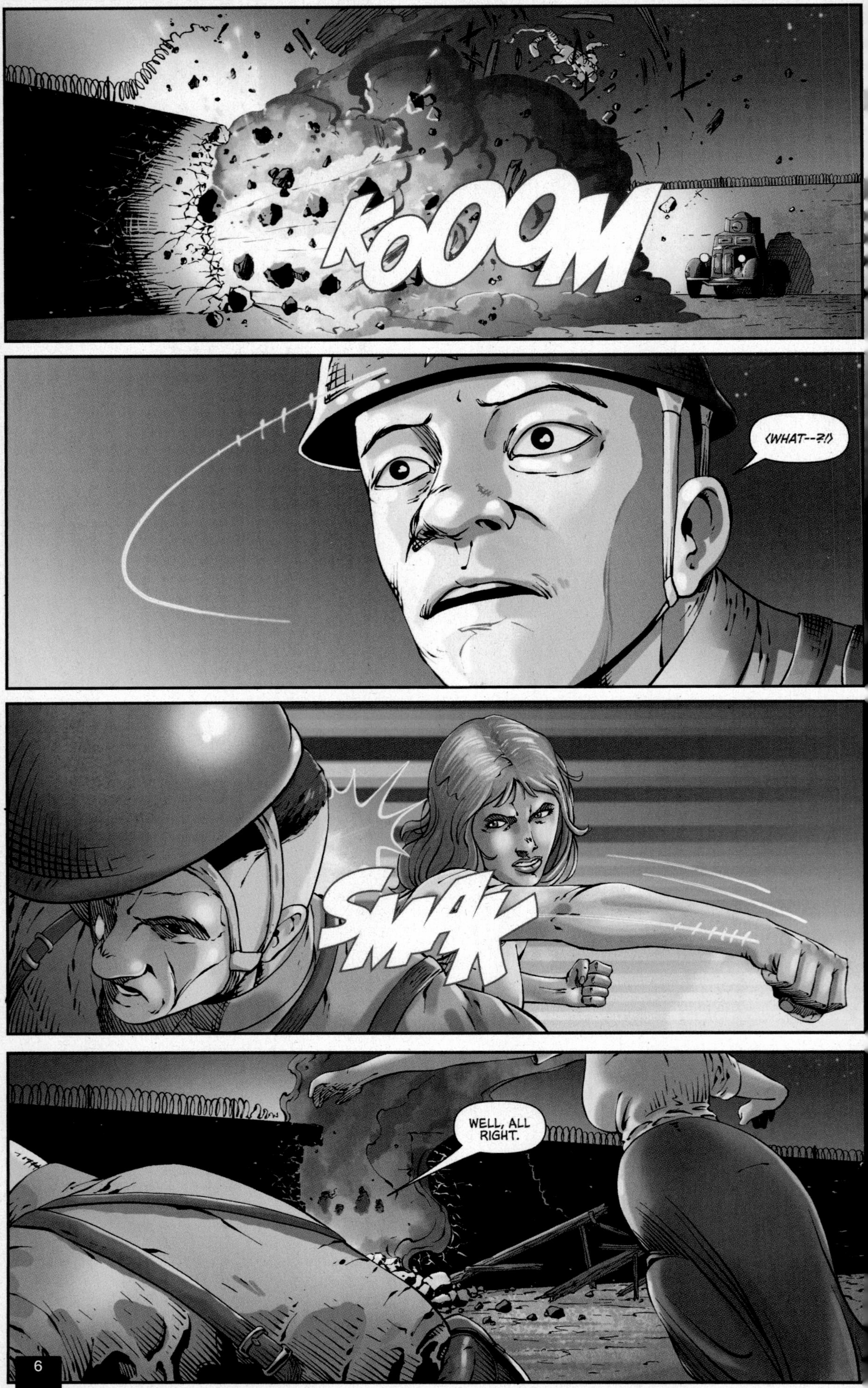
KOOOM
⟨WHAT--?!⟩
SMAK
WELL, ALL RIGHT.

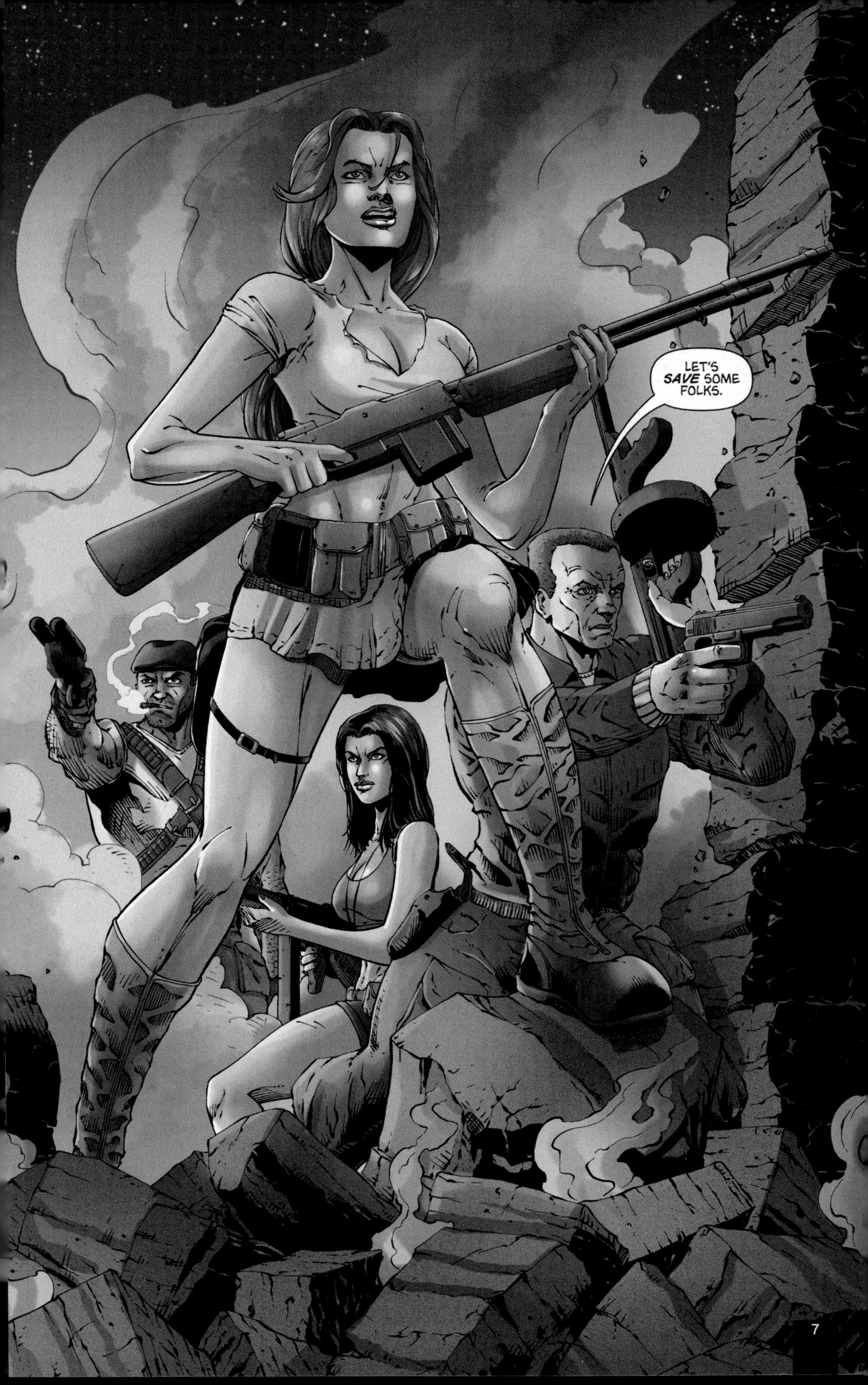
LET'S SAVE SOME FOLKS.

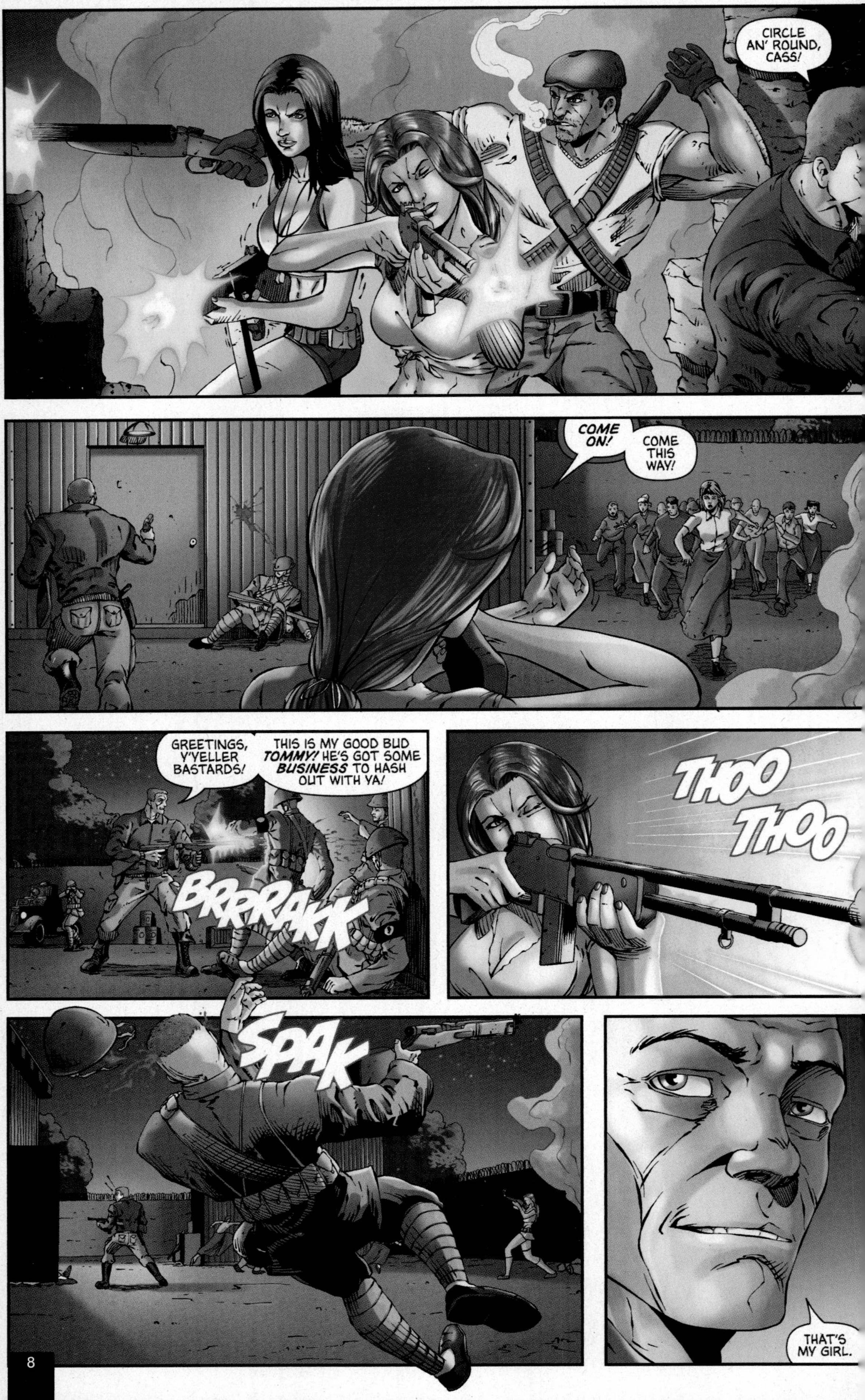
CIRCLE AN' ROUND, CASS!
COME ON!
COME THIS WAY!
GREETINGS, Y'YELLER BASTARDS!
THIS IS MY GOOD BUD *TOMMY!* HE'S GOT SOME *BUSINESS* TO HASH OUT WITH YA!
BRRRAKK
THOO
THOO
SPAK
THAT'S MY GIRL.

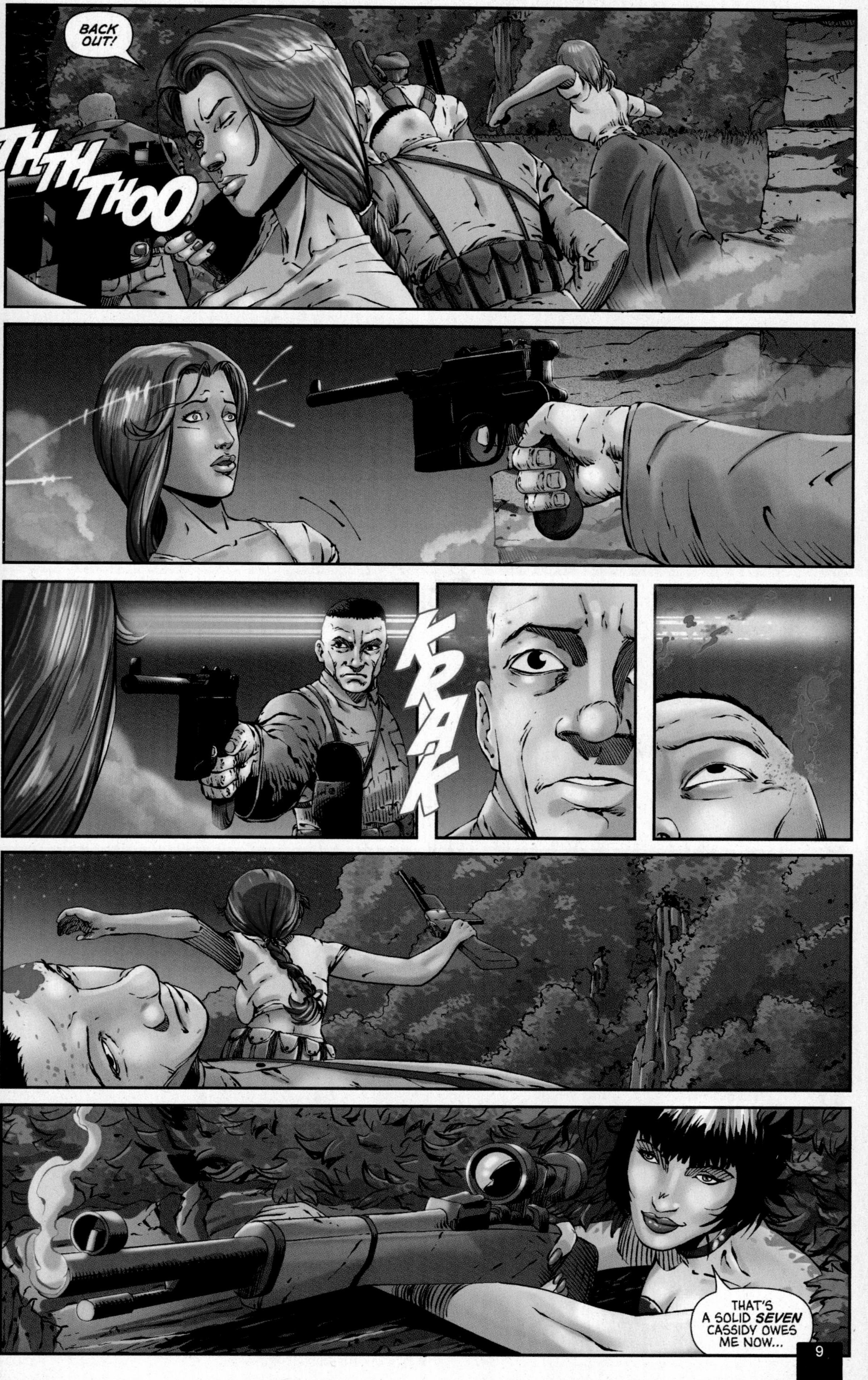
BACK OUT!
THTHTHOO
KRAK
THAT'S A SOLID SEVEN CASSIDY OWES ME NOW...

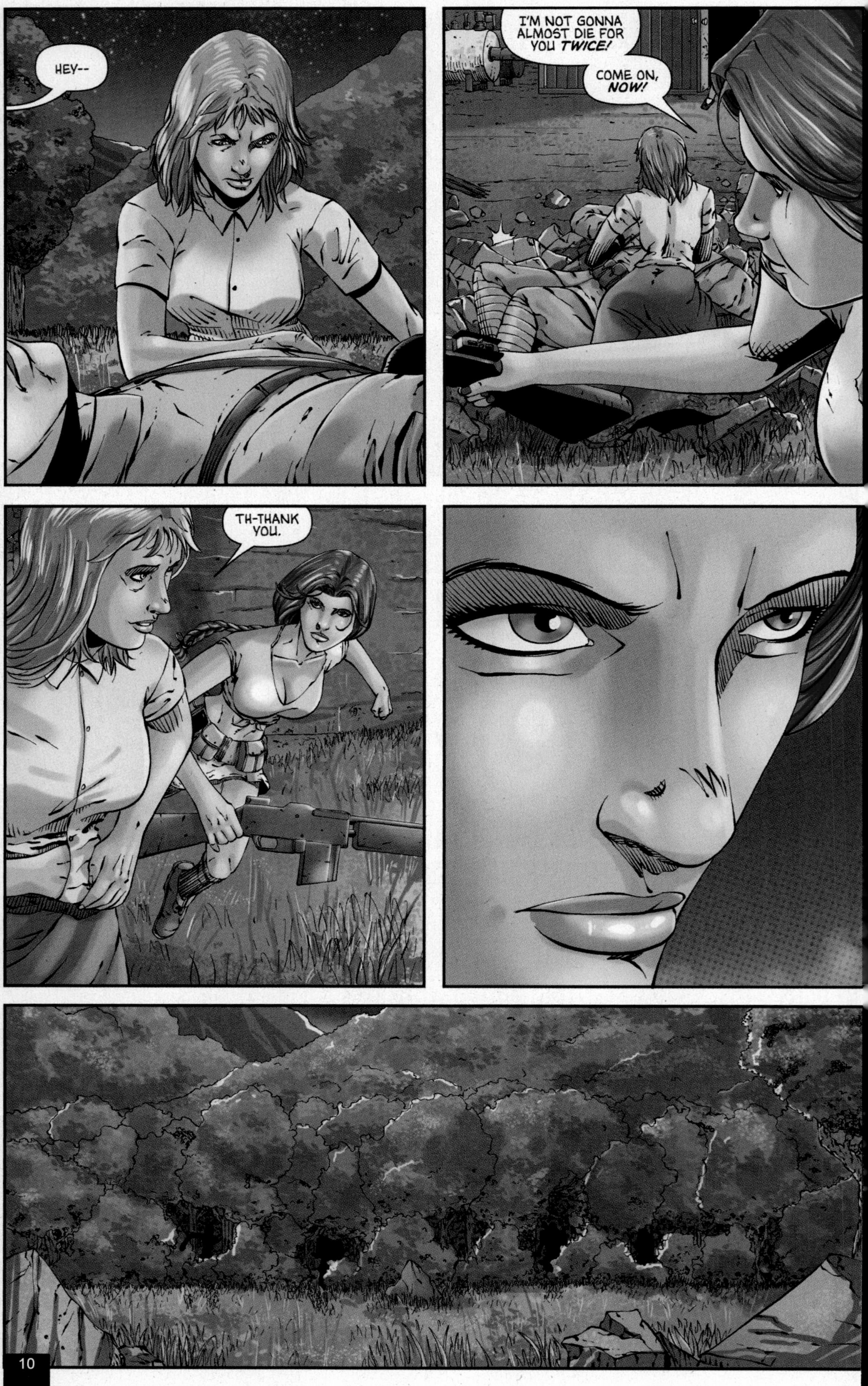
HEY--
I'M NOT GONNA ALMOST DIE FOR YOU TWICE!
COME ON, NOW!
TH-THANK YOU.

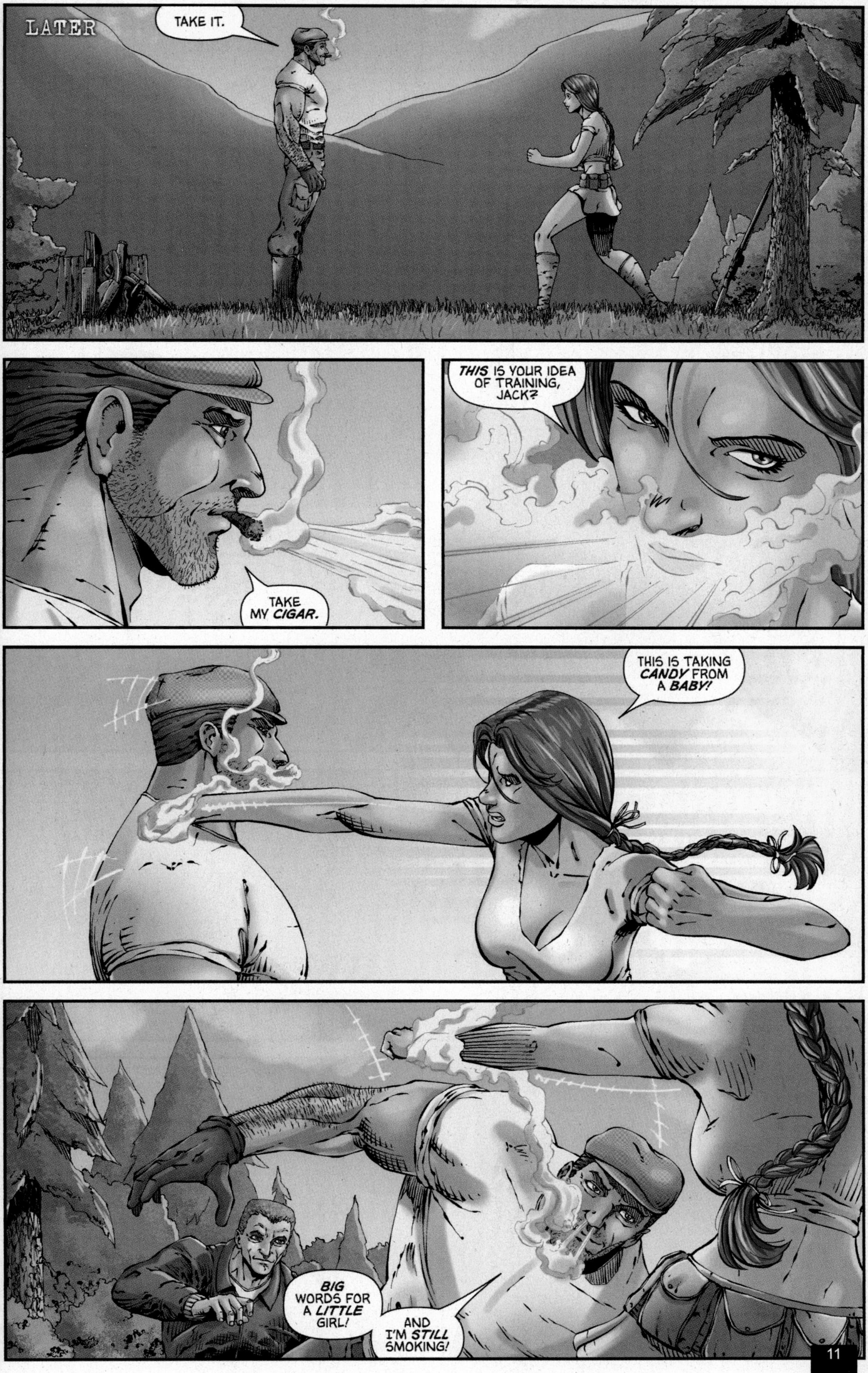
LATER
TAKE IT.
TAKE MY *CIGAR*.
THIS IS YOUR IDEA OF TRAINING, JACK?
THIS IS TAKING *CANDY* FROM A *BABY!*
BIG WORDS FOR A *LITTLE* GIRL!
AND I'M *STILL* SMOKING!

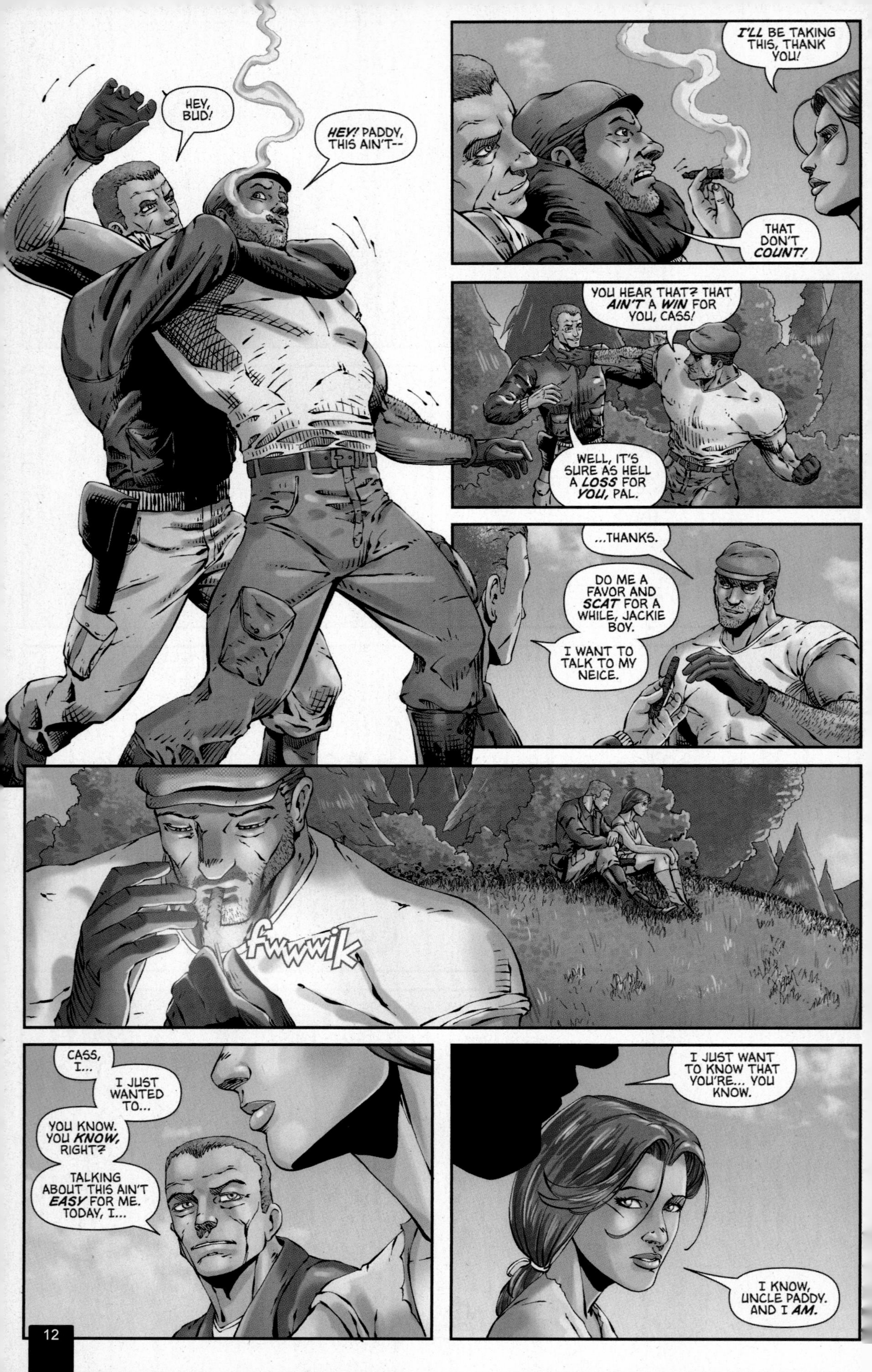
HEY, BUD!
HEY! PADDY, THIS AIN'T--
I'LL BE TAKING THIS, THANK YOU!
THAT DON'T COUNT!
YOU HEAR THAT? THAT AIN'T A WIN FOR YOU, CASS!
WELL, IT'S SURE AS HELL A LOSS FOR YOU, PAL.
...THANKS.
DO ME A FAVOR AND SCAT FOR A WHILE, JACKIE BOY.
I WANT TO TALK TO MY NEICE.
fwwwik
CASS, I...
I JUST WANTED TO...
YOU KNOW. YOU KNOW, RIGHT?
TALKING ABOUT THIS AIN'T EASY FOR ME. TODAY, I...
I JUST WANT TO KNOW THAT YOU'RE... YOU KNOW.
I KNOW, UNCLE PADDY. AND I AM.

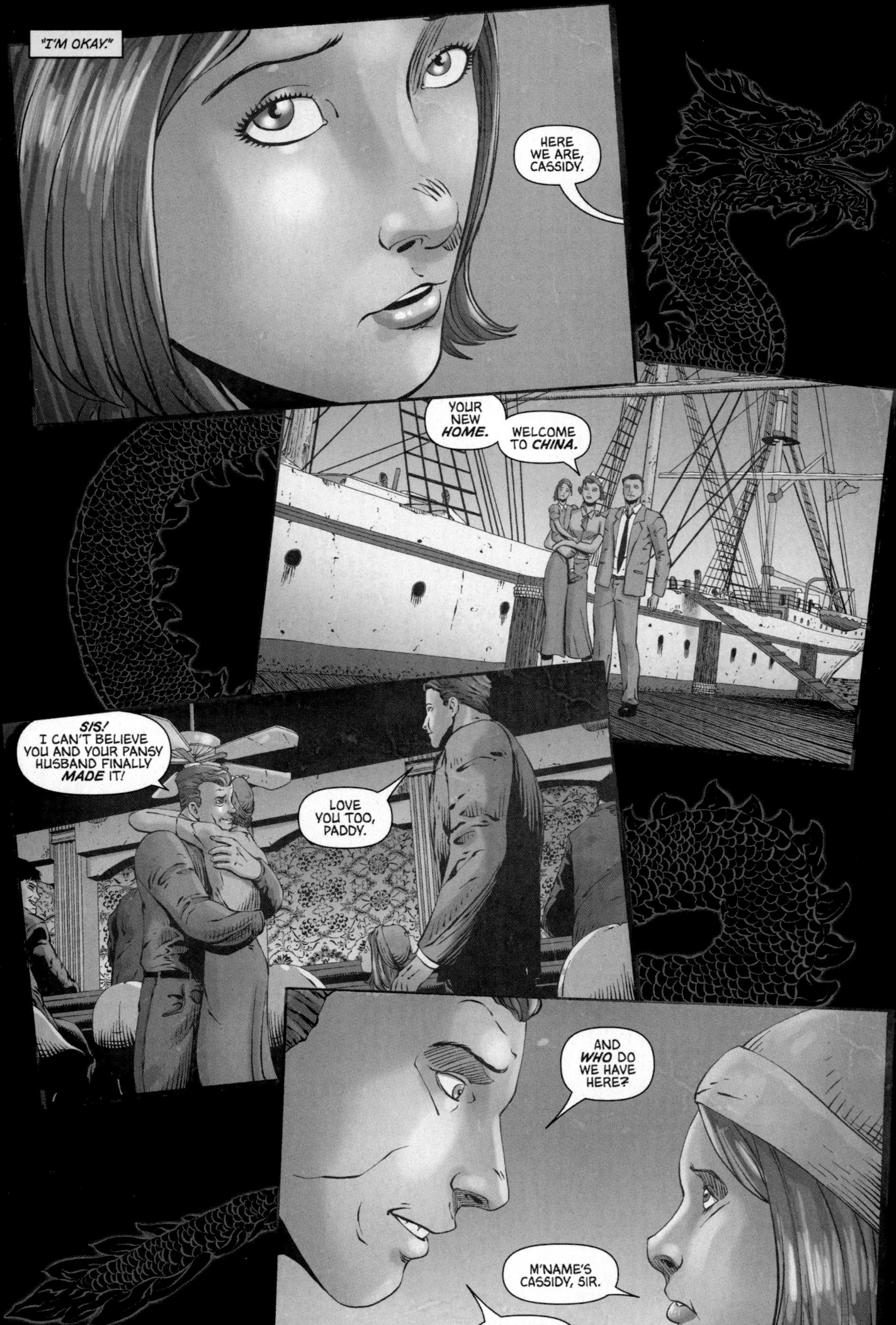
"I'M OKAY."
HERE WE ARE, CASSIDY.
YOUR NEW HOME.
WELCOME TO CHINA.
SIS! I CAN'T BELIEVE YOU AND YOUR PANSY HUSBAND FINALLY MADE IT!
LOVE YOU TOO, PADDY.
AND WHO DO WE HAVE HERE?
M'NAME'S CASSIDY, SIR.
I AIN'T NO SIR, CASS! I'M YOUR UNCLE!

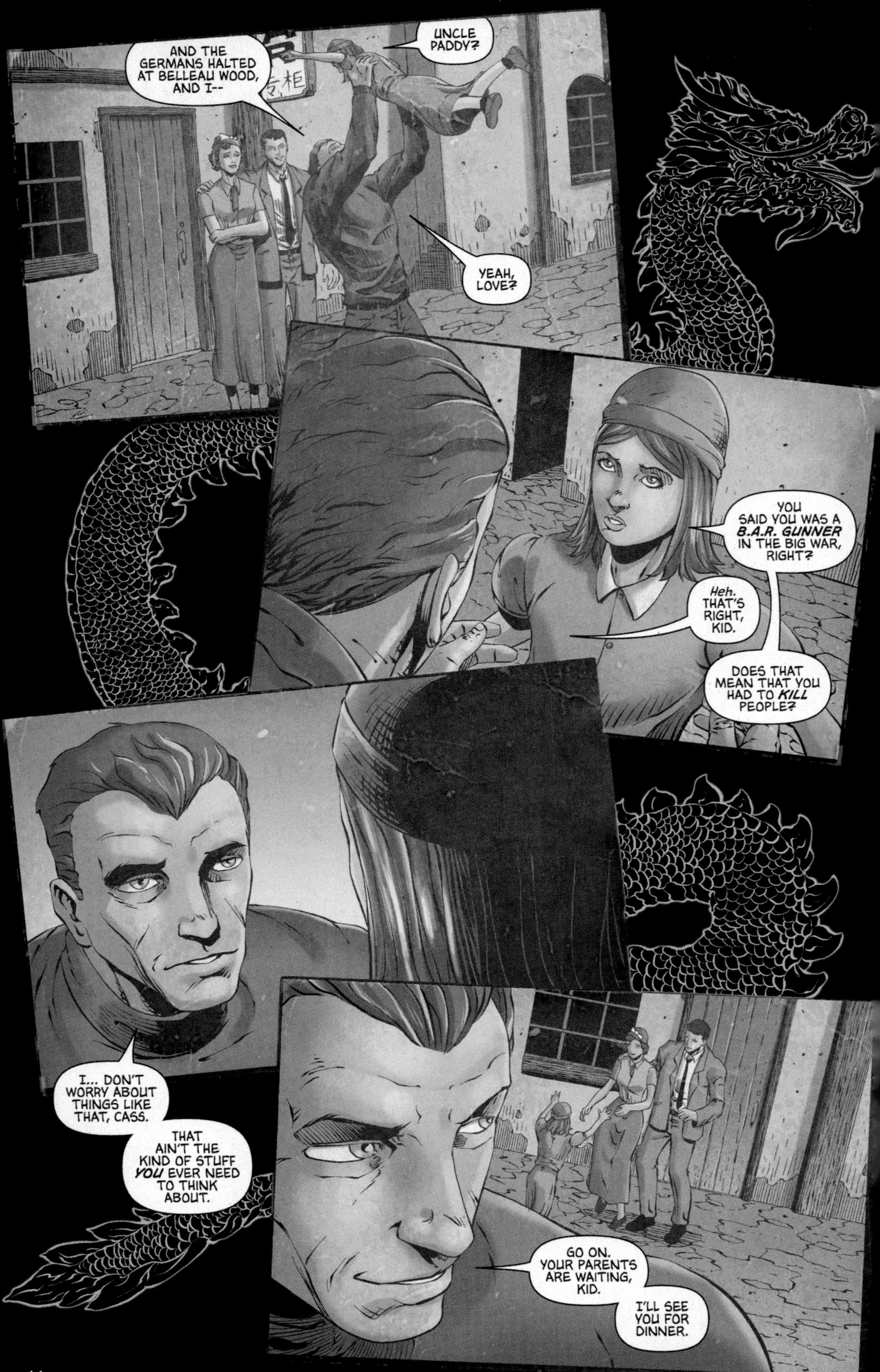
AND THE GERMANS HALTED AT BELLEAU WOOD, AND I--
UNCLE PADDY?
YEAH, LOVE?
YOU SAID YOU WAS A *B.A.R. GUNNER* IN THE BIG WAR, RIGHT?
Heh. THAT'S RIGHT, KID.
DOES THAT MEAN THAT YOU HAD TO *KILL* PEOPLE?
I... DON'T WORRY ABOUT THINGS LIKE THAT, CASS.
THAT AIN'T THE KIND OF STUFF *YOU* EVER NEED TO THINK ABOUT.
GO ON. YOUR PARENTS ARE WAITING, KID.
I'LL SEE YOU FOR DINNER.

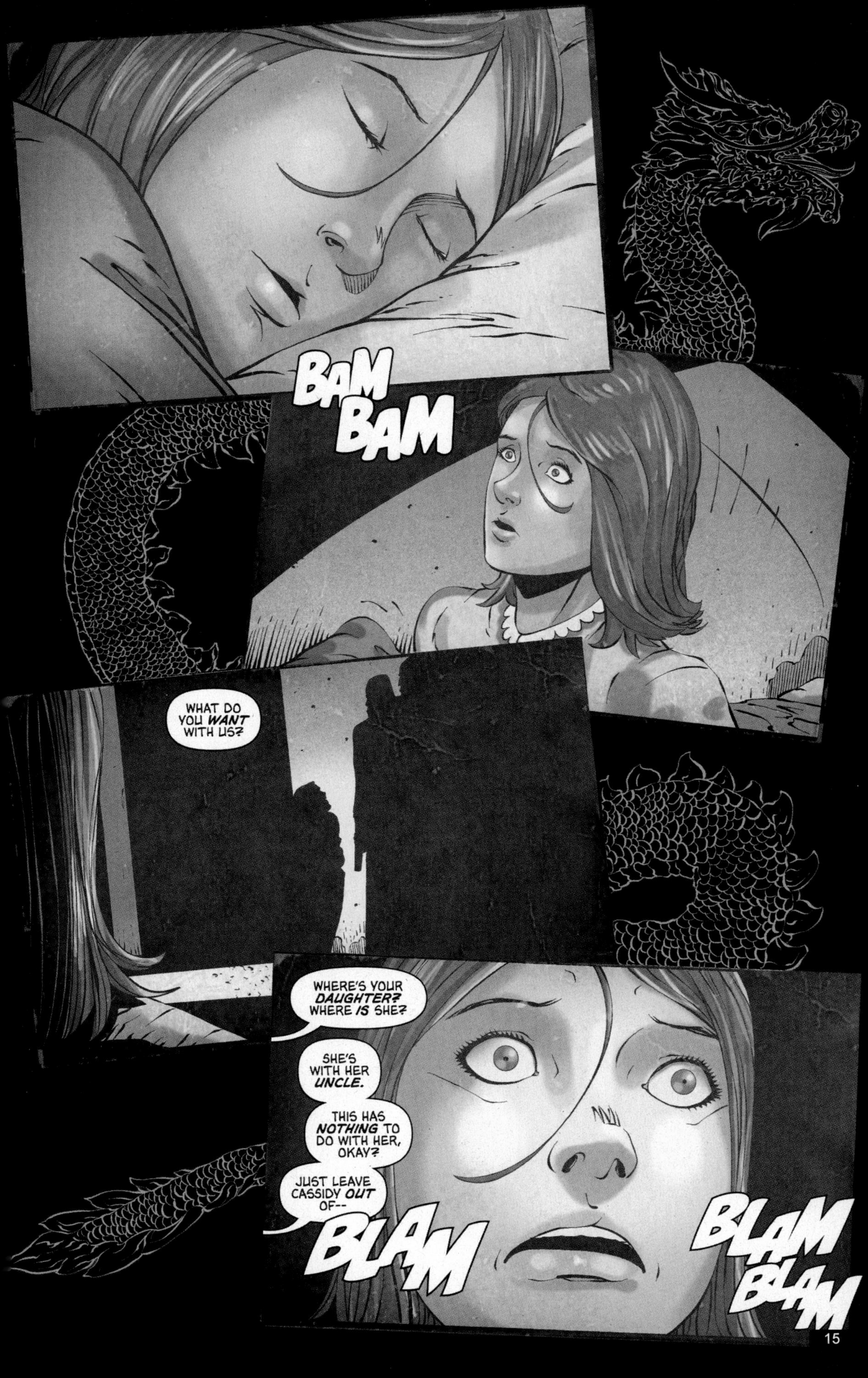
BAM BAM
WHAT DO YOU *WANT* WITH US?
WHERE'S YOUR *DAUGHTER?* WHERE *IS* SHE?
SHE'S WITH HER *UNCLE.*
THIS HAS *NOTHING* TO DO WITH HER, OKAY?
JUST LEAVE CASSIDY *OUT* OF--
BLAM
BLAM BLAM

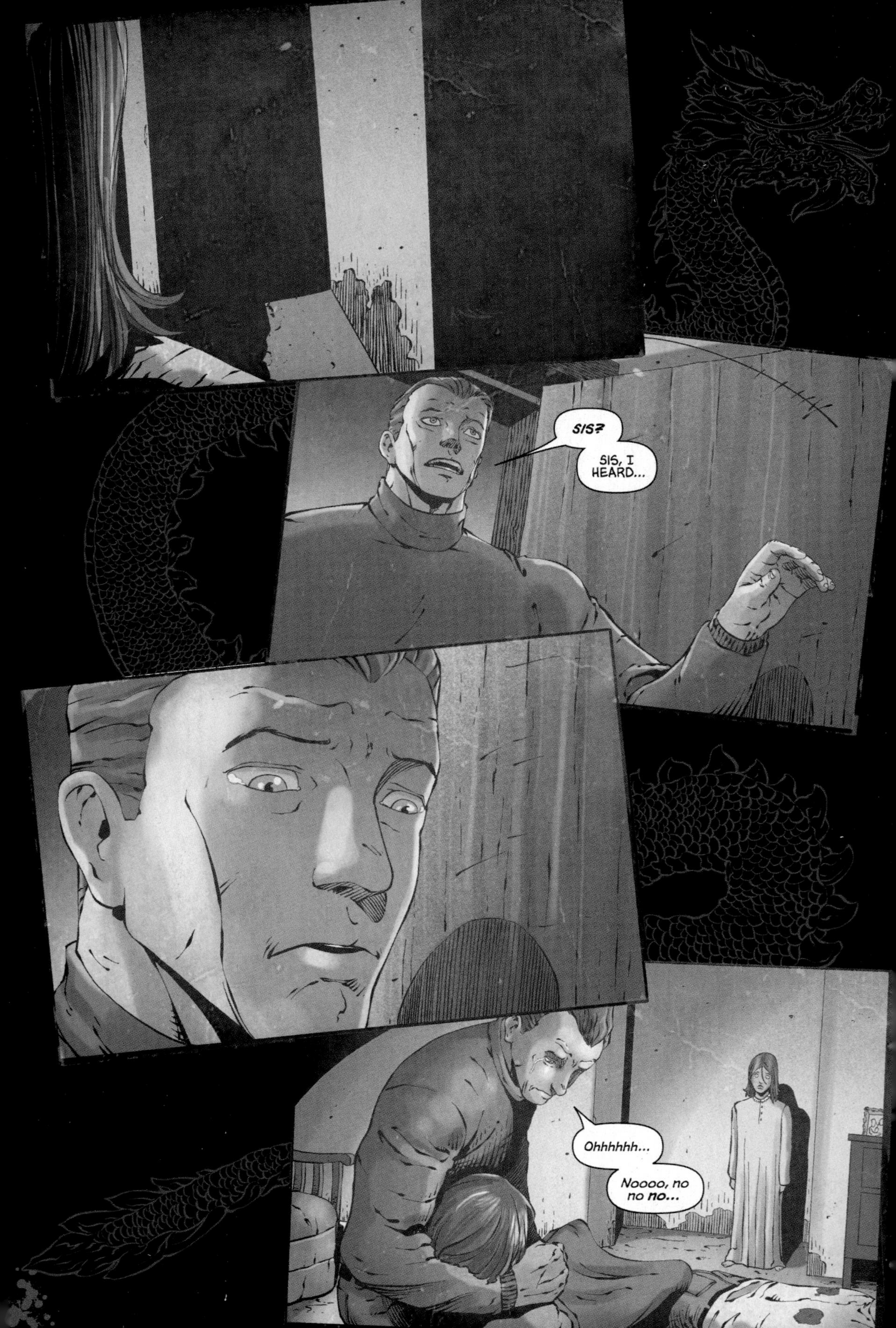
SIS?
SIS, I HEARD...
Ohhhhhh...
Noooo, no no no...

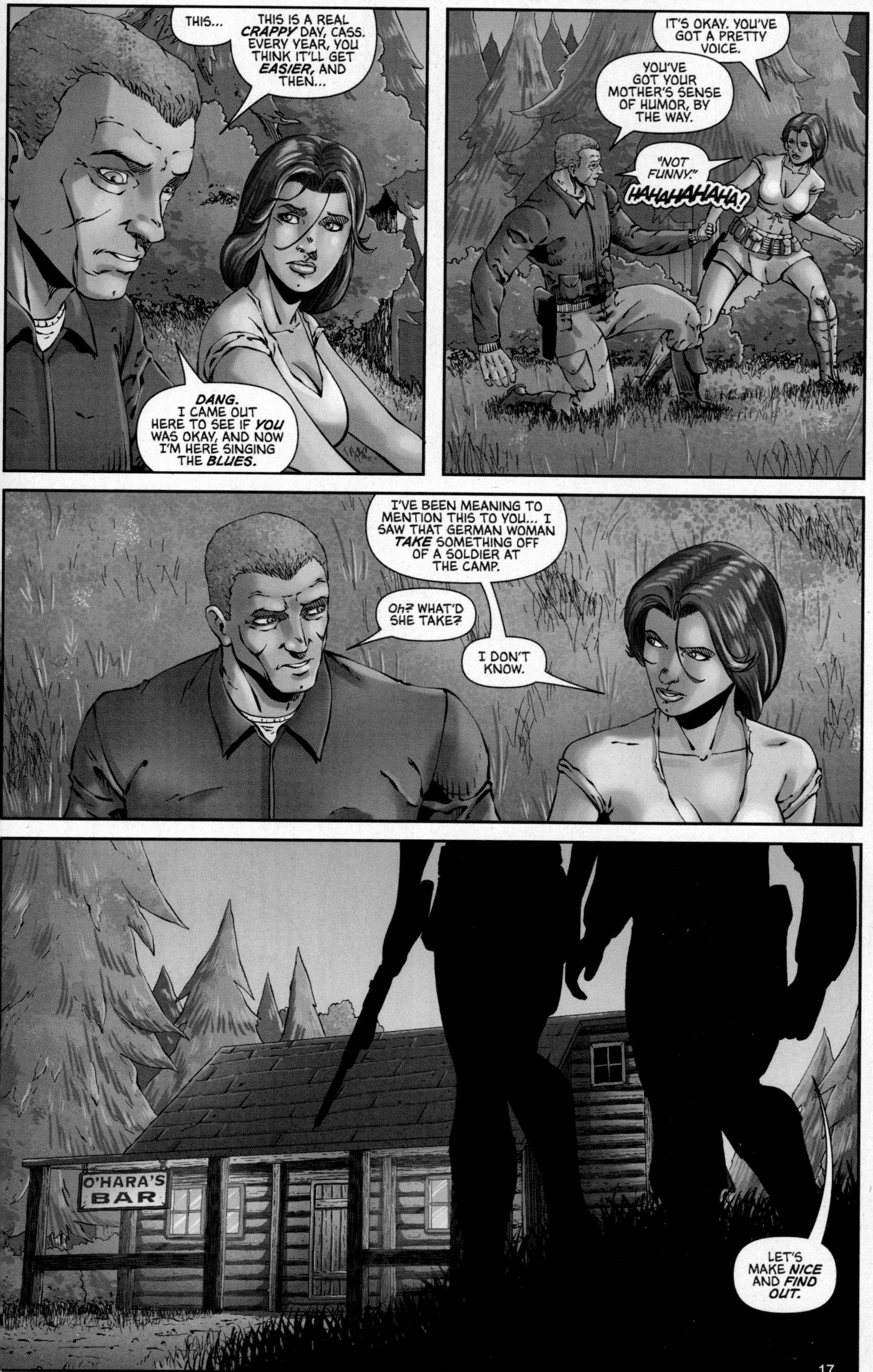
THIS...
THIS IS A REAL CRAPPY DAY, CASS. EVERY YEAR, YOU THINK IT'LL GET EASIER, AND THEN...
DANG. I CAME OUT HERE TO SEE IF YOU WAS OKAY, AND NOW I'M HERE SINGING THE BLUES.
IT'S OKAY. YOU'VE GOT A PRETTY VOICE.
YOU'VE GOT YOUR MOTHER'S SENSE OF HUMOR, BY THE WAY.
"NOT FUNNY."
HAHAHAHAHA!
I'VE BEEN MEANING TO MENTION THIS TO YOU... I SAW THAT GERMAN WOMAN TAKE SOMETHING OFF OF A SOLDIER AT THE CAMP.
Oh? WHAT'D SHE TAKE?
I DON'T KNOW.
O'HARA'S BAR
LET'S MAKE NICE AND FIND OUT.

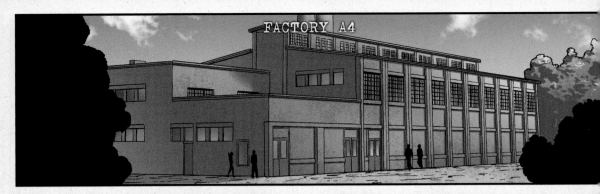

FACTORY A4

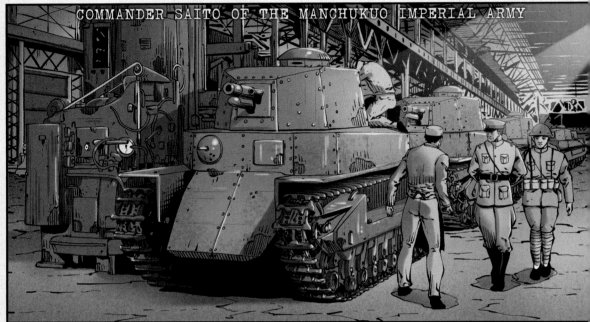

COMMANDER SAITO OF THE MANCHUKUO IMPERIAL ARMY

...

⟨PROCEED.⟩

⟨STAY OUTSIDE.⟩

⟨YES, SIR.⟩

⟨ASSHOLE.⟩

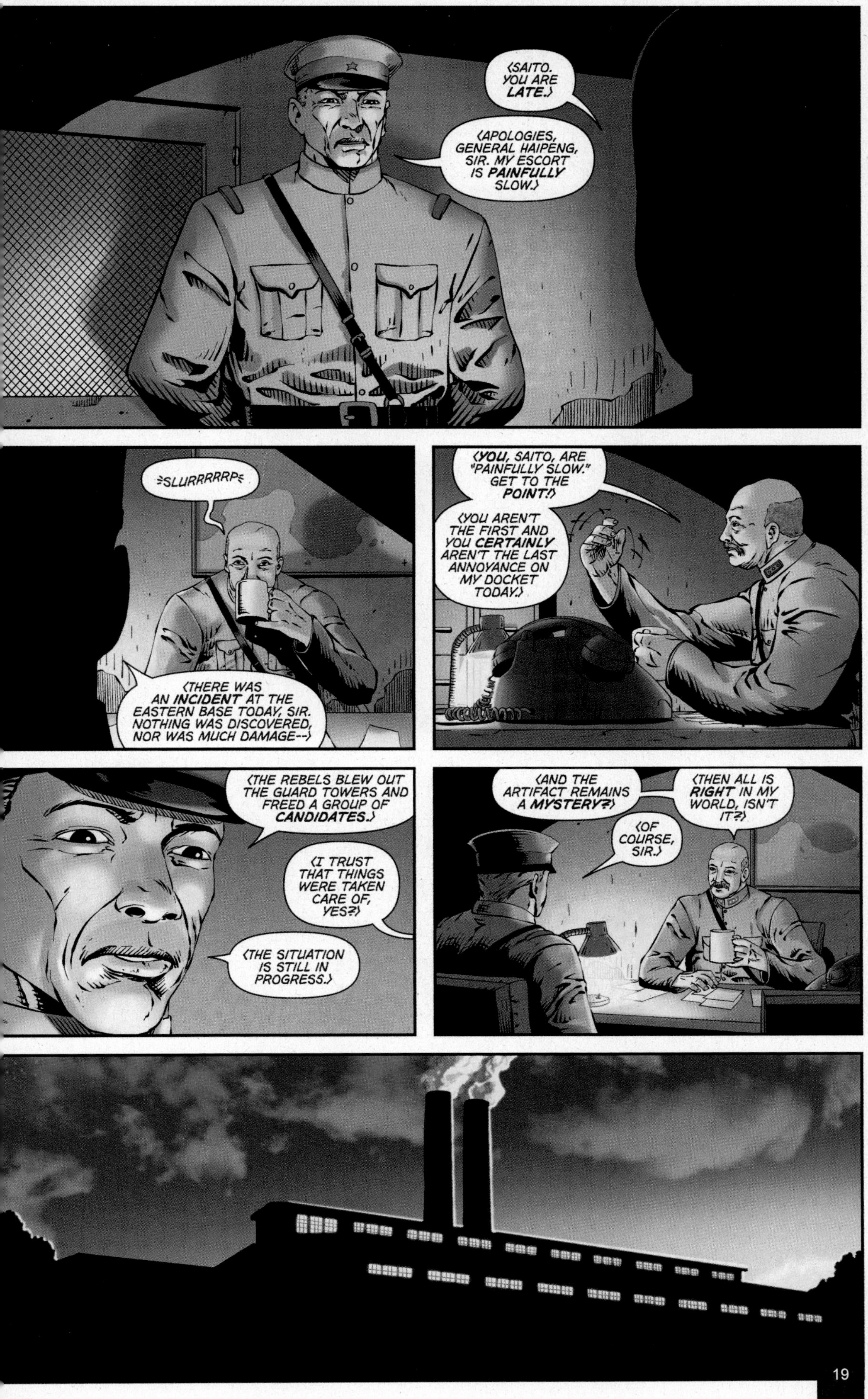
‹SAITO. YOU ARE LATE.›
‹APOLOGIES, GENERAL HAIPENG, SIR. MY ESCORT IS PAINFULLY SLOW.›
≶SLURRRRRP≶
‹THERE WAS AN INCIDENT AT THE EASTERN BASE TODAY, SIR. NOTHING WAS DISCOVERED, NOR WAS MUCH DAMAGE--›
‹YOU, SAITO, ARE "PAINFULLY SLOW." GET TO THE POINT!›
‹YOU AREN'T THE FIRST AND YOU CERTAINLY AREN'T THE LAST ANNOYANCE ON MY DOCKET TODAY.›
‹THE REBELS BLEW OUT THE GUARD TOWERS AND FREED A GROUP OF CANDIDATES.›
‹I TRUST THAT THINGS WERE TAKEN CARE OF, YES?›
‹THE SITUATION IS STILL IN PROGRESS.›
‹AND THE ARTIFACT REMAINS A MYSTERY?›
‹THEN ALL IS RIGHT IN MY WORLD, ISN'T IT?›
‹OF COURSE, SIR.›

GIVE IT TO ME.

O'HARA'S BAR

WHY BOTHER PLAYING? YOU CANNOT *HOPE* TO SURVIVE.

MY DEAR YING LEE... THOUGH LOOKS MAY DECEIVE, I AM LIKE THE *CUCARACHA*. SURVIVAL -- IT IS MY *HOBBY*.

ALL RIGHT, MY PRETTY LITTLE BUG. HERE IS YOUR SITUATION.

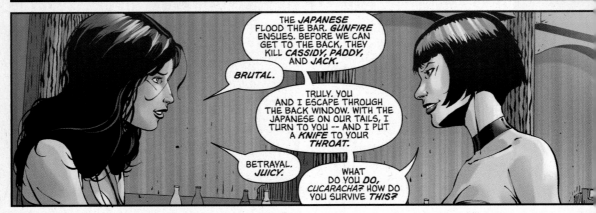

THE *JAPANESE* FLOOD THE BAR. *GUNFIRE* ENSUES. BEFORE WE CAN GET TO THE BACK, THEY KILL *CASSIDY*, *PADDY*, AND *JACK*.

BRUTAL.

TRULY. YOU AND I ESCAPE THROUGH THE BACK WINDOW. WITH THE JAPANESE ON OUR TAILS, I TURN TO YOU -- AND I PUT A *KNIFE* TO YOUR *THROAT*.

BETRAYAL. *JUICY.*

WHAT DO YOU *DO*, *CUCARACHA*? HOW DO YOU SURVIVE *THIS*?

I'M *RESOURCEFUL*, YING.

I HAVE KNOWN ABOUT YOUR *TRUE* ALLEGIANCE FOR SOME TIME. YOUR DRINK? *POISONED*. I HAVE THE TIME TO *WINK* AT YOU BEFORE YOU DROP DEAD, AND I STEAL OFF INTO THE *NIGHT*.

RIDICULOUS, ELENA. YOU DIE AT *MY* HAND.

WHAT DOES CASSIDY SAY TO YOU? "SORE LOSER," YES?

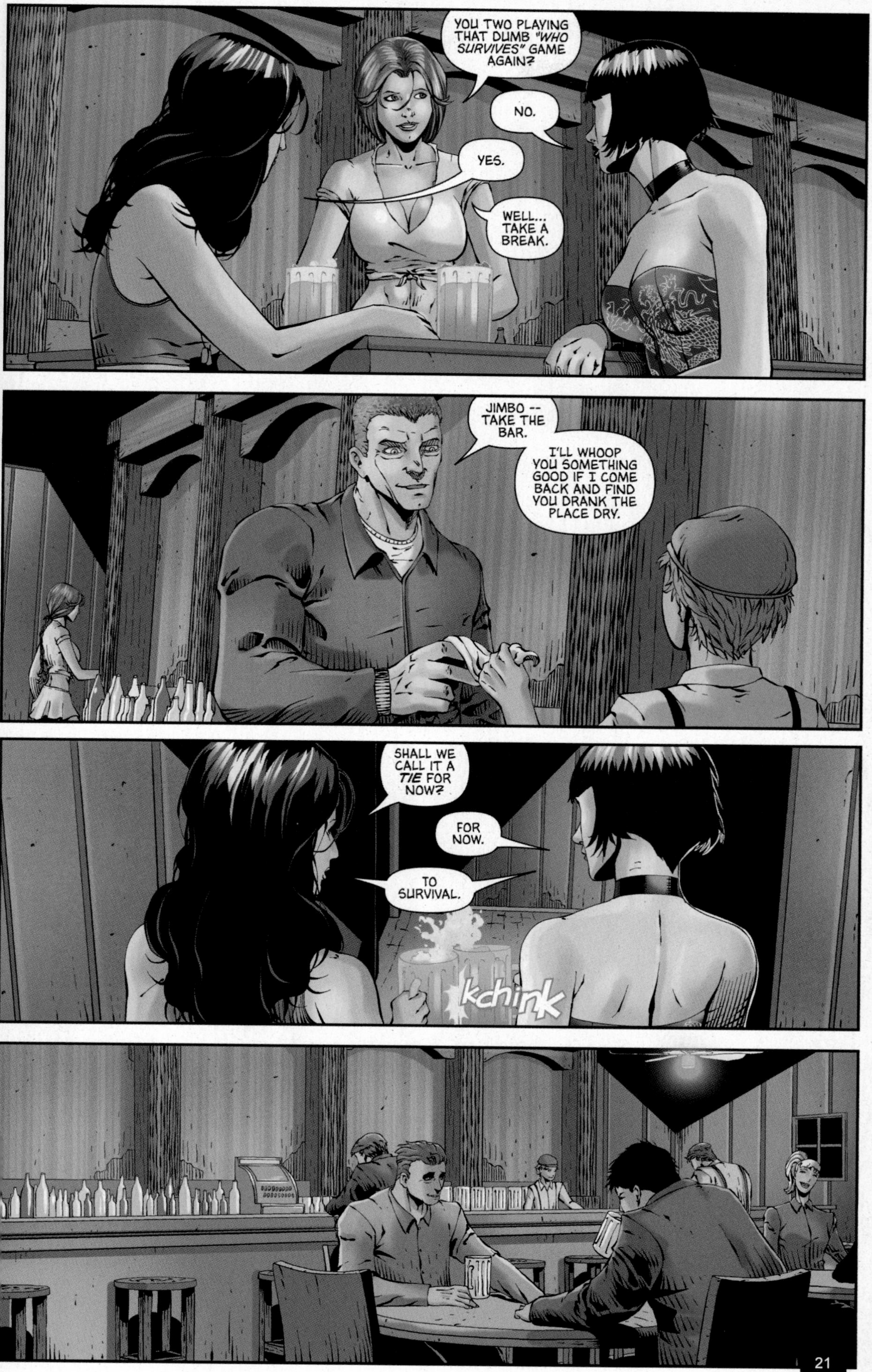
YOU TWO PLAYING THAT DUMB "*WHO SURVIVES*" GAME AGAIN?
NO.
YES.
WELL... TAKE A BREAK.
JIMBO -- TAKE THE BAR.
I'LL WHOOP YOU SOMETHING GOOD IF I COME BACK AND FIND YOU DRANK THE PLACE DRY.
SHALL WE CALL IT A *TIE* FOR NOW?
FOR NOW.
TO SURVIVAL.
kchink

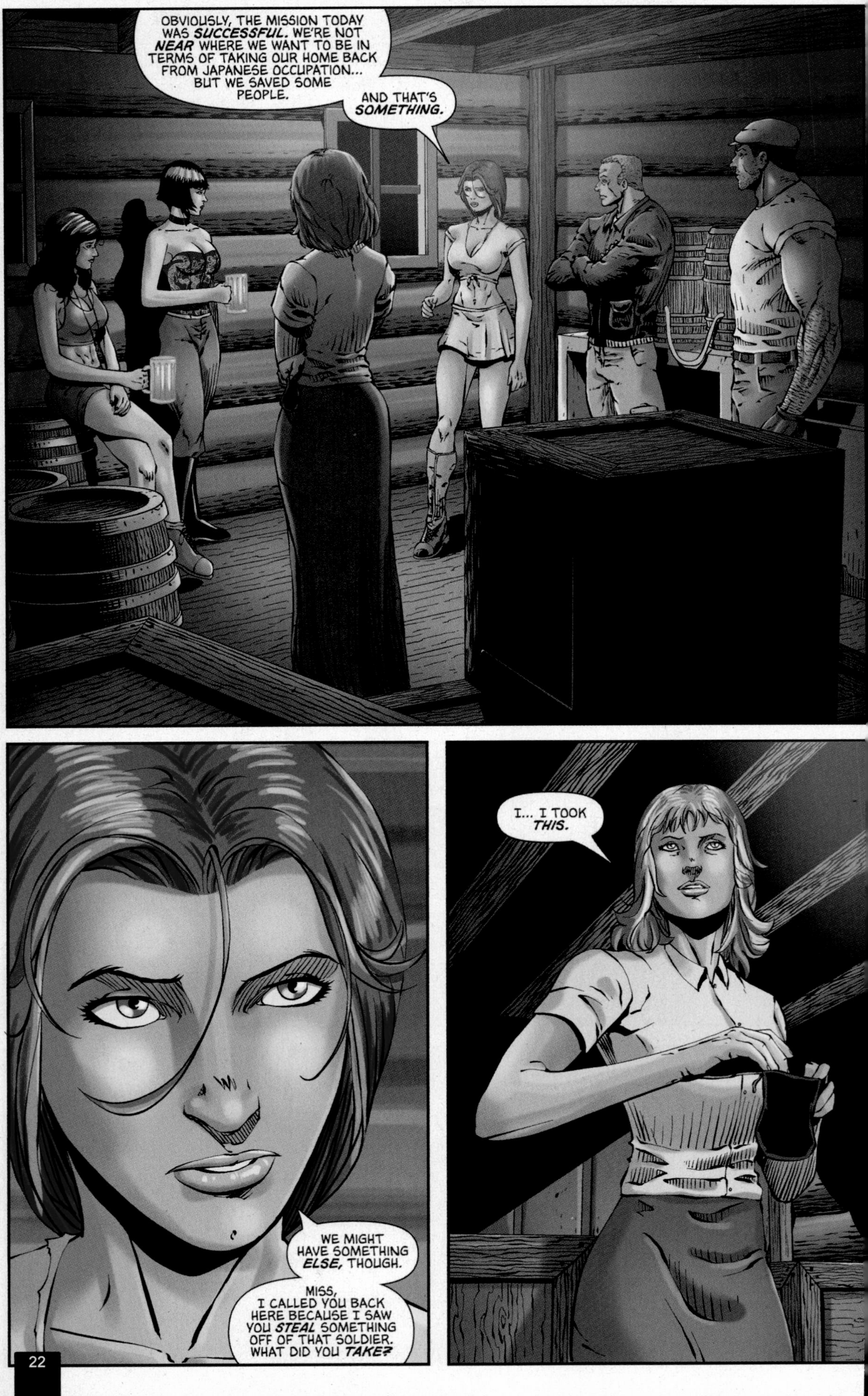

OBVIOUSLY, THE MISSION TODAY WAS SUCCESSFUL. WE'RE NOT NEAR WHERE WE WANT TO BE IN TERMS OF TAKING OUR HOME BACK FROM JAPANESE OCCUPATION... BUT WE SAVED SOME PEOPLE.
AND THAT'S SOMETHING.
WE MIGHT HAVE SOMETHING ELSE, THOUGH.
MISS, I CALLED YOU BACK HERE BECAUSE I SAW YOU STEAL SOMETHING OFF OF THAT SOLDIER. WHAT DID YOU TAKE?
I... I TOOK THIS.

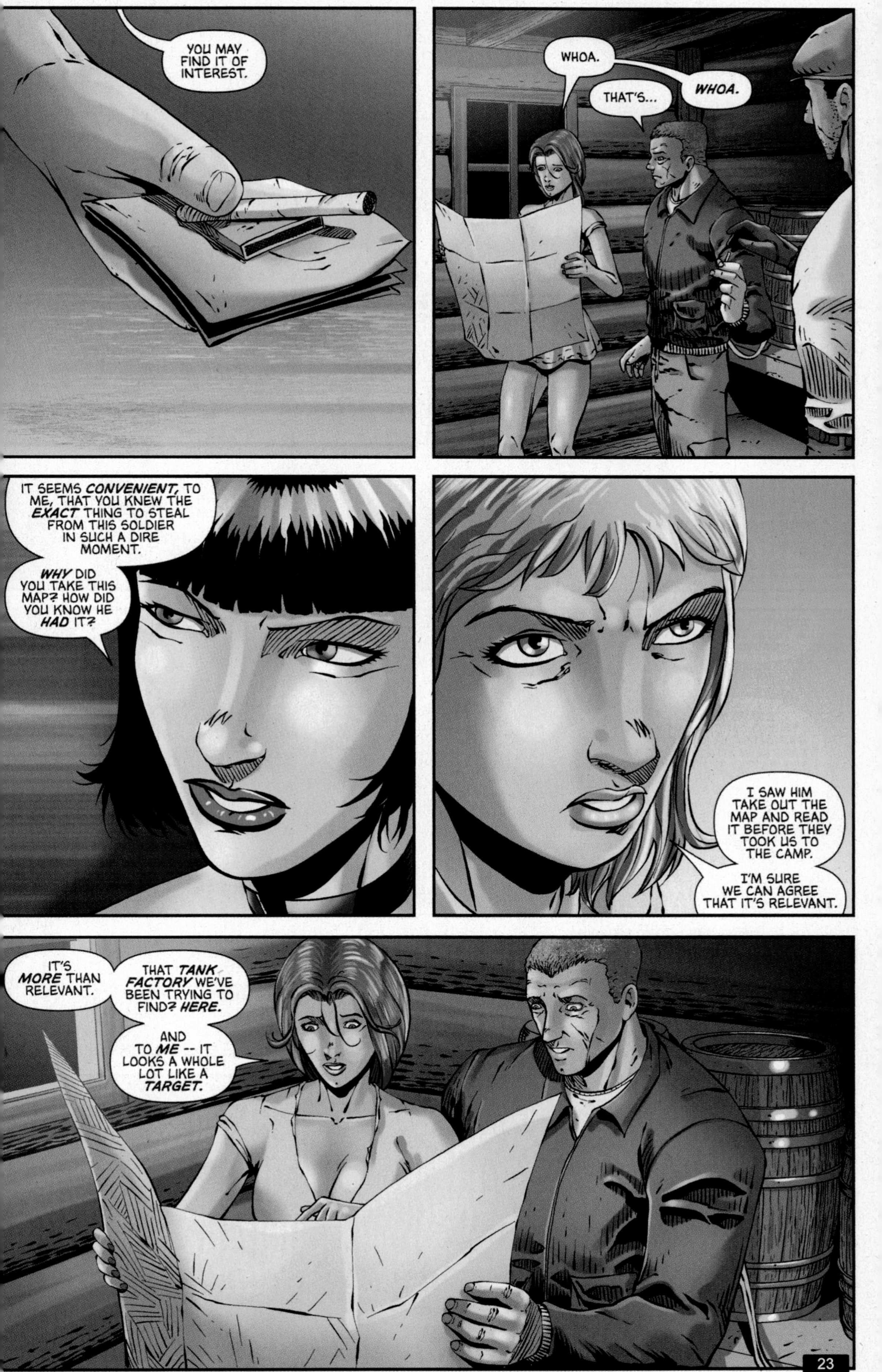

YOU MAY FIND IT OF INTEREST.
WHOA.
THAT'S...
WHOA.
IT SEEMS CONVENIENT, TO ME, THAT YOU KNEW THE EXACT THING TO STEAL FROM THIS SOLDIER IN SUCH A DIRE MOMENT.
WHY DID YOU TAKE THIS MAP? HOW DID YOU KNOW HE HAD IT?
I SAW HIM TAKE OUT THE MAP AND READ IT BEFORE THEY TOOK US TO THE CAMP.
I'M SURE WE CAN AGREE THAT IT'S RELEVANT.
IT'S MORE THAN RELEVANT.
THAT TANK FACTORY WE'VE BEEN TRYING TO FIND? HERE.
AND TO ME -- IT LOOKS A WHOLE LOT LIKE A TARGET.

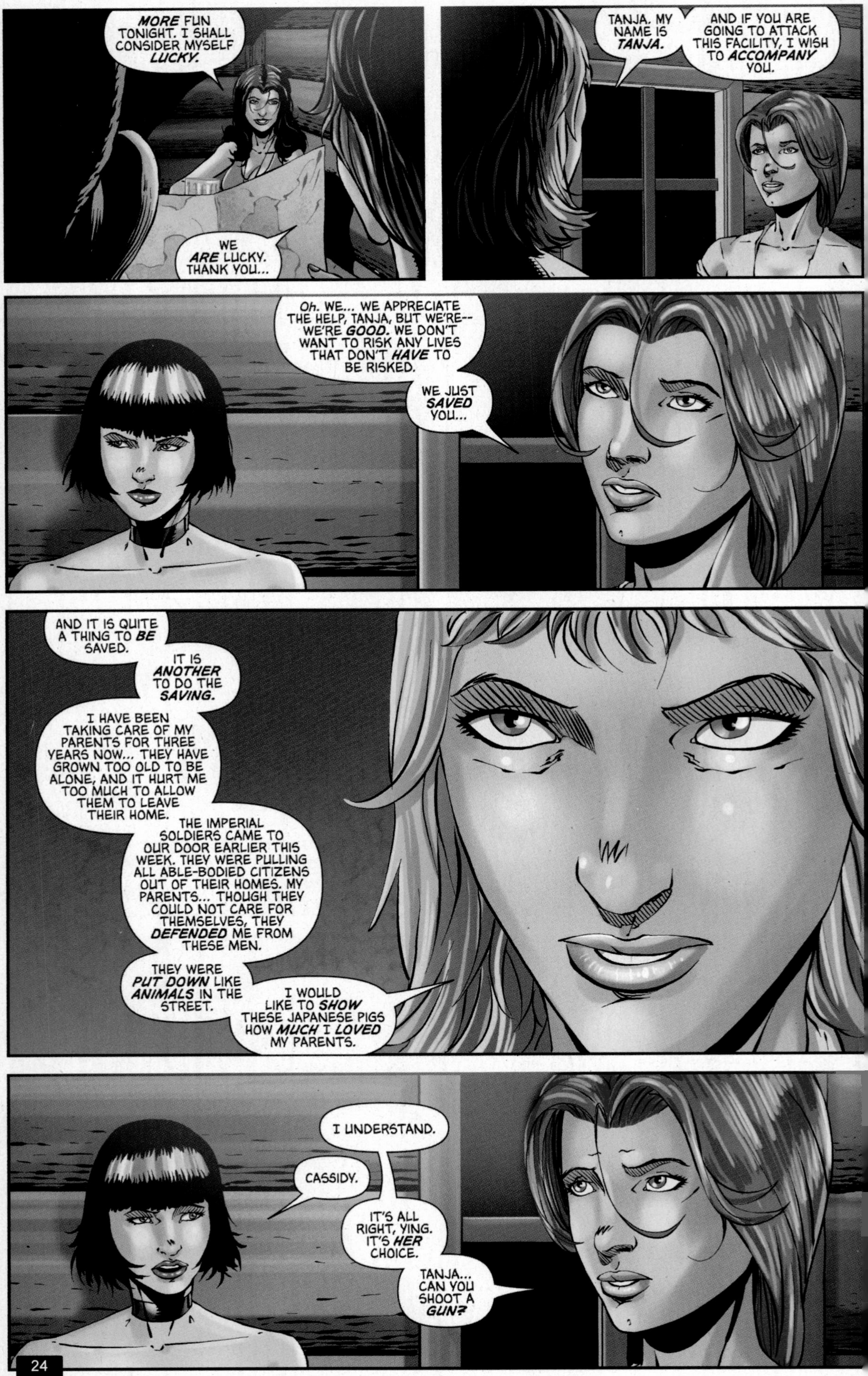

MORE FUN TONIGHT. I SHALL CONSIDER MYSELF LUCKY.
WE ARE LUCKY. THANK YOU...
TANJA. MY NAME IS TANJA.
AND IF YOU ARE GOING TO ATTACK THIS FACILITY, I WISH TO ACCOMPANY YOU.
Oh. WE... WE APPRECIATE THE HELP, TANJA, BUT WE'RE-- WE'RE GOOD. WE DON'T WANT TO RISK ANY LIVES THAT DON'T HAVE TO BE RISKED.
WE JUST SAVED YOU...
AND IT IS QUITE A THING TO BE SAVED.
IT IS ANOTHER TO DO THE SAVING.
I HAVE BEEN TAKING CARE OF MY PARENTS FOR THREE YEARS NOW... THEY HAVE GROWN TOO OLD TO BE ALONE, AND IT HURT ME TOO MUCH TO ALLOW THEM TO LEAVE THEIR HOME.
THE IMPERIAL SOLDIERS CAME TO OUR DOOR EARLIER THIS WEEK. THEY WERE PULLING ALL ABLE-BODIED CITIZENS OUT OF THEIR HOMES. MY PARENTS... THOUGH THEY COULD NOT CARE FOR THEMSELVES, THEY DEFENDED ME FROM THESE MEN.
THEY WERE PUT DOWN LIKE ANIMALS IN THE STREET.
I WOULD LIKE TO SHOW THESE JAPANESE PIGS HOW MUCH I LOVED MY PARENTS.
I UNDERSTAND.
CASSIDY.
IT'S ALL RIGHT, YING. IT'S HER CHOICE.
TANJA... CAN YOU SHOOT A GUN?

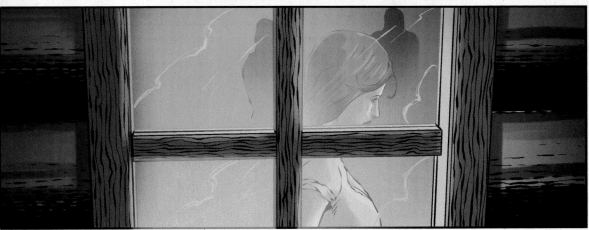

〈THERE SHE IS.〉

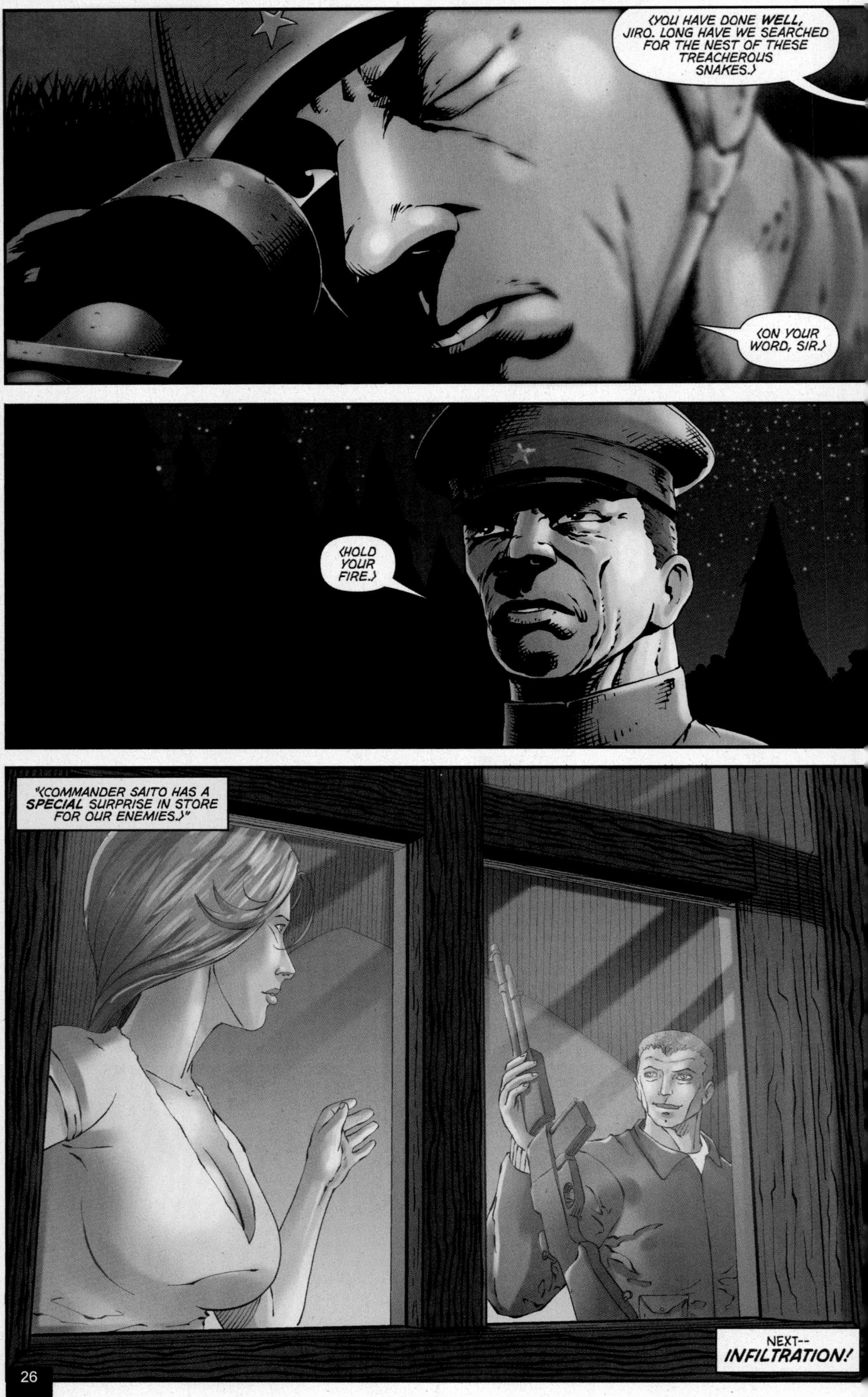
‹YOU HAVE DONE WELL, JIRO. LONG HAVE WE SEARCHED FOR THE NEST OF THESE TREACHEROUS SNAKES.›
‹ON YOUR WORD, SIR.›
‹HOLD YOUR FIRE.›
"‹COMMANDER SAITO HAS A SPECIAL SURPRISE IN STORE FOR OUR ENEMIES.›"
NEXT-- INFILTRATION!

B.A.R Maid

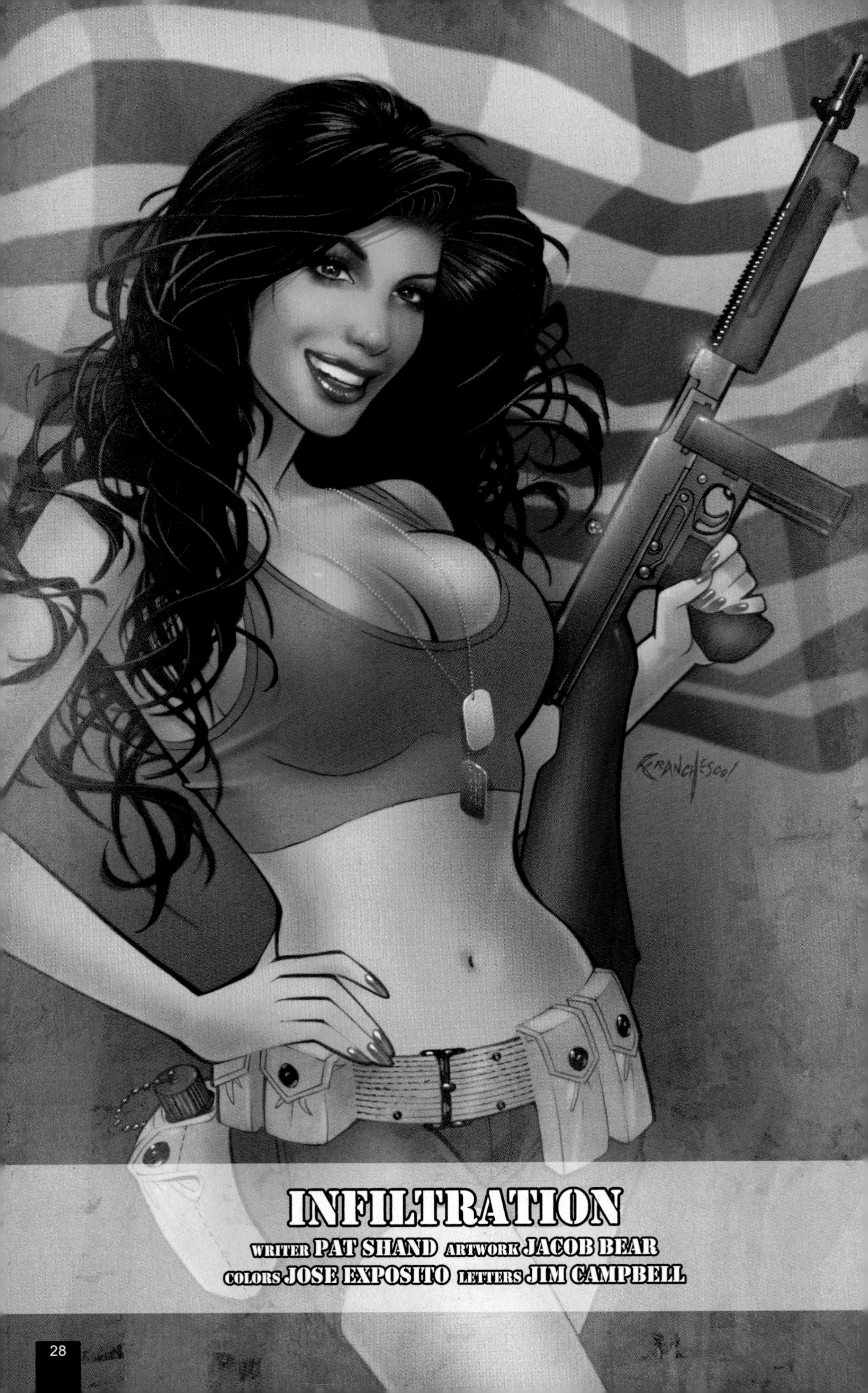

INFILTRATION

WRITER PAT SHAND ARTWORK JACOB BEAR
COLORS JOSE EXPOSITO LETTERS JIM CAMPBELL

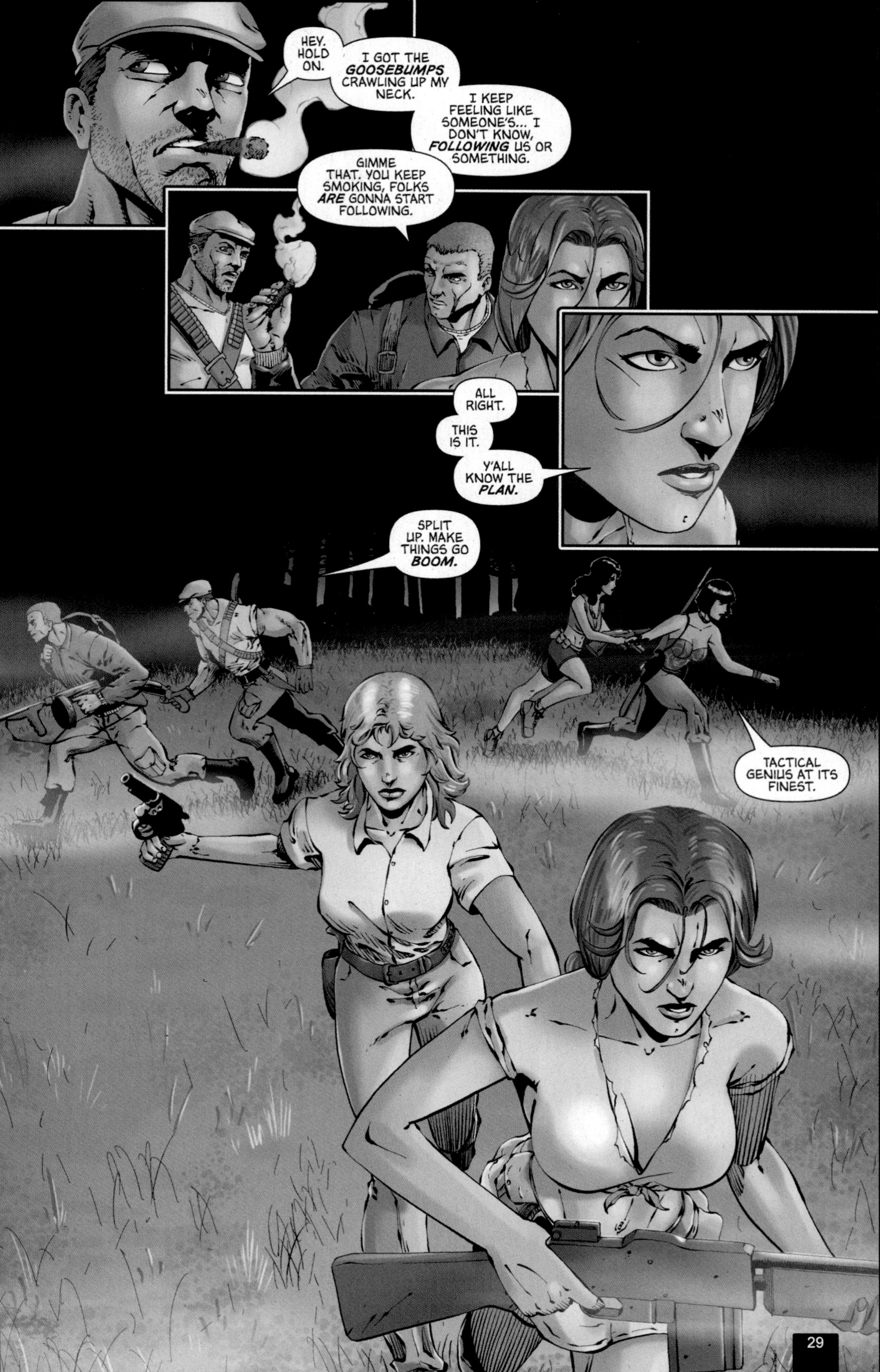
HEY. HOLD ON.
I GOT THE GOOSEBUMPS CRAWLING UP MY NECK.
I KEEP FEELING LIKE SOMEONE'S... I DON'T KNOW, FOLLOWING US OR SOMETHING.
GIMME THAT. YOU KEEP SMOKING, FOLKS ARE GONNA START FOLLOWING.
ALL RIGHT.
THIS IS IT.
Y'ALL KNOW THE PLAN.
SPLIT UP. MAKE THINGS GO BOOM.
TACTICAL GENIUS AT ITS FINEST.

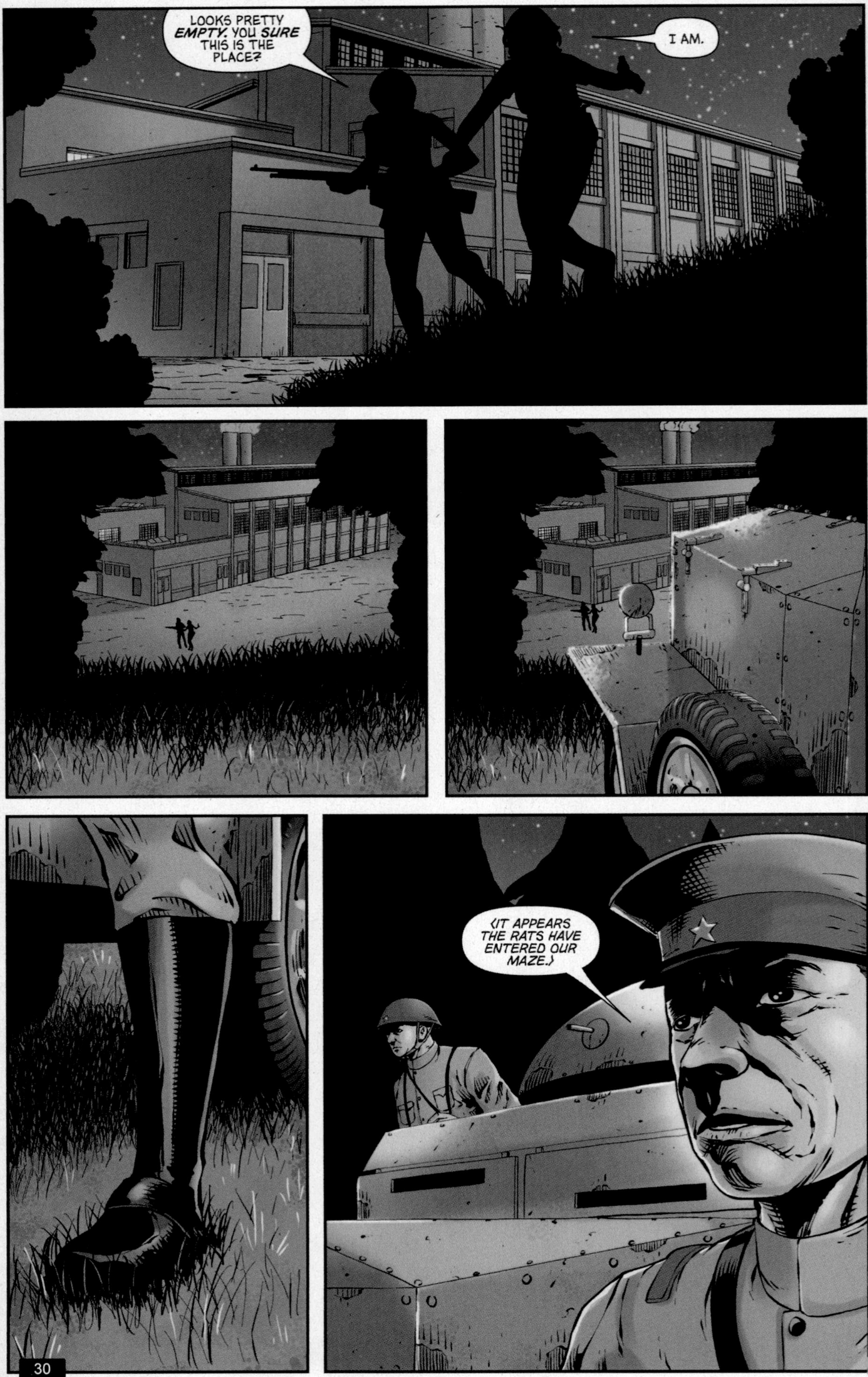

LOOKS PRETTY EMPTY. YOU SURE THIS IS THE PLACE?
I AM.
‹IT APPEARS THE RATS HAVE ENTERED OUR MAZE.›

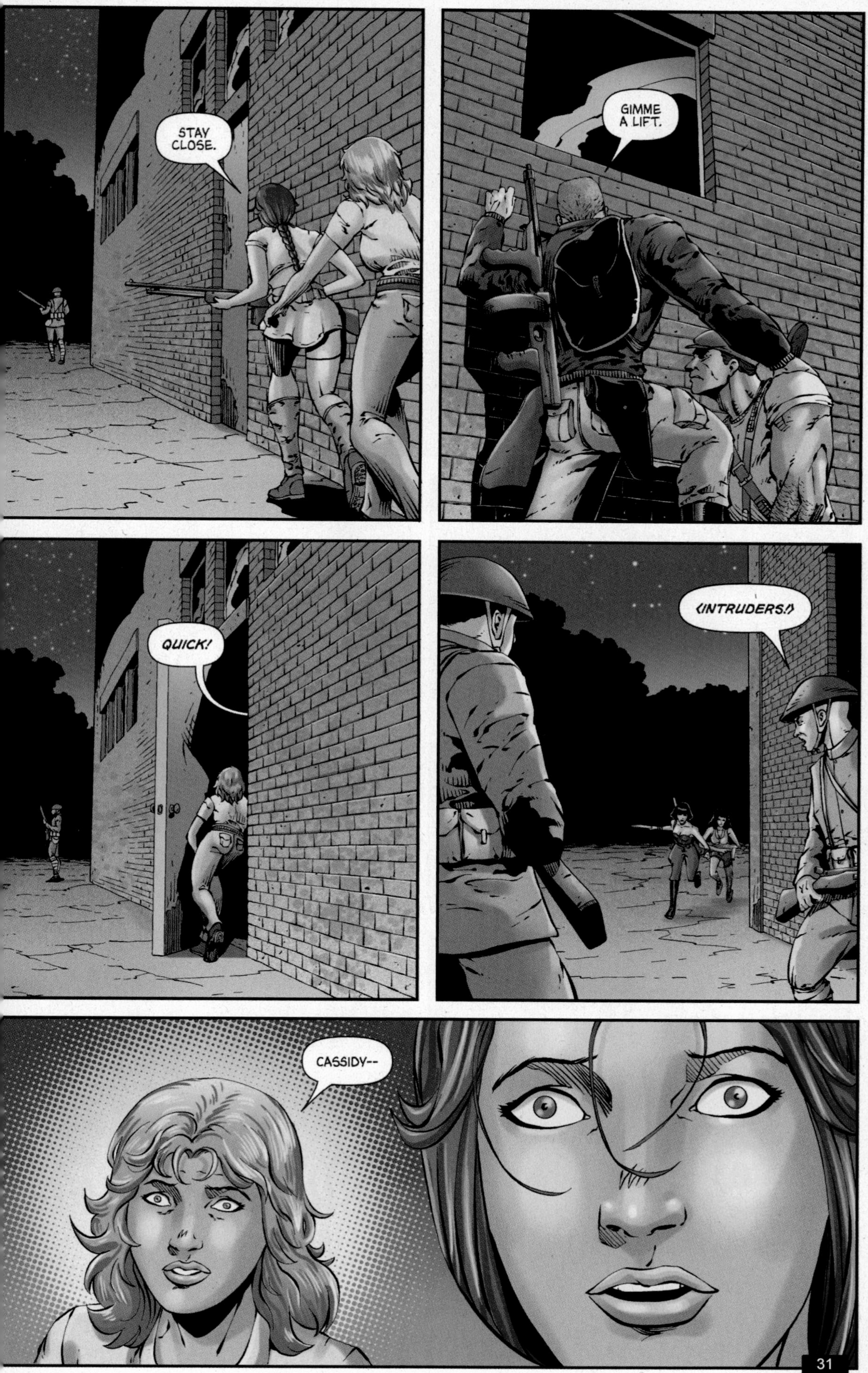
STAY CLOSE.
GIMME A LIFT.
QUICK!
‹INTRUDERS!›
CASSIDY--

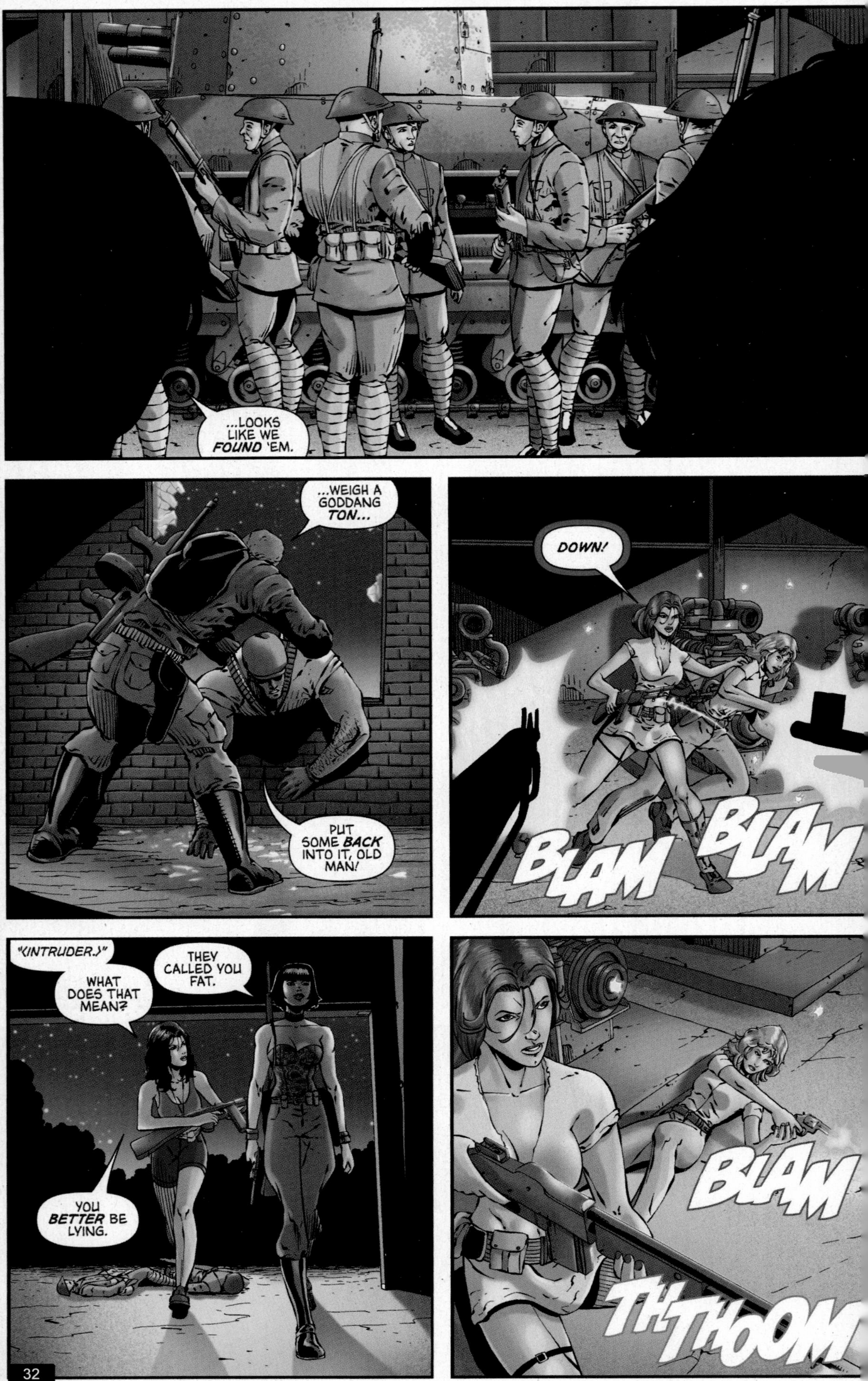
...LOOKS LIKE WE FOUND 'EM.
...WEIGH A GODDANG TON...
PUT SOME BACK INTO IT, OLD MAN!
DOWN!
BLAM BLAM
"‹INTRUDER.›"
WHAT DOES THAT MEAN?
THEY CALLED YOU FAT.
YOU BETTER BE LYING.
BLAM
THTHOOM

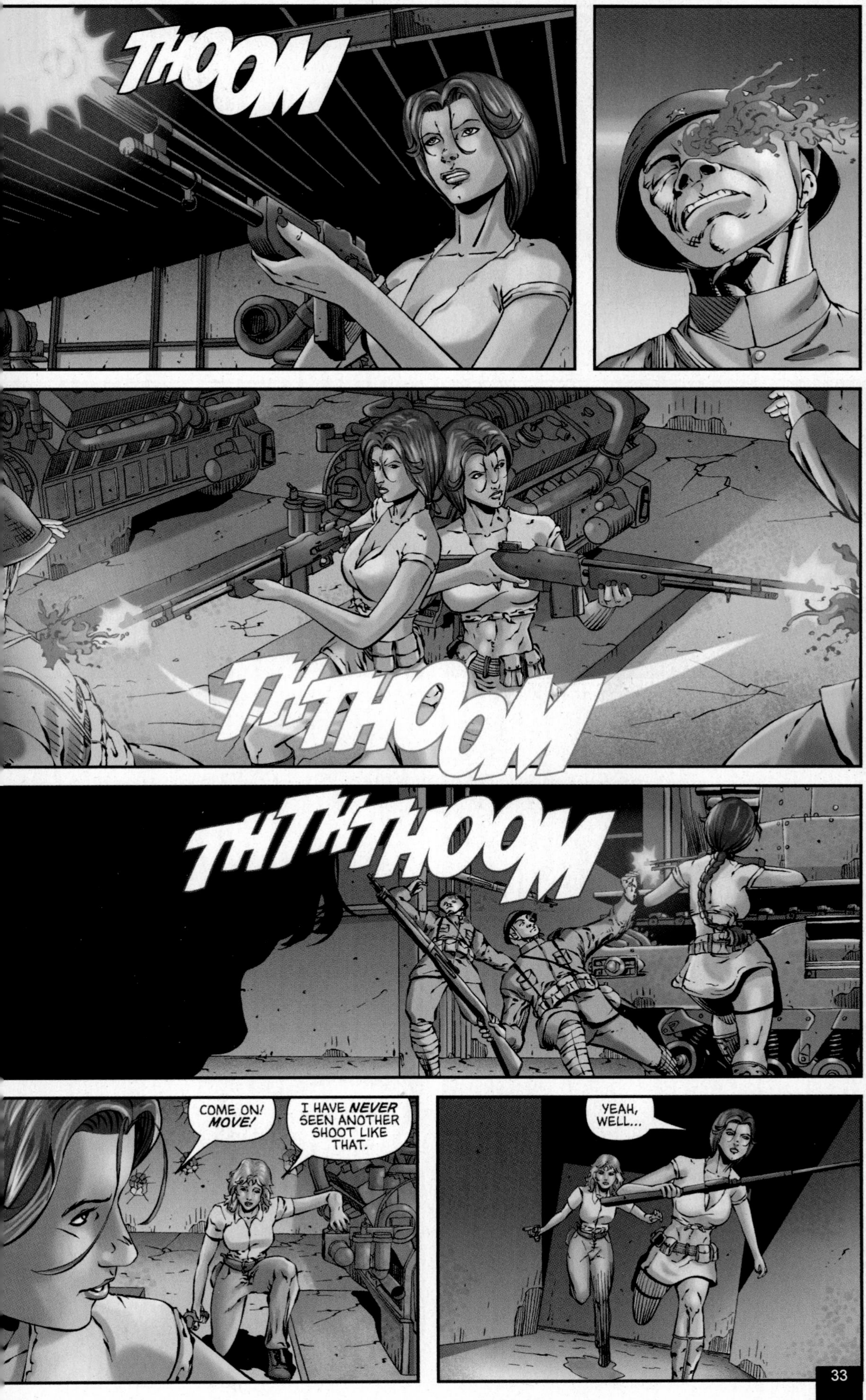
THOOM
THTHOOM
THTHTHOOM
COME ON! MOVE!
I HAVE NEVER SEEN ANOTHER SHOOT LIKE THAT.
YEAH, WELL...

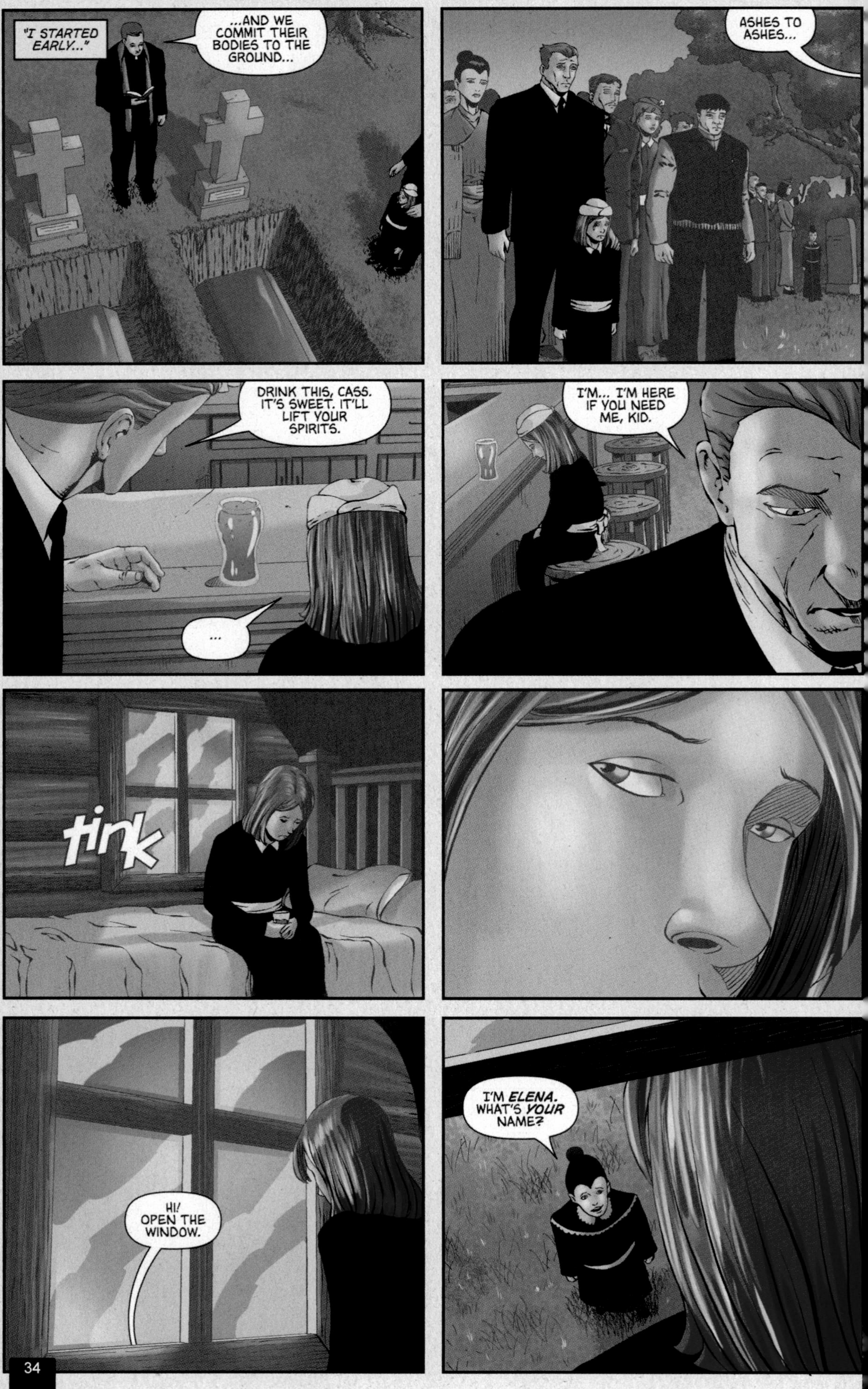
"I STARTED EARLY..."
...AND WE COMMIT THEIR BODIES TO THE GROUND...
ASHES TO ASHES...
DRINK THIS, CASS. IT'S SWEET. IT'LL LIFT YOUR SPIRITS.
...
I'M... I'M HERE IF YOU NEED ME, KID.
tink
HI! OPEN THE WINDOW.
I'M ELENA. WHAT'S YOUR NAME?

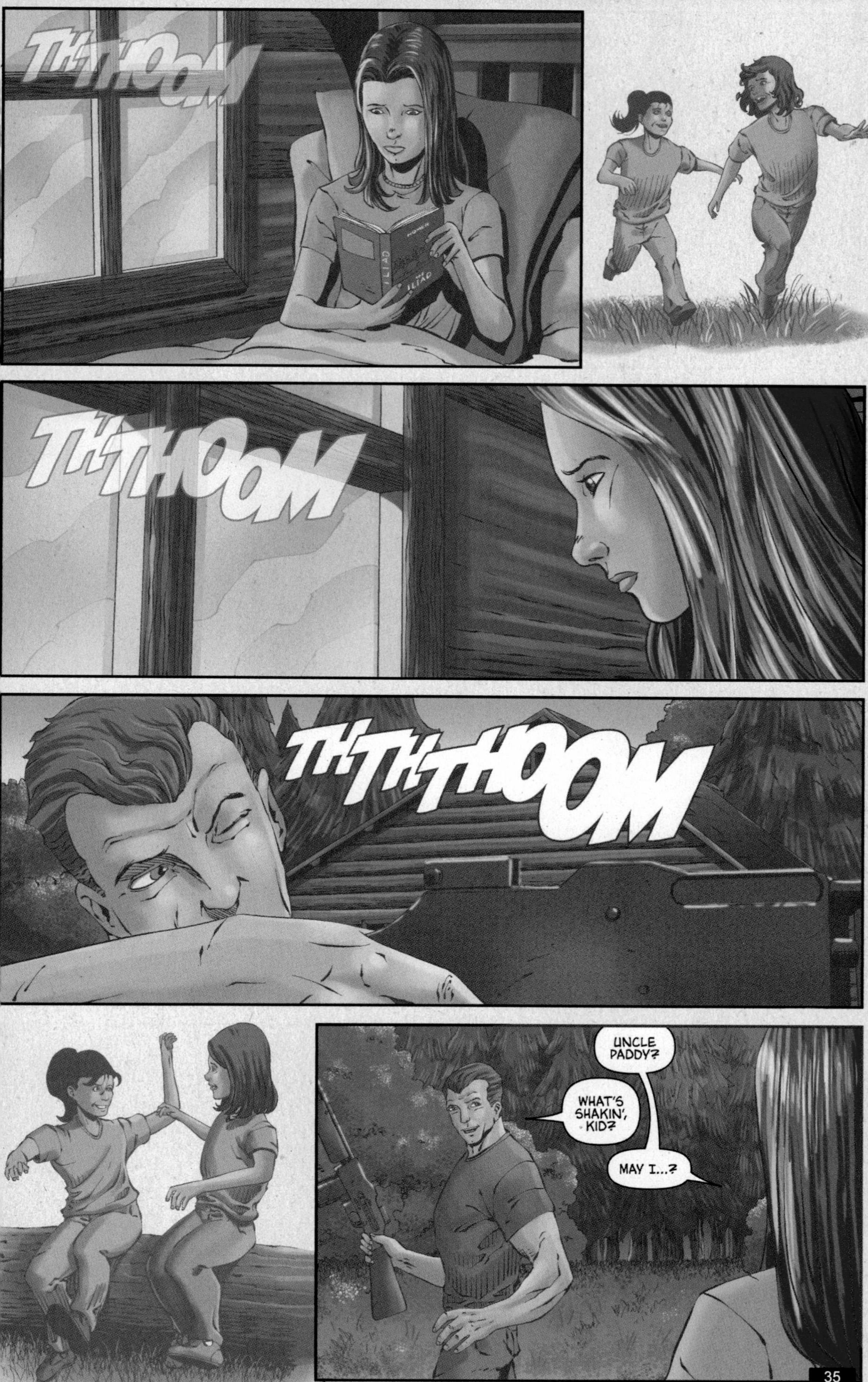
THTHOOM
ILIAD
THTHOOM
THTHTHOOM
UNCLE PADDY?
WHAT'S SHAKIN', KID?
MAY I...?

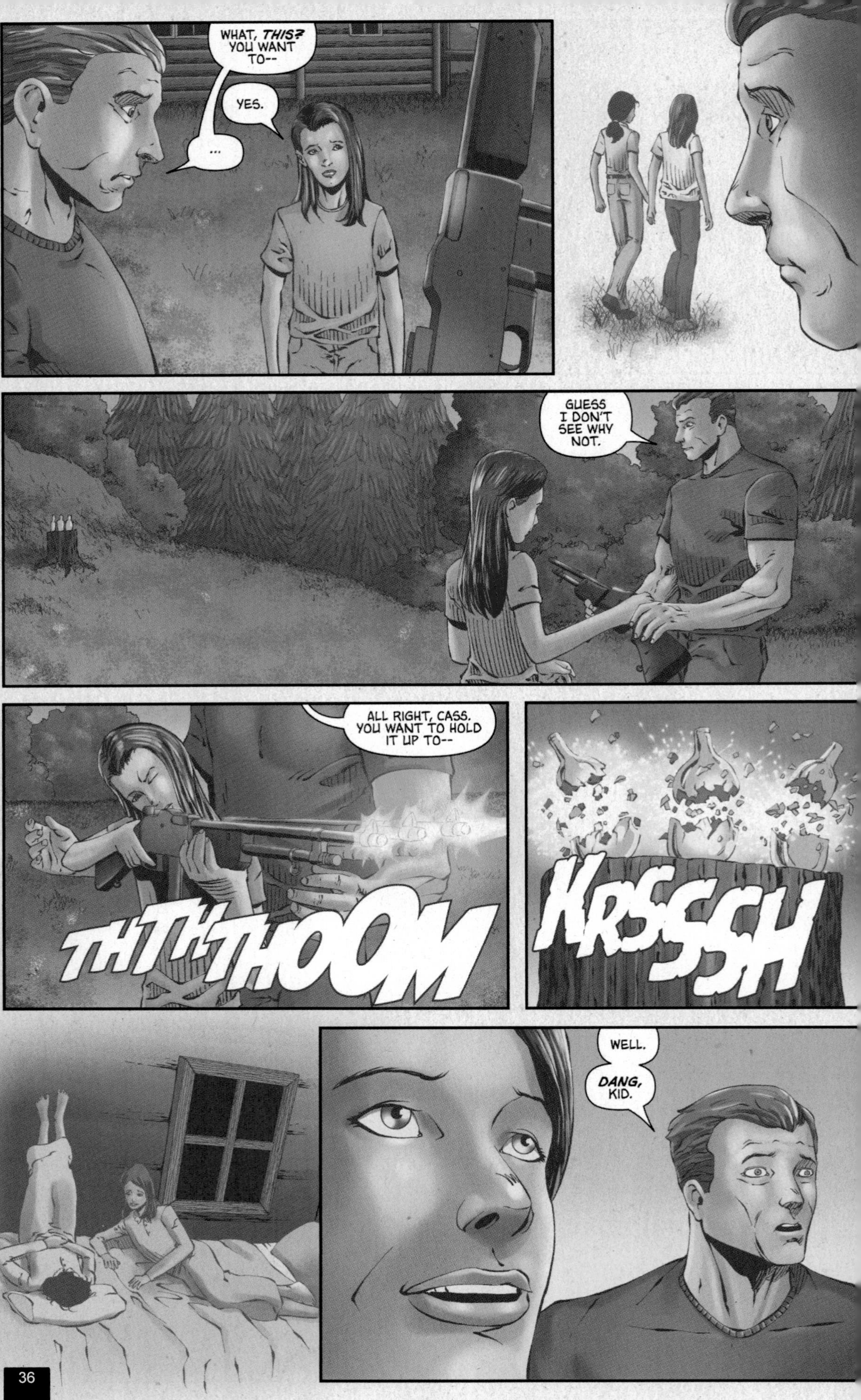
WHAT, *THIS?* YOU WANT TO--
YES.
...
GUESS I DON'T SEE WHY NOT.
ALL RIGHT, CASS. YOU WANT TO HOLD IT UP TO--
THTHTHOOM
KRSSSH
WELL.
DANG, KID.

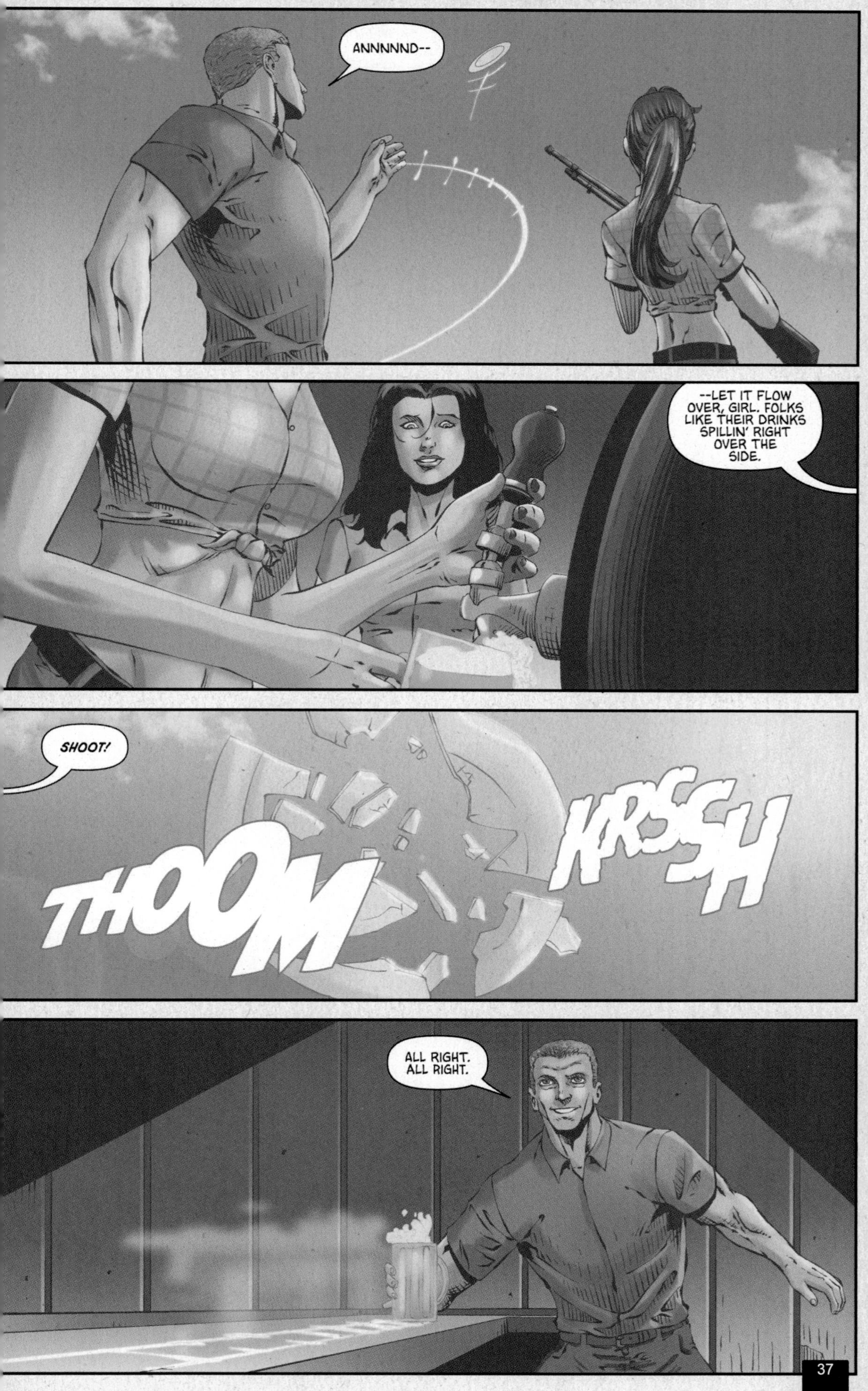
ANNNNND--
--LET IT FLOW OVER, GIRL. FOLKS LIKE THEIR DRINKS SPILLIN' RIGHT OVER THE SIDE.
SHOOT!
THOOM
KRSSH
ALL RIGHT. ALL RIGHT.

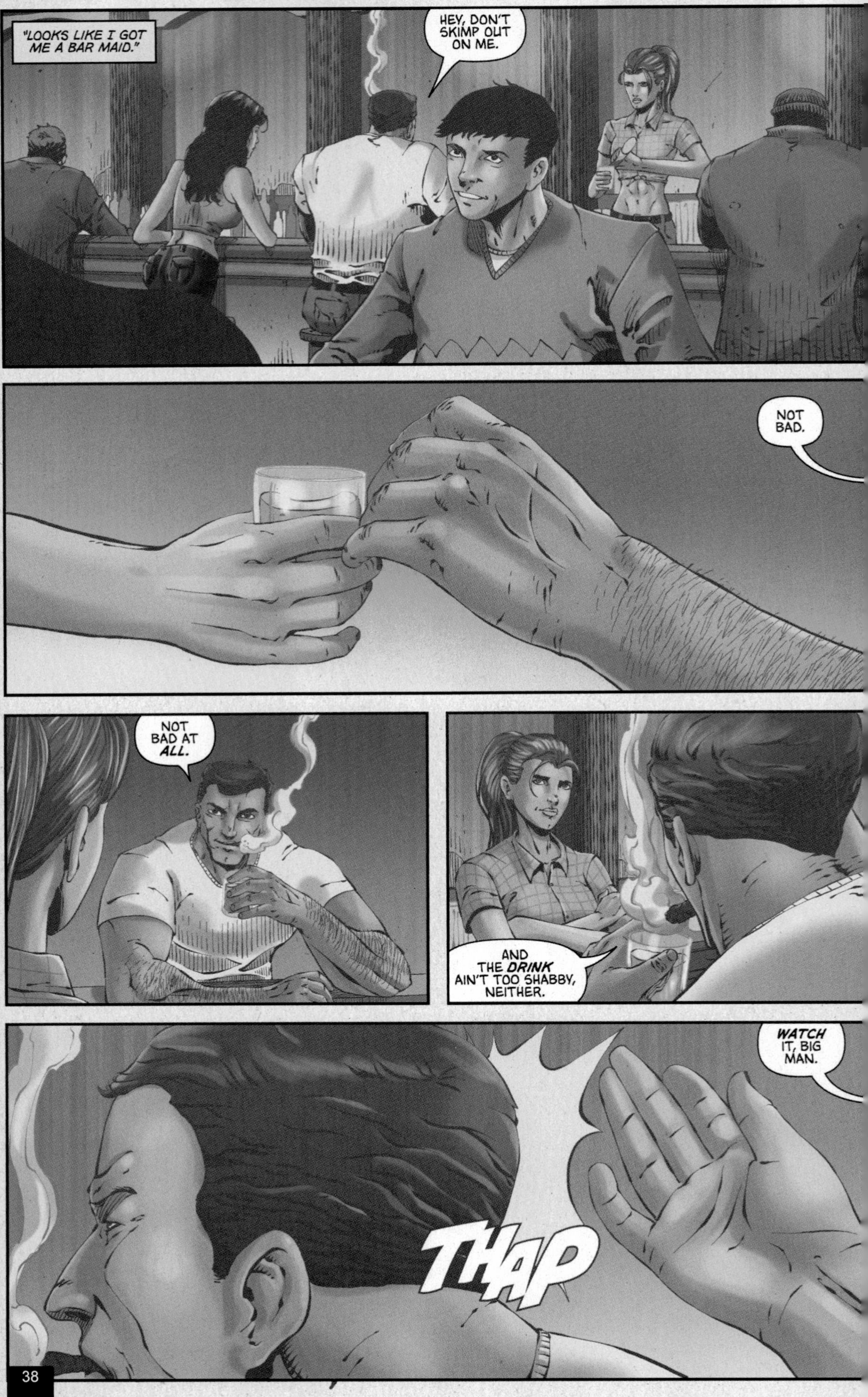
"LOOKS LIKE I GOT ME A BAR MAID."
HEY, DON'T SKIMP OUT ON ME.
NOT BAD.
NOT BAD AT ALL.
AND THE DRINK AIN'T TOO SHABBY, NEITHER.
WATCH IT, BIG MAN.
THAP

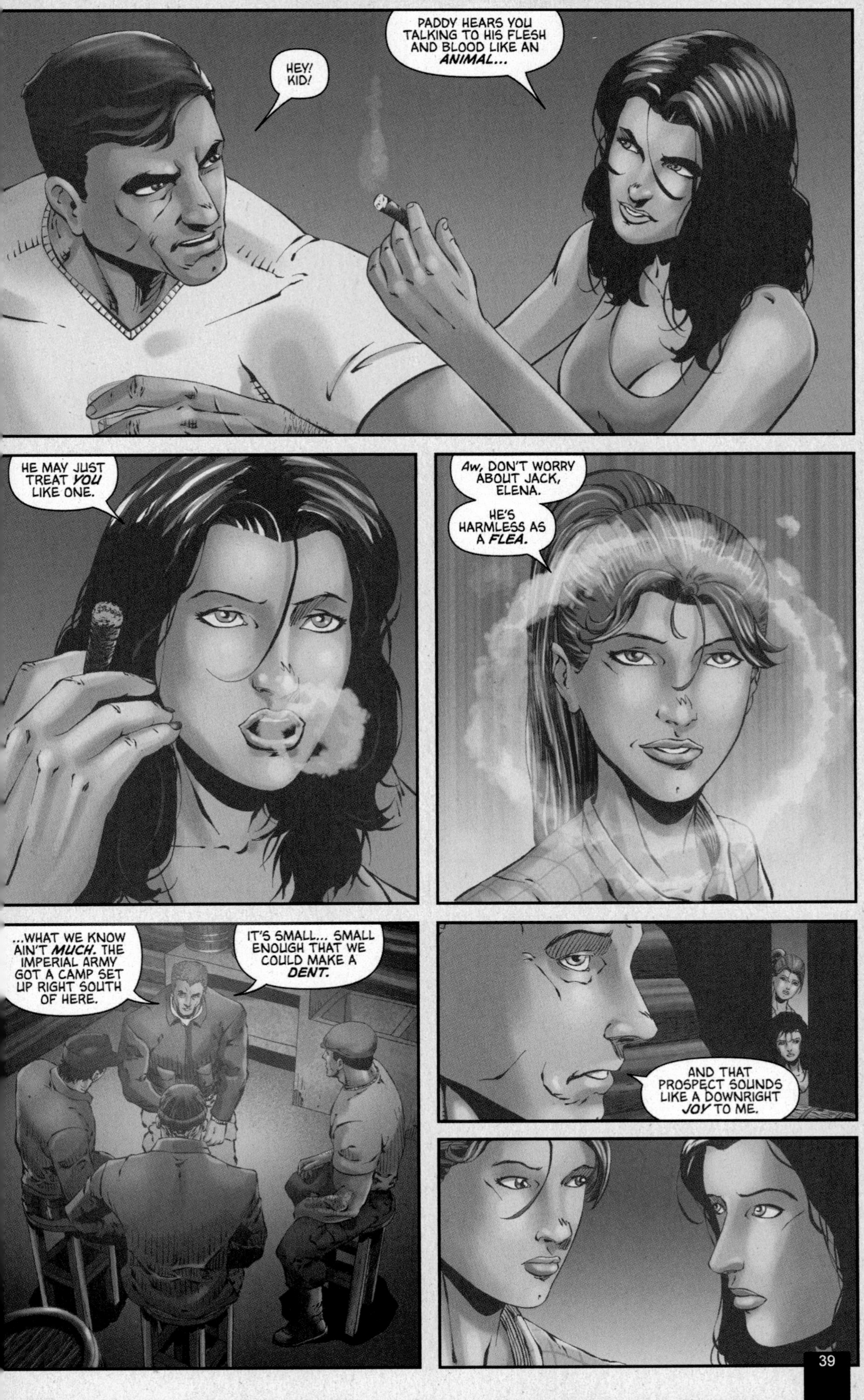
HEY! KID!
PADDY HEARS YOU TALKING TO HIS FLESH AND BLOOD LIKE AN *ANIMAL...*
HE MAY JUST TREAT *YOU* LIKE ONE.
Aw, DON'T WORRY ABOUT JACK, ELENA.
HE'S HARMLESS AS A *FLEA.*
...WHAT WE KNOW AIN'T *MUCH.* THE IMPERIAL ARMY GOT A CAMP SET UP RIGHT SOUTH OF HERE.
IT'S SMALL... SMALL ENOUGH THAT WE COULD MAKE A *DENT.*
AND THAT PROSPECT SOUNDS LIKE A DOWNRIGHT *JOY* TO ME.

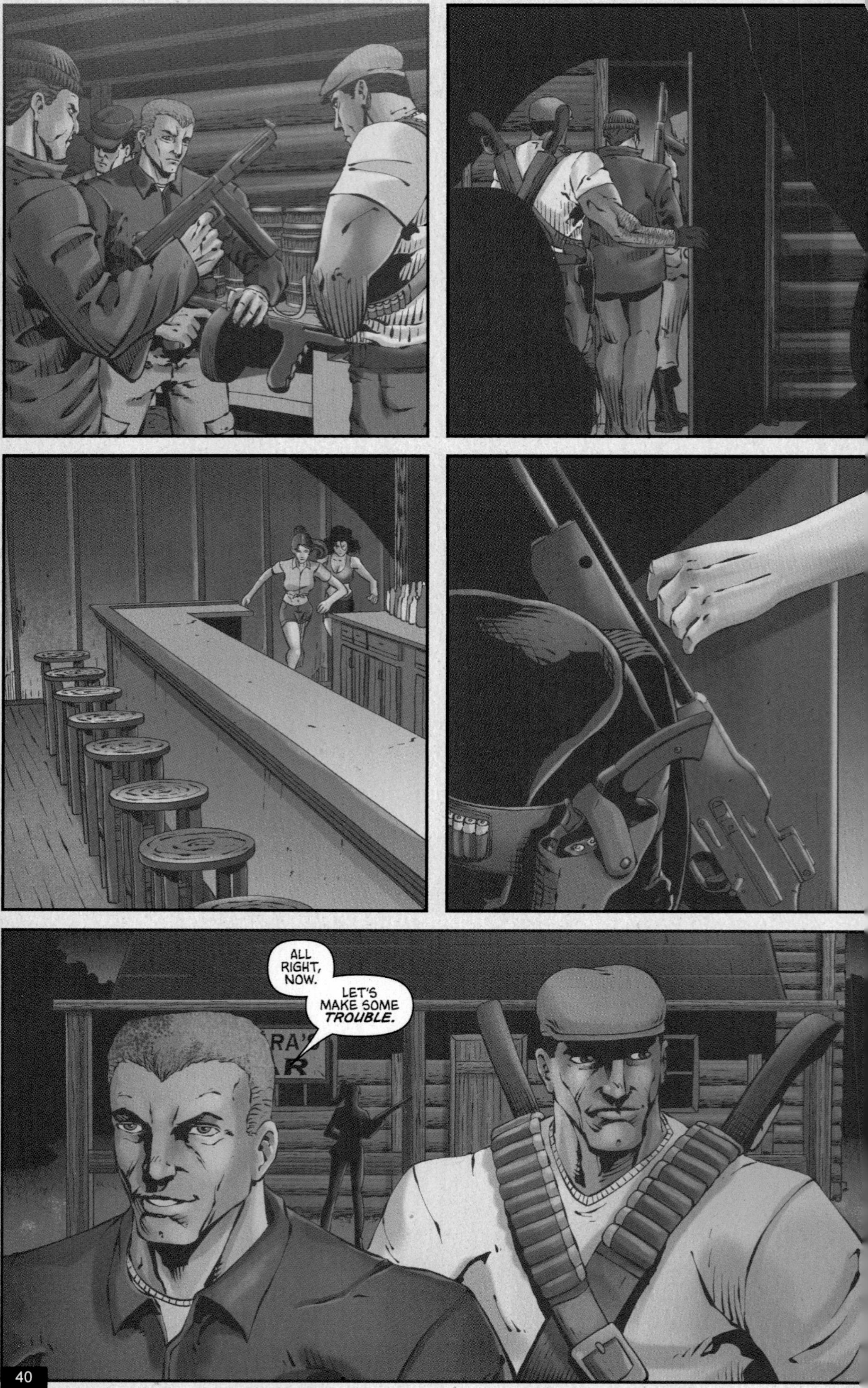
ALL RIGHT, NOW.
LET'S MAKE SOME *TROUBLE.*

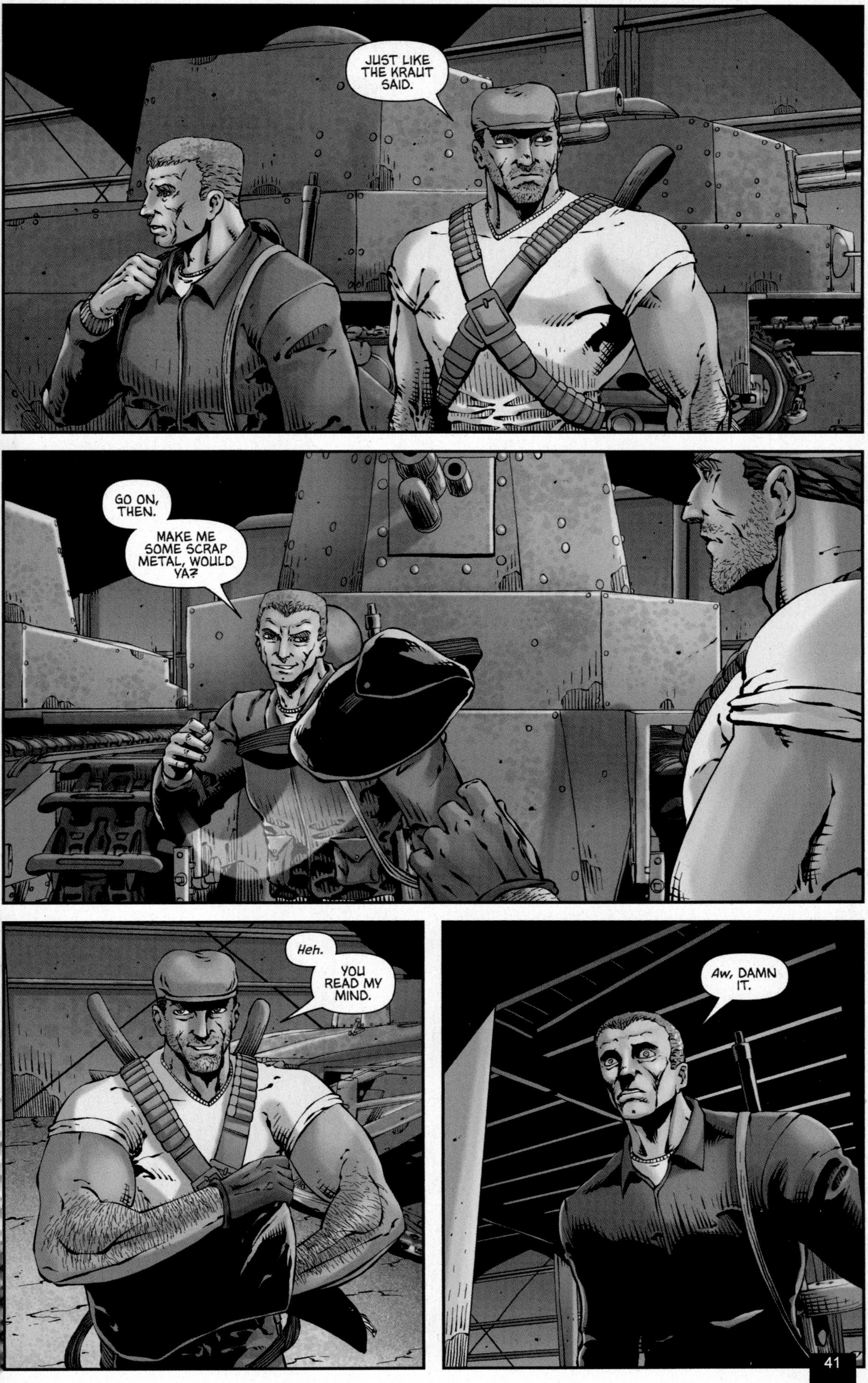
JUST LIKE THE KRAUT SAID.
GO ON, THEN.
MAKE ME SOME SCRAP METAL, WOULD YA?
Heh.
YOU READ MY MIND.
Aw, DAMN IT.

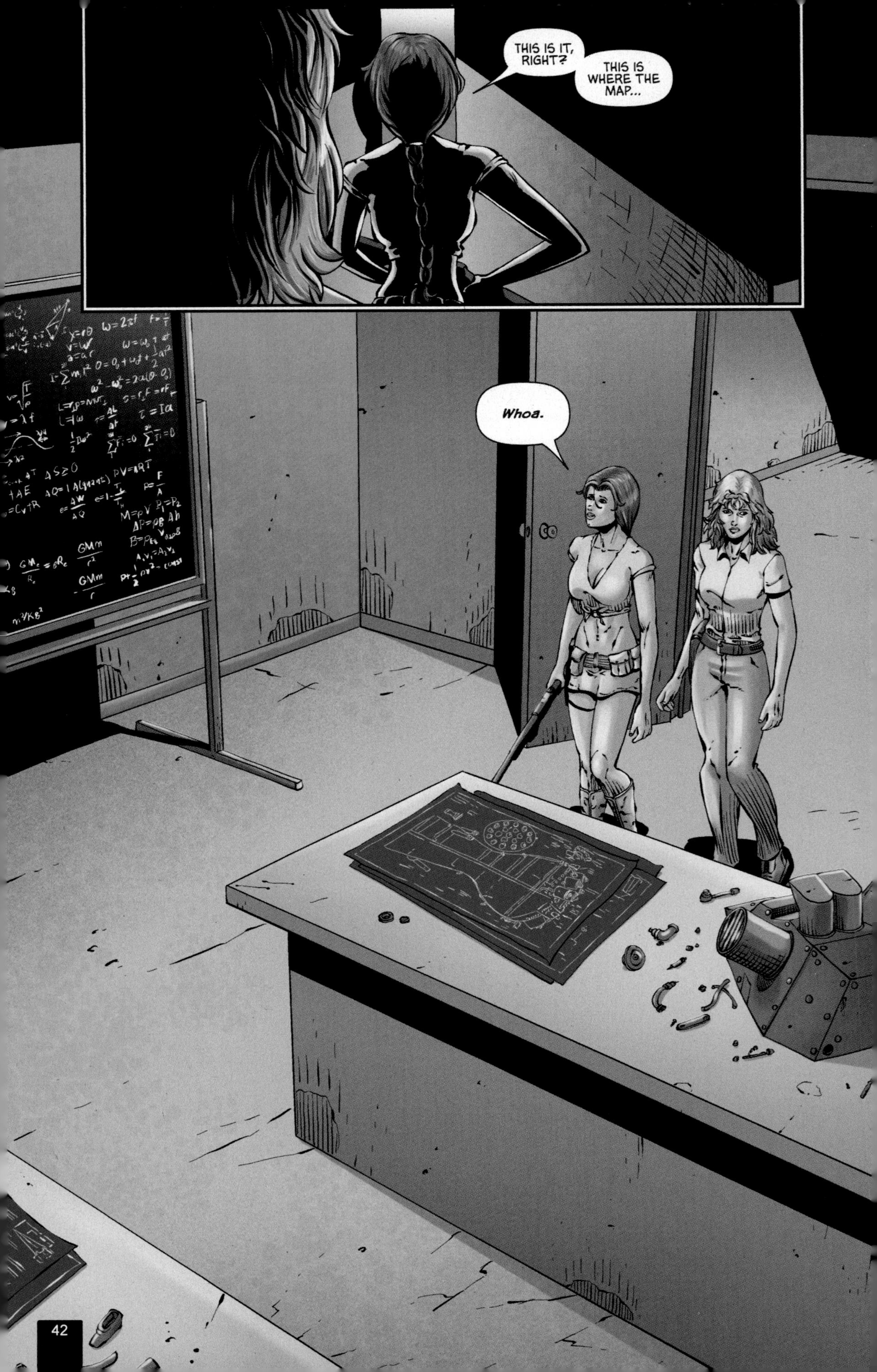
THIS IS IT, RIGHT?
THIS IS WHERE THE MAP...
Whoa.

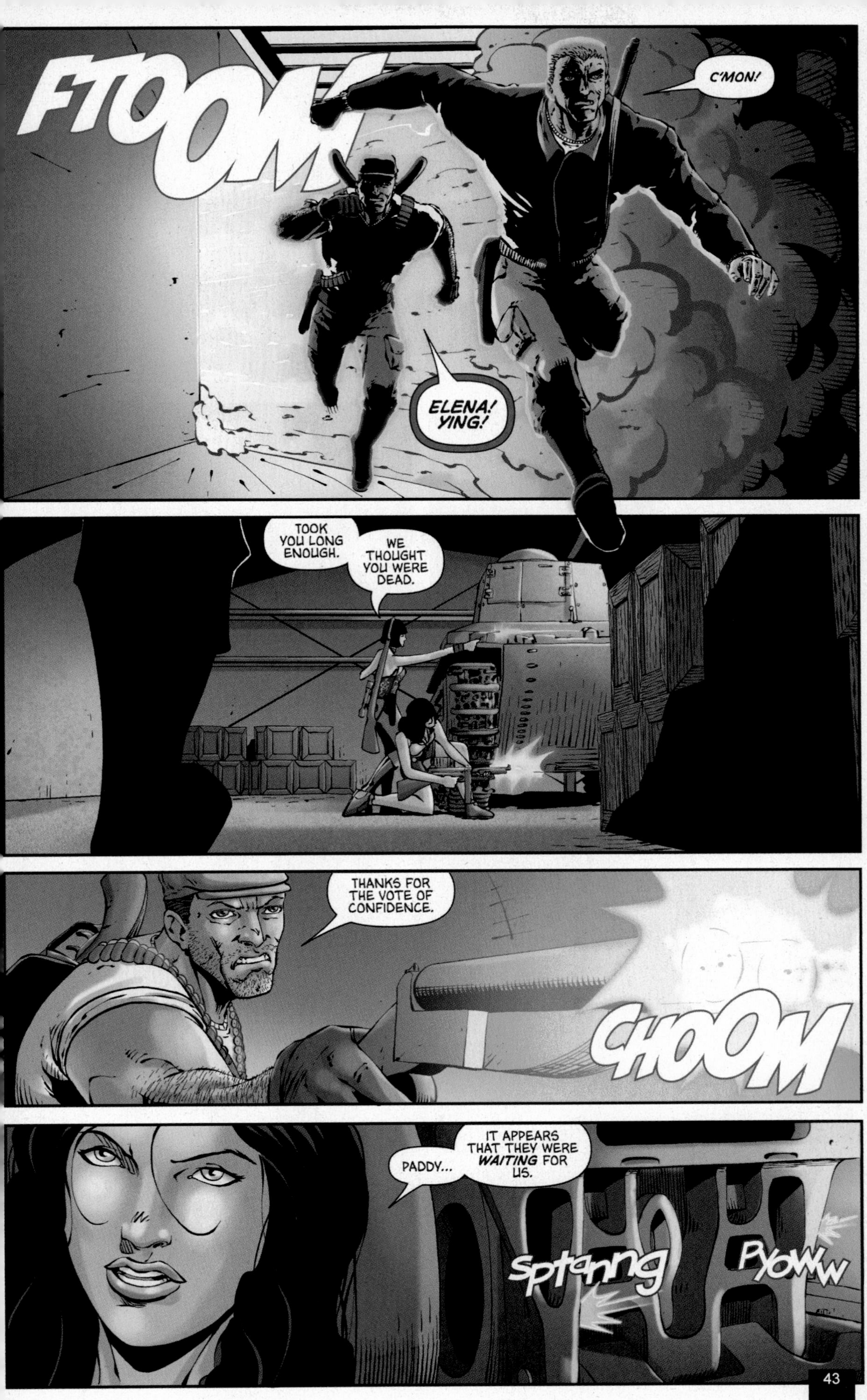
FTOOM
C'MON!
ELENA! YING!
TOOK YOU LONG ENOUGH.
WE THOUGHT YOU WERE DEAD.
THANKS FOR THE VOTE OF CONFIDENCE.
CHOOM
PADDY...
IT APPEARS THAT THEY WERE *WAITING* FOR US.
Sptanng
Pyoww

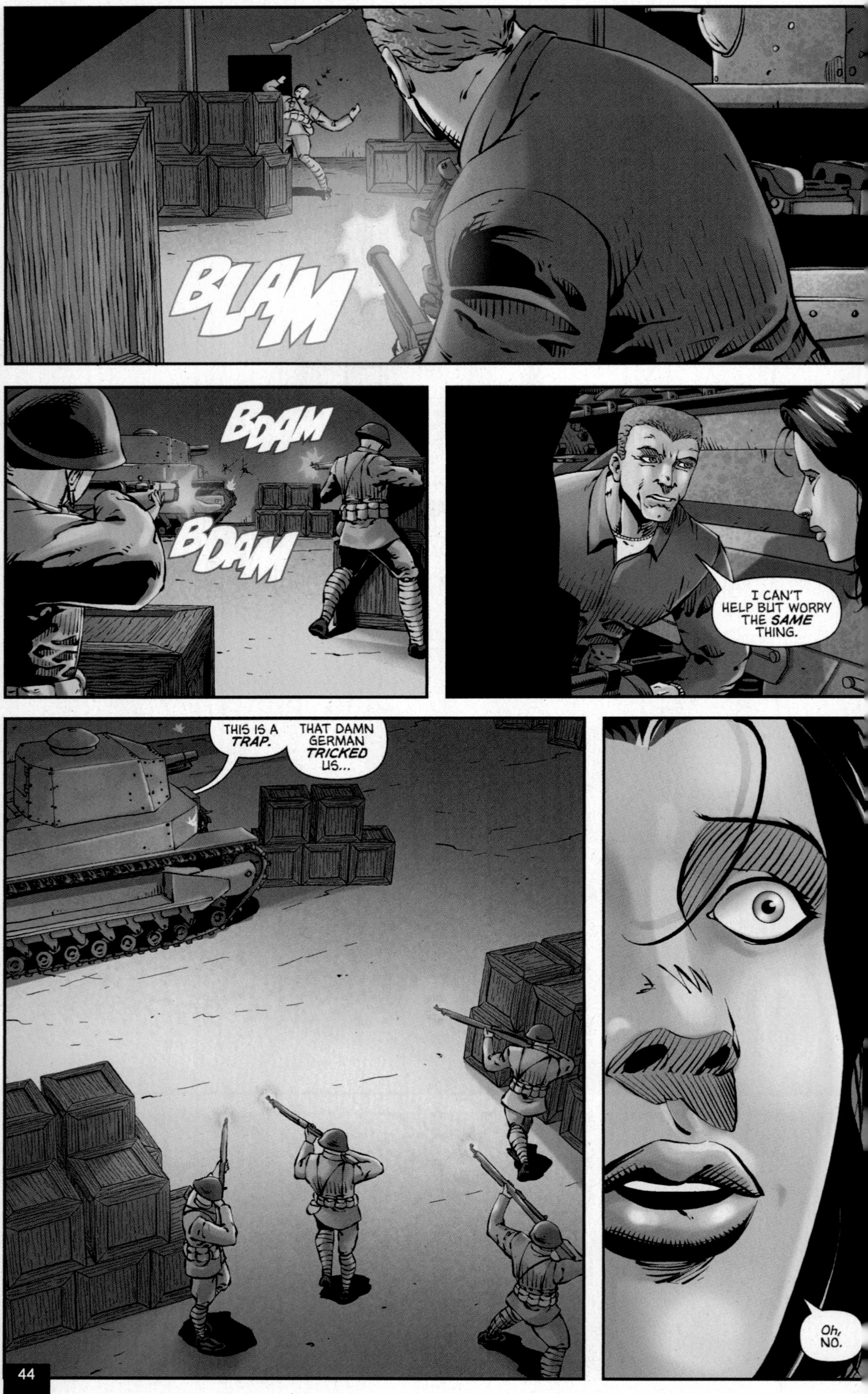
BLAM
BDAM
BDAM
I CAN'T HELP BUT WORRY THE *SAME* THING.
THIS IS A *TRAP.*
THAT DAMN GERMAN *TRICKED* US...
Oh, NO.

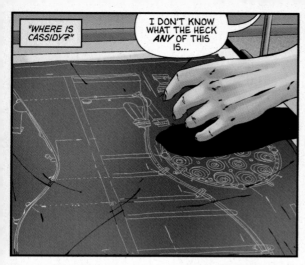

"WHERE IS CASSIDY?"

I DON'T KNOW WHAT THE HECK *ANY* OF THIS IS...

BUT IT LOOKS LIKE SOMETHING OUT OF ONE OF MY UNCLE'S SCI-FI BOOKS.

IT IS A *SHAME*, CASSIDY--

--THAT YOU WILL NEVER KNOW THE *TRUTH* OF OUR PLAN!

OUR PLAN?

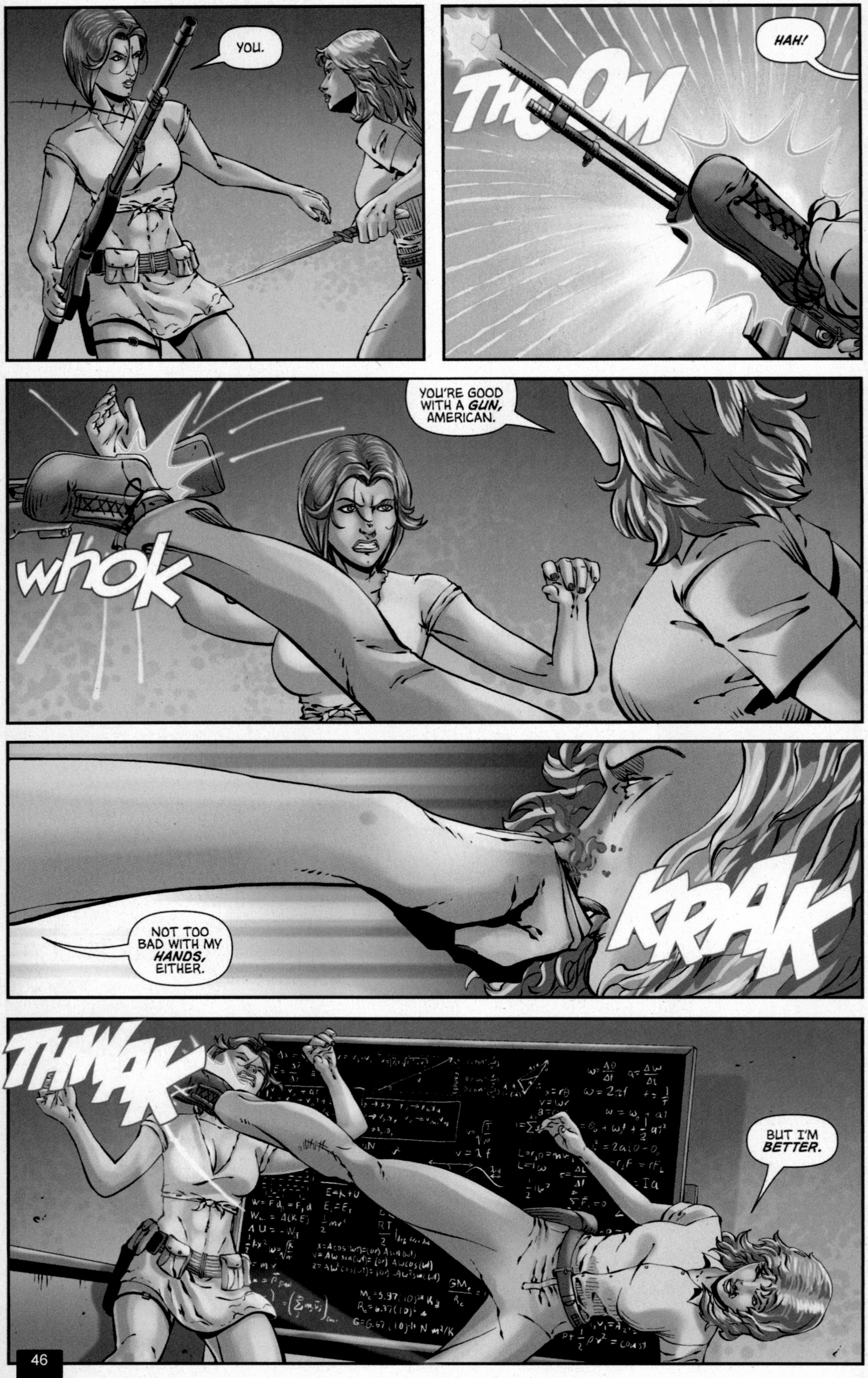
YOU.
THOOM
HAH!
YOU'RE GOOD WITH A *GUN*, AMERICAN.
whok
NOT TOO BAD WITH MY *HANDS*, EITHER.
KRAK
THWAK
BUT I'M *BETTER.*

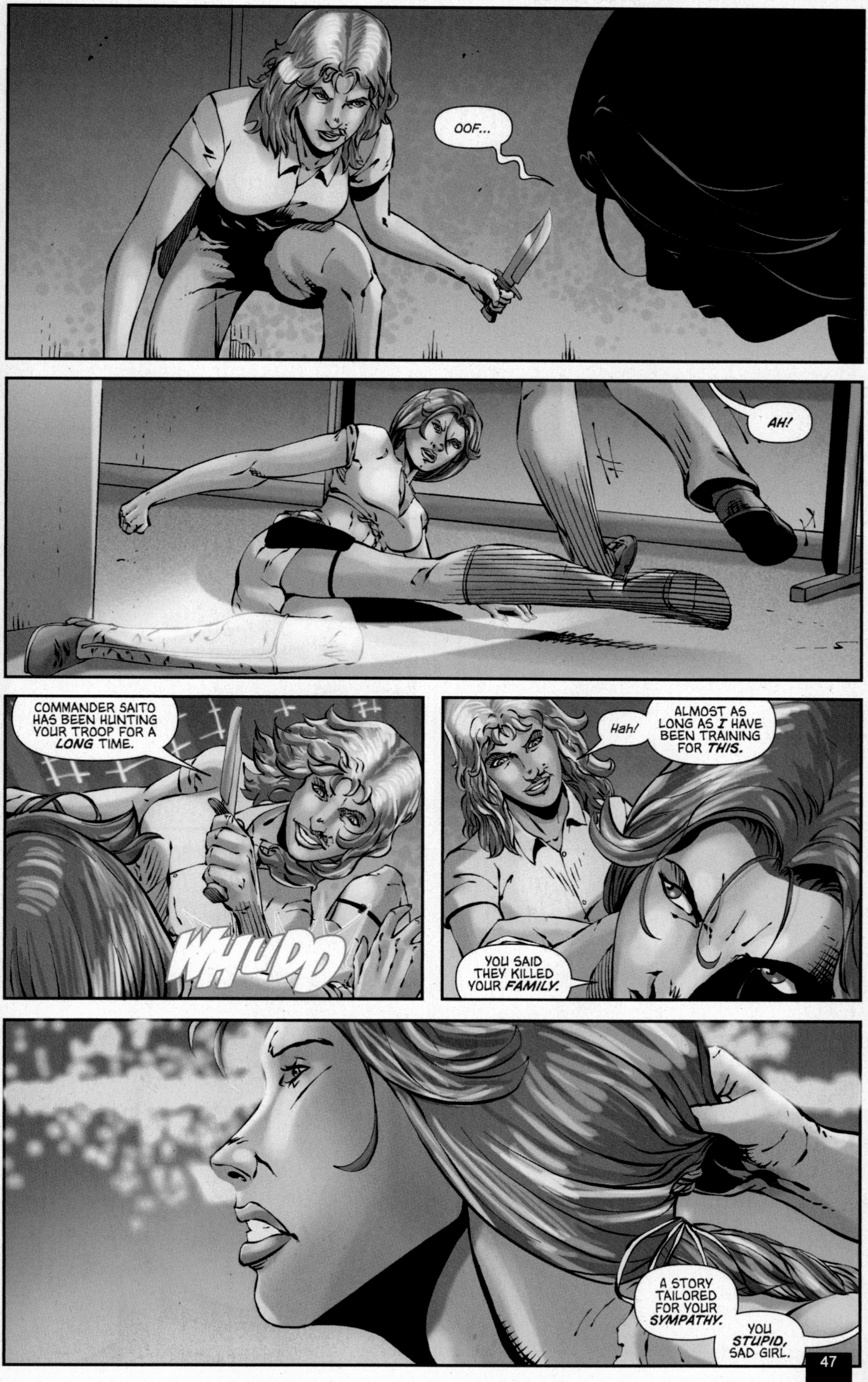
OOF...
AH!
COMMANDER SAITO HAS BEEN HUNTING YOUR TROOP FOR A LONG TIME.
WHUDD
Hah!
ALMOST AS LONG AS I HAVE BEEN TRAINING FOR THIS.
YOU SAID THEY KILLED YOUR FAMILY.
A STORY TAILORED FOR YOUR SYMPATHY.
YOU STUPID, SAD GIRL.

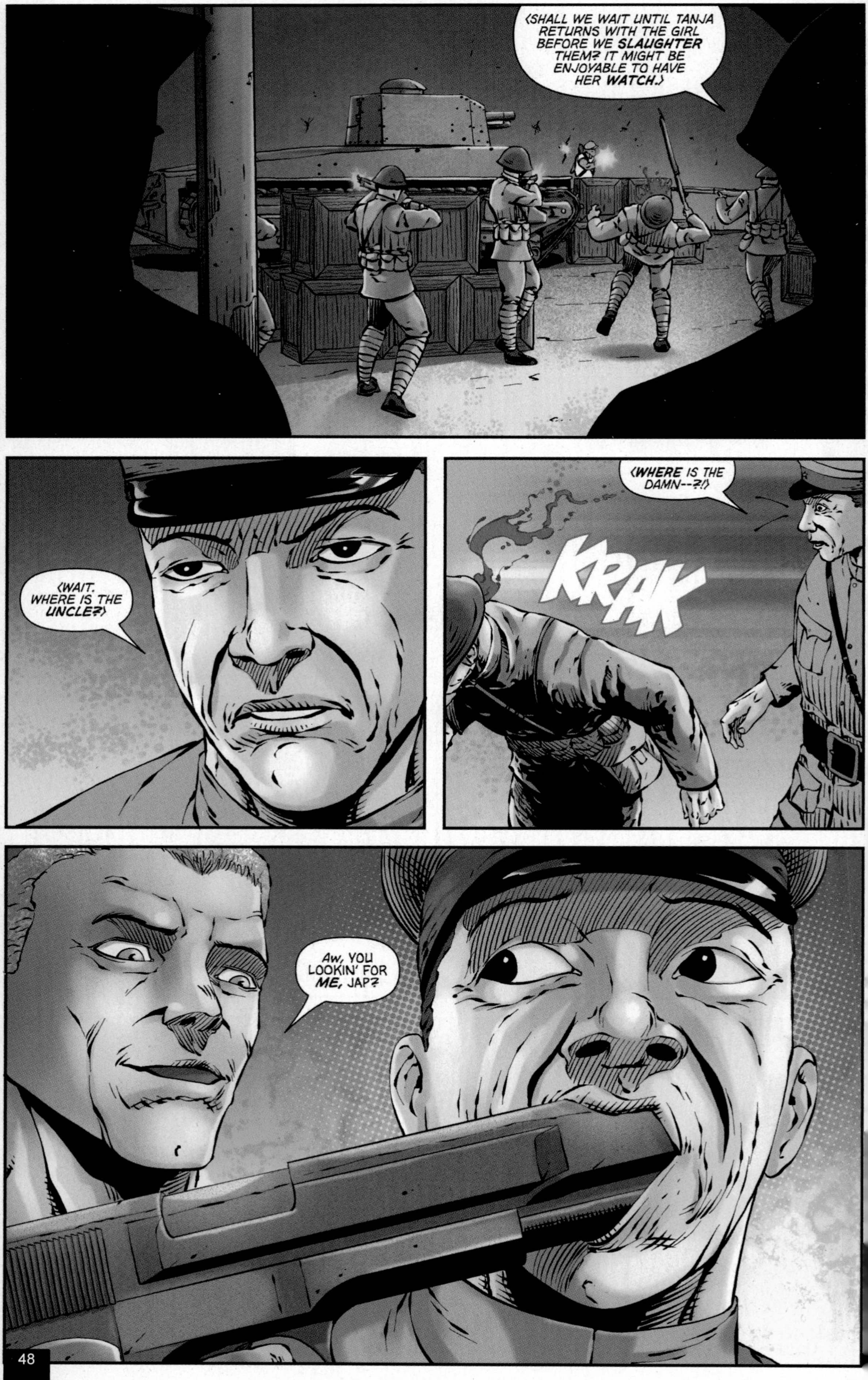
‹SHALL WE WAIT UNTIL TANJA RETURNS WITH THE GIRL BEFORE WE SLAUGHTER THEM? IT MIGHT BE ENJOYABLE TO HAVE HER WATCH.›
‹WAIT. WHERE IS THE UNCLE?›
‹WHERE IS THE DAMN--?!›
KRAK
Aw, YOU LOOKIN' FOR ME, JAP?

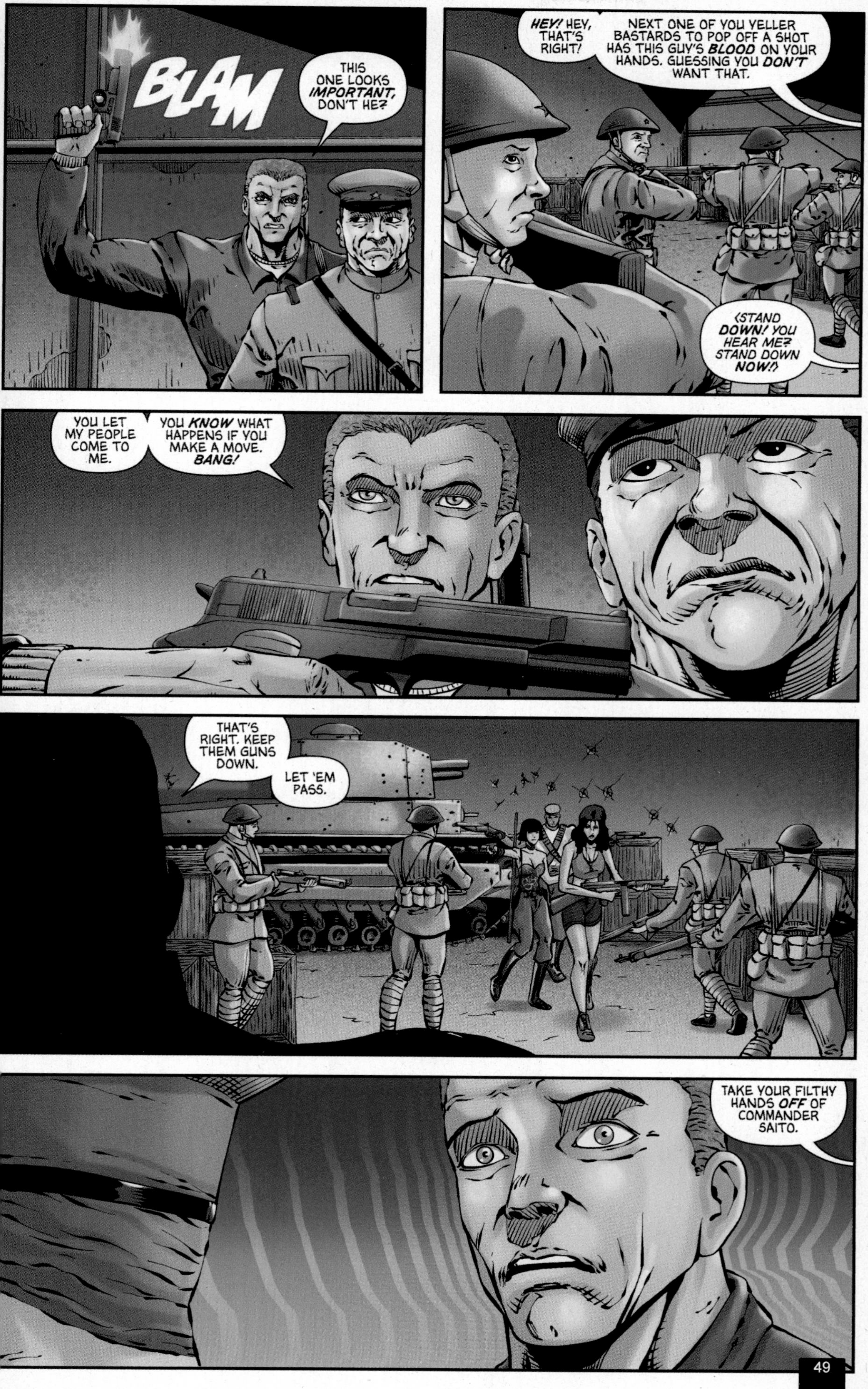
BLAM
THIS ONE LOOKS IMPORTANT, DON'T HE?
HEY! HEY, THAT'S RIGHT!
NEXT ONE OF YOU YELLER BASTARDS TO POP OFF A SHOT HAS THIS GUY'S BLOOD ON YOUR HANDS. GUESSING YOU DON'T WANT THAT.
‹STAND DOWN! YOU HEAR ME? STAND DOWN NOW!›
YOU LET MY PEOPLE COME TO ME.
YOU KNOW WHAT HAPPENS IF YOU MAKE A MOVE. BANG!
THAT'S RIGHT. KEEP THEM GUNS DOWN.
LET 'EM PASS.
TAKE YOUR FILTHY HANDS OFF OF COMMANDER SAITO.

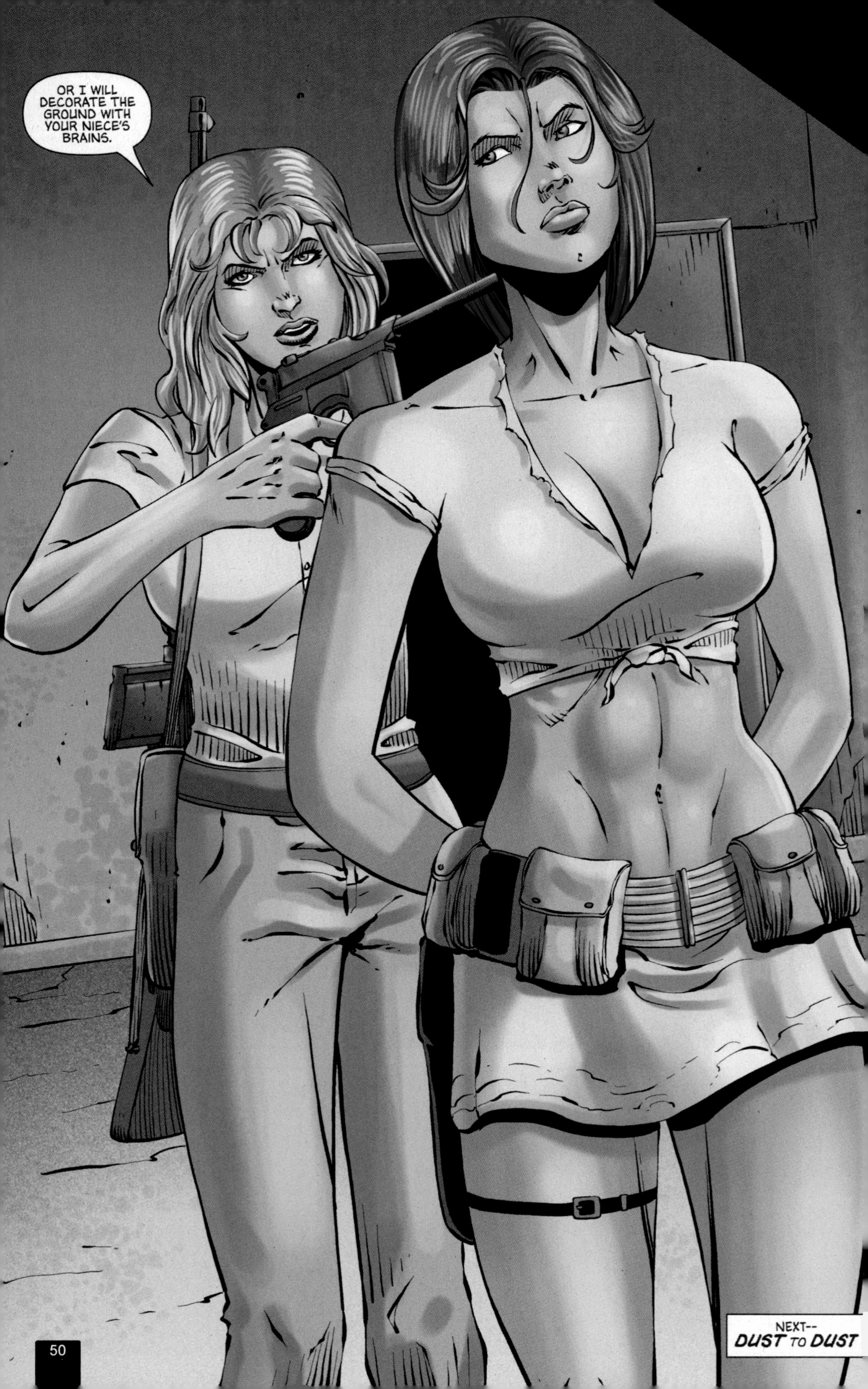
OR I WILL DECORATE THE GROUND WITH YOUR NIECE'S BRAINS.
NEXT-- DUST TO DUST

B.A.R. Maid

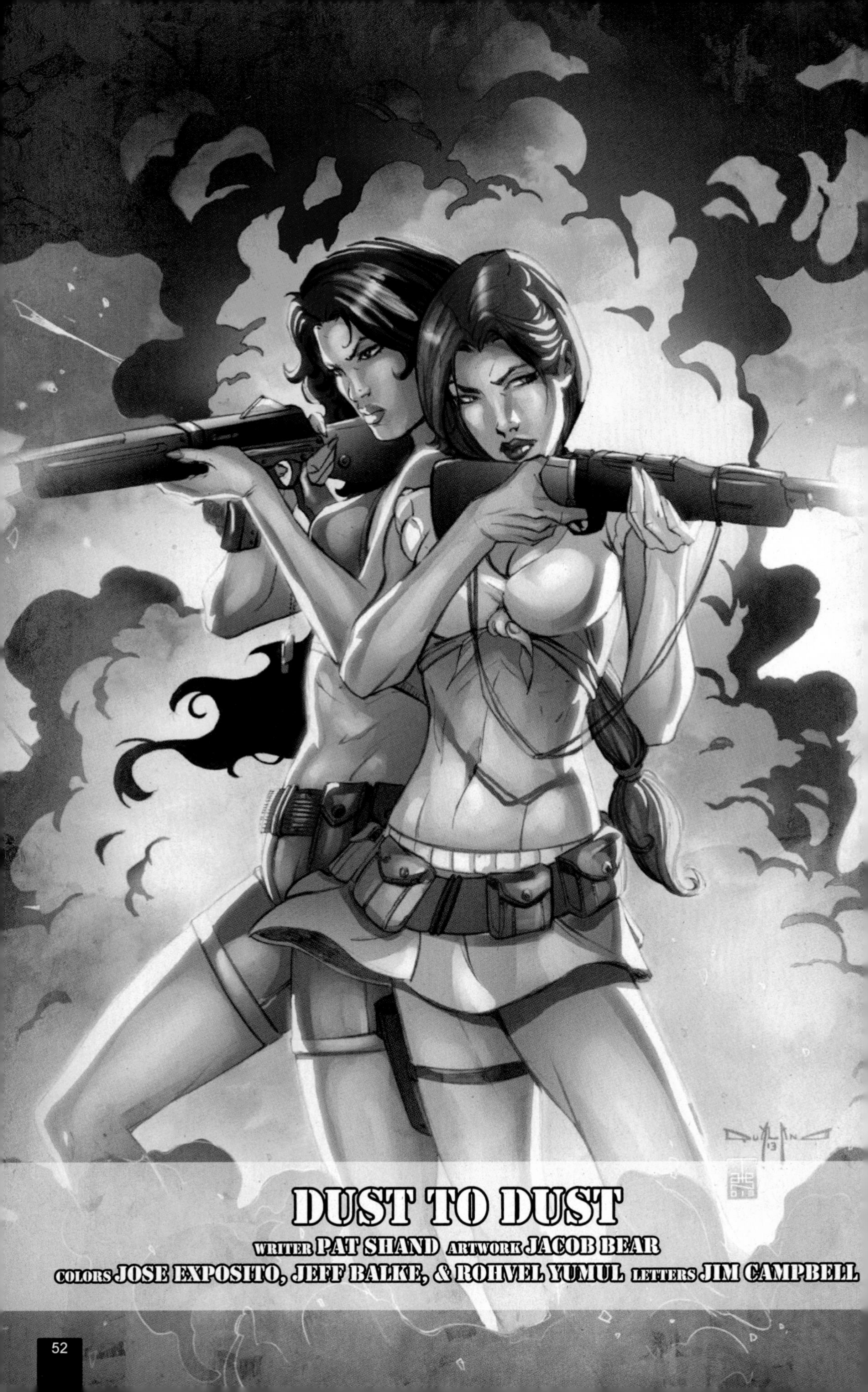

DUST TO DUST

WRITER PAT SHAND ARTWORK JACOB BEAR
COLORS JOSE EXPOSITO, JEFF BALKE, & ROHVEL YUMUL LETTERS JIM CAMPBELL

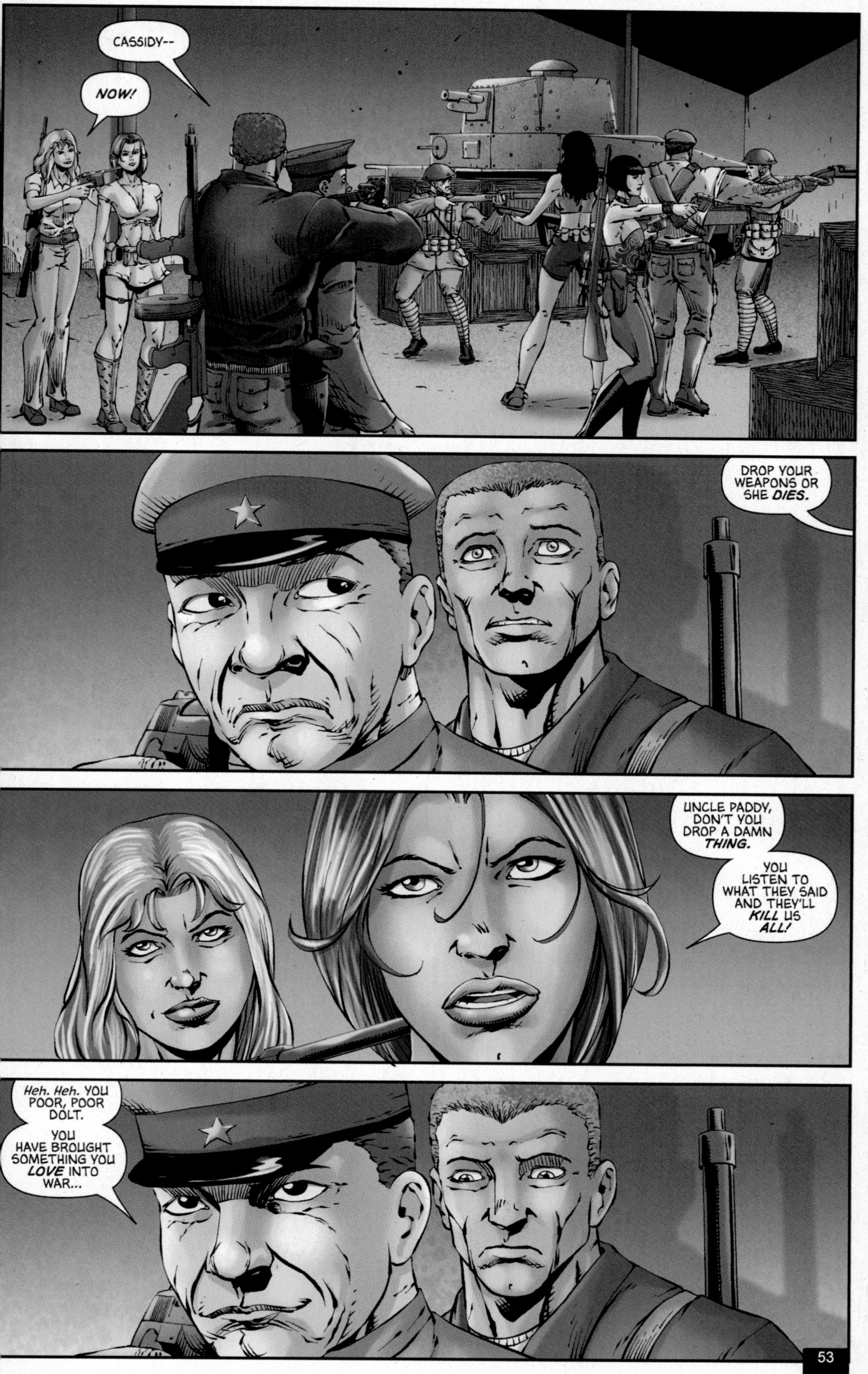
CASSIDY--
NOW!
DROP YOUR WEAPONS OR SHE DIES.
UNCLE PADDY, DON'T YOU DROP A DAMN THING.
YOU LISTEN TO WHAT THEY SAID AND THEY'LL KILL US ALL!
Heh. Heh. YOU POOR, POOR DOLT.
YOU HAVE BROUGHT SOMETHING YOU LOVE INTO WAR...

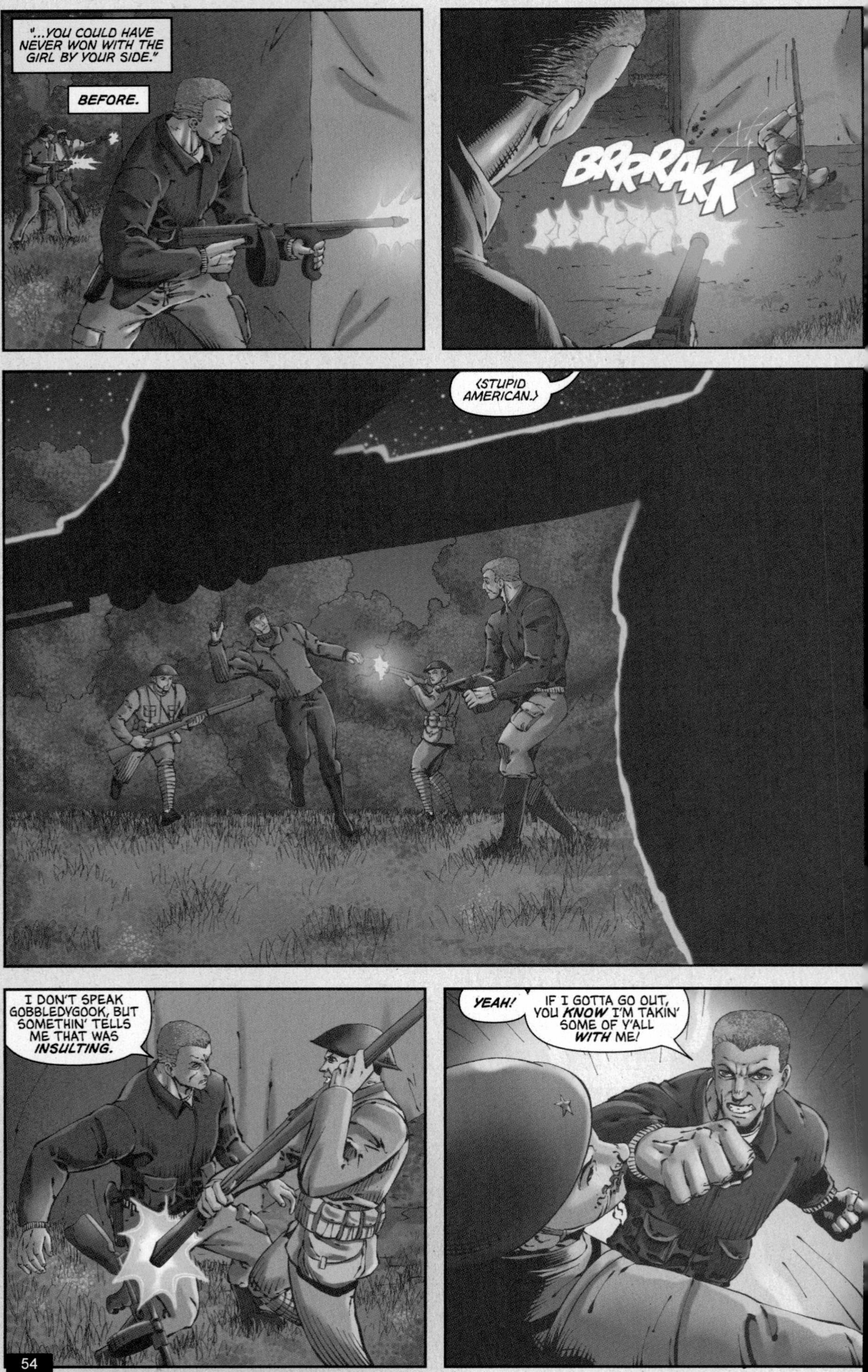
"...YOU COULD HAVE NEVER WON WITH THE GIRL BY YOUR SIDE."
BEFORE.
BRRRAKK
‹STUPID AMERICAN.›
I DON'T SPEAK GOBBLEDYGOOK, BUT SOMETHIN' TELLS ME THAT WAS *INSULTING.*
YEAH!
IF I GOTTA GO OUT, YOU *KNOW* I'M TAKIN' SOME OF Y'ALL *WITH* ME!

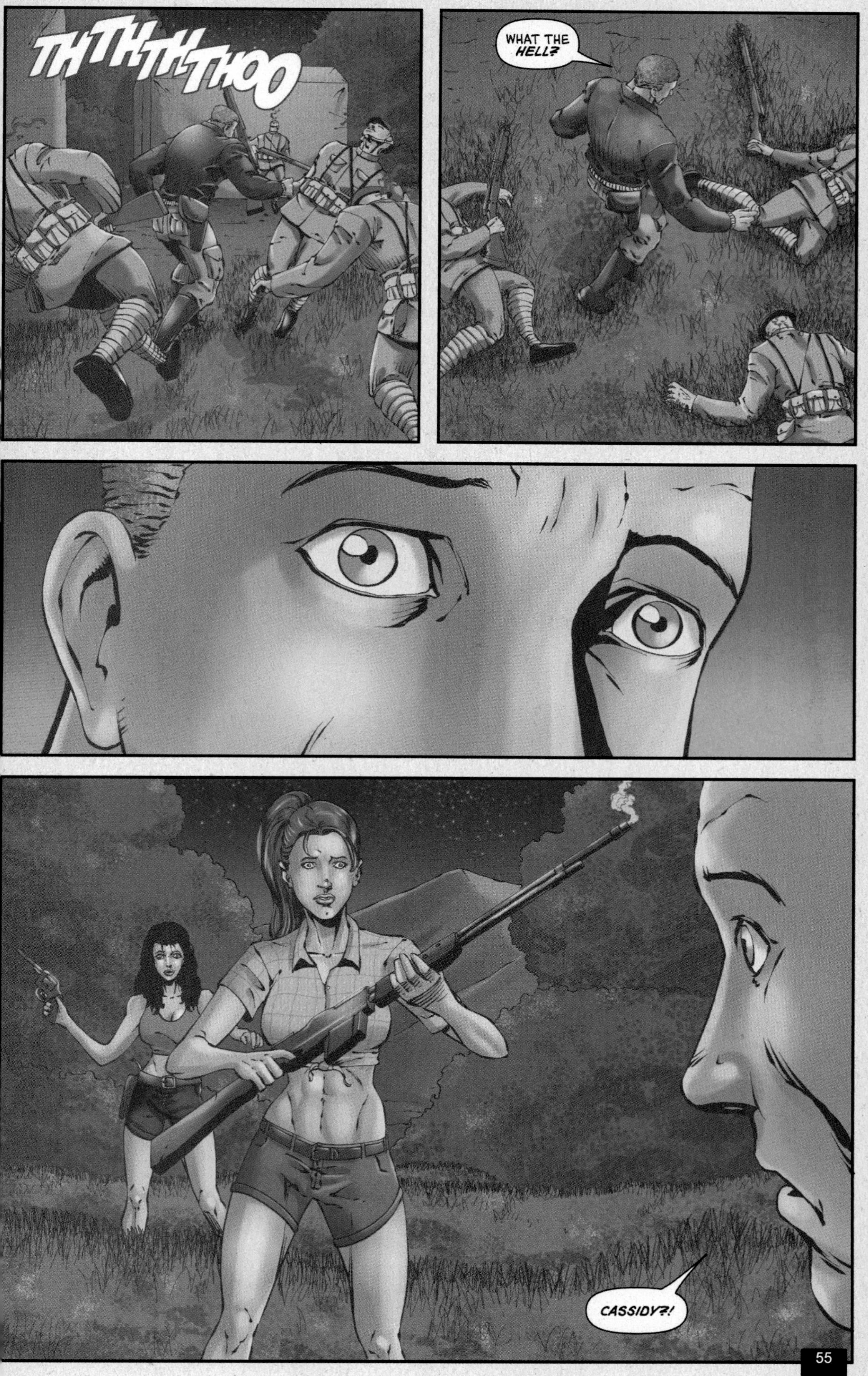
THTHTHTHOO
WHAT THE HELL?
CASSIDY?!

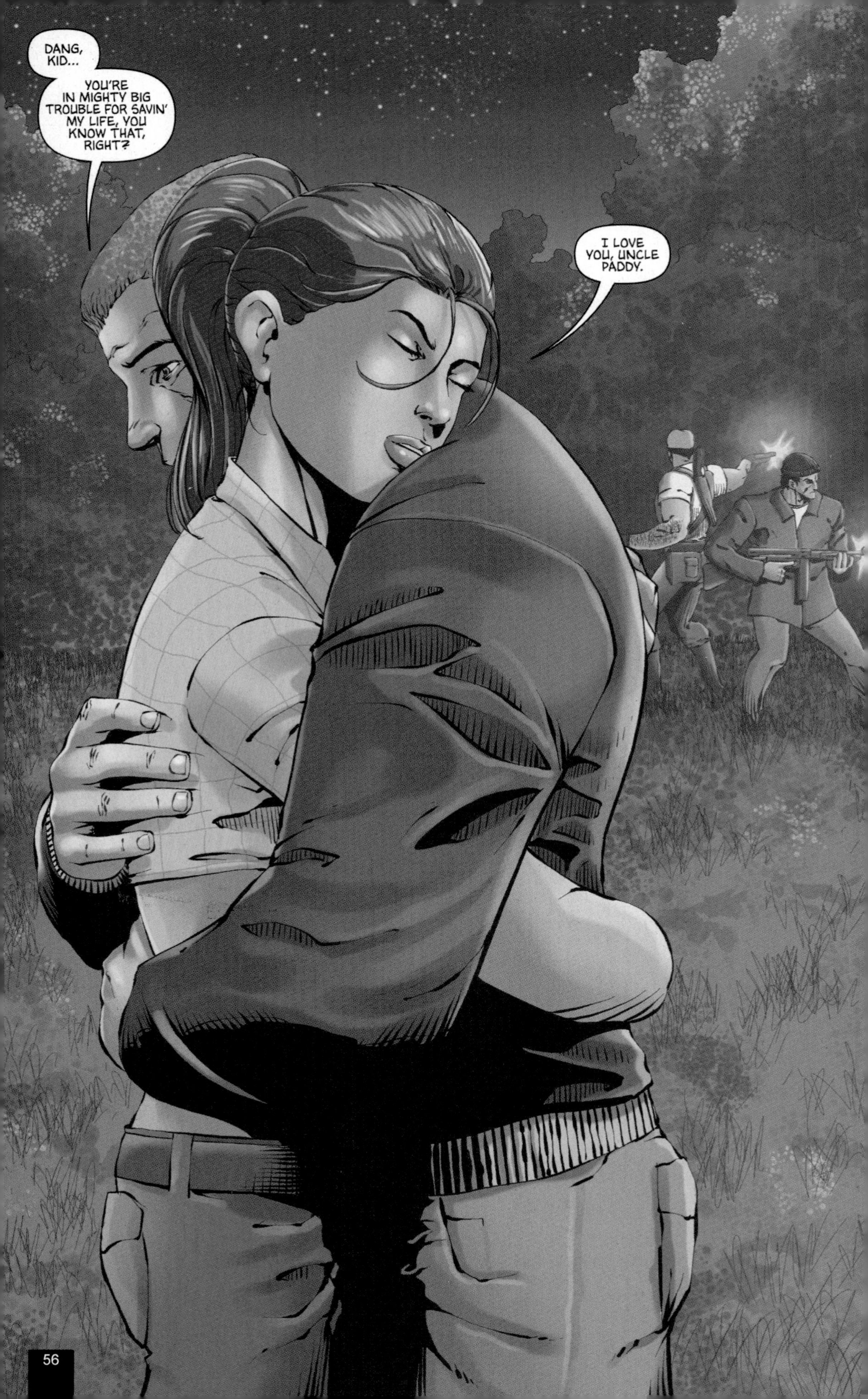
DANG, KID...
YOU'RE IN MIGHTY BIG TROUBLE FOR SAVIN' MY LIFE, YOU KNOW THAT, RIGHT?
I LOVE YOU, UNCLE PADDY.

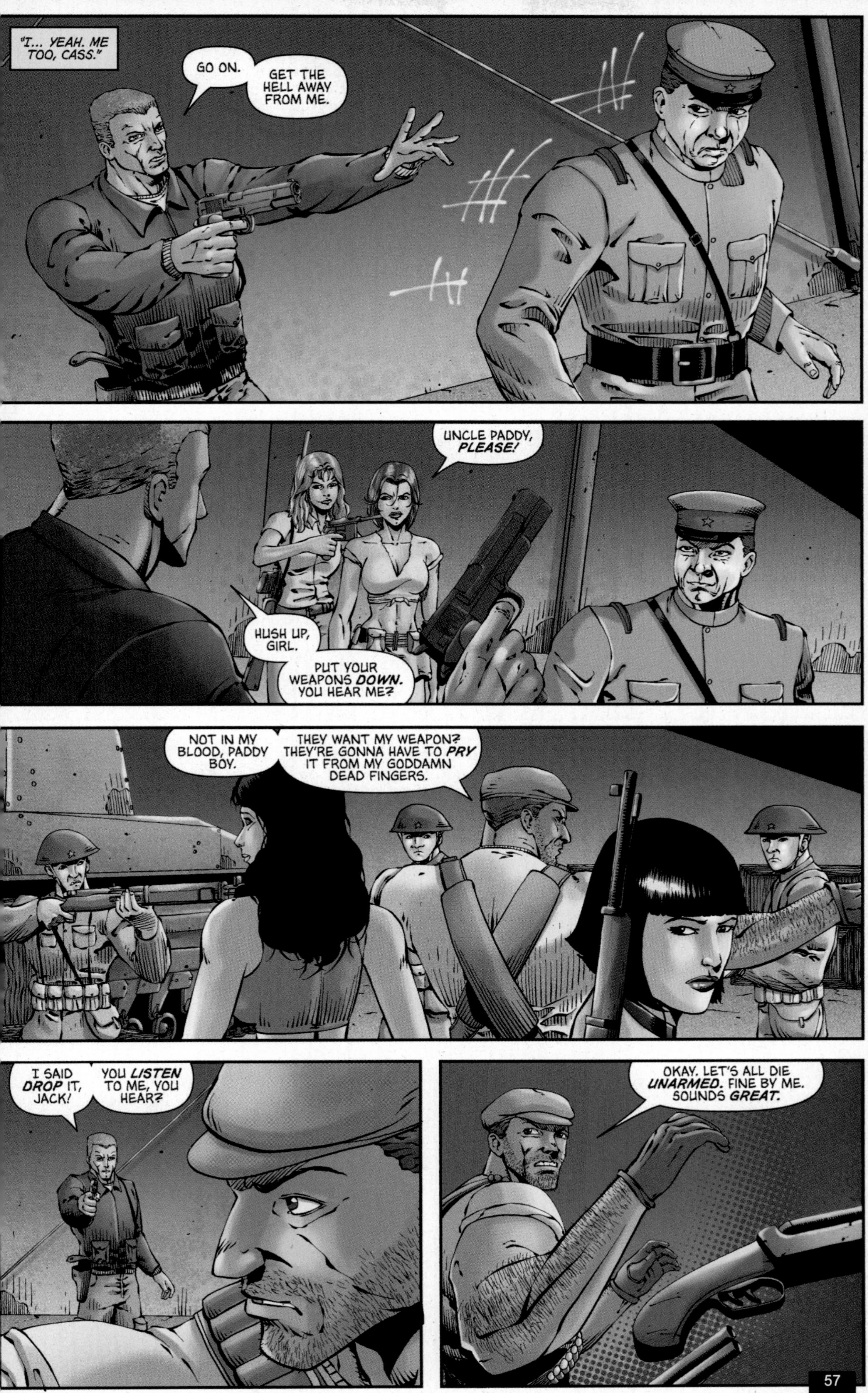
"I... YEAH. ME TOO, CASS."
GO ON.
GET THE HELL AWAY FROM ME.
UNCLE PADDY, *PLEASE!*
HUSH UP, GIRL.
PUT YOUR WEAPONS *DOWN.* YOU HEAR ME?
NOT IN MY BLOOD, PADDY BOY.
THEY WANT MY WEAPON? THEY'RE GONNA HAVE TO *PRY* IT FROM MY GODDAMN DEAD FINGERS.
I SAID *DROP* IT, JACK!
YOU *LISTEN* TO ME, YOU HEAR?
OKAY. LET'S ALL DIE *UNARMED.* FINE BY ME. SOUNDS *GREAT.*

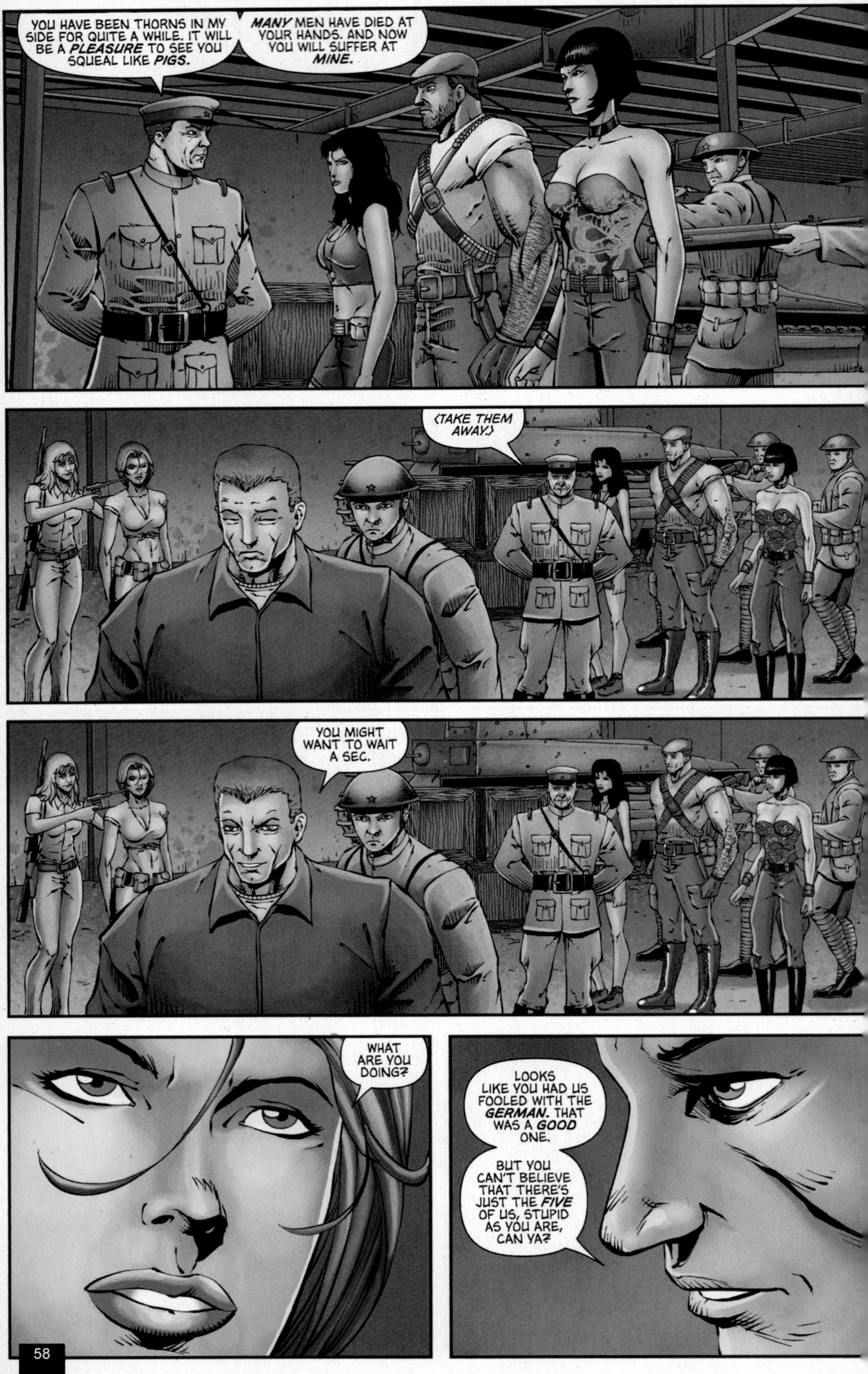
YOU HAVE BEEN THORNS IN MY SIDE FOR QUITE A WHILE. IT WILL BE A *PLEASURE* TO SEE YOU SQUEAL LIKE *PIGS*.
MANY MEN HAVE DIED AT YOUR HANDS. AND NOW YOU WILL SUFFER AT *MINE*.
<*TAKE THEM AWAY.*>
YOU MIGHT WANT TO WAIT A SEC.
WHAT ARE YOU DOING?
LOOKS LIKE YOU HAD US FOOLED WITH THE *GERMAN*. THAT WAS A *GOOD* ONE.
BUT YOU CAN'T BELIEVE THAT THERE'S JUST THE *FIVE* OF US, STUPID AS YOU ARE, CAN YA?

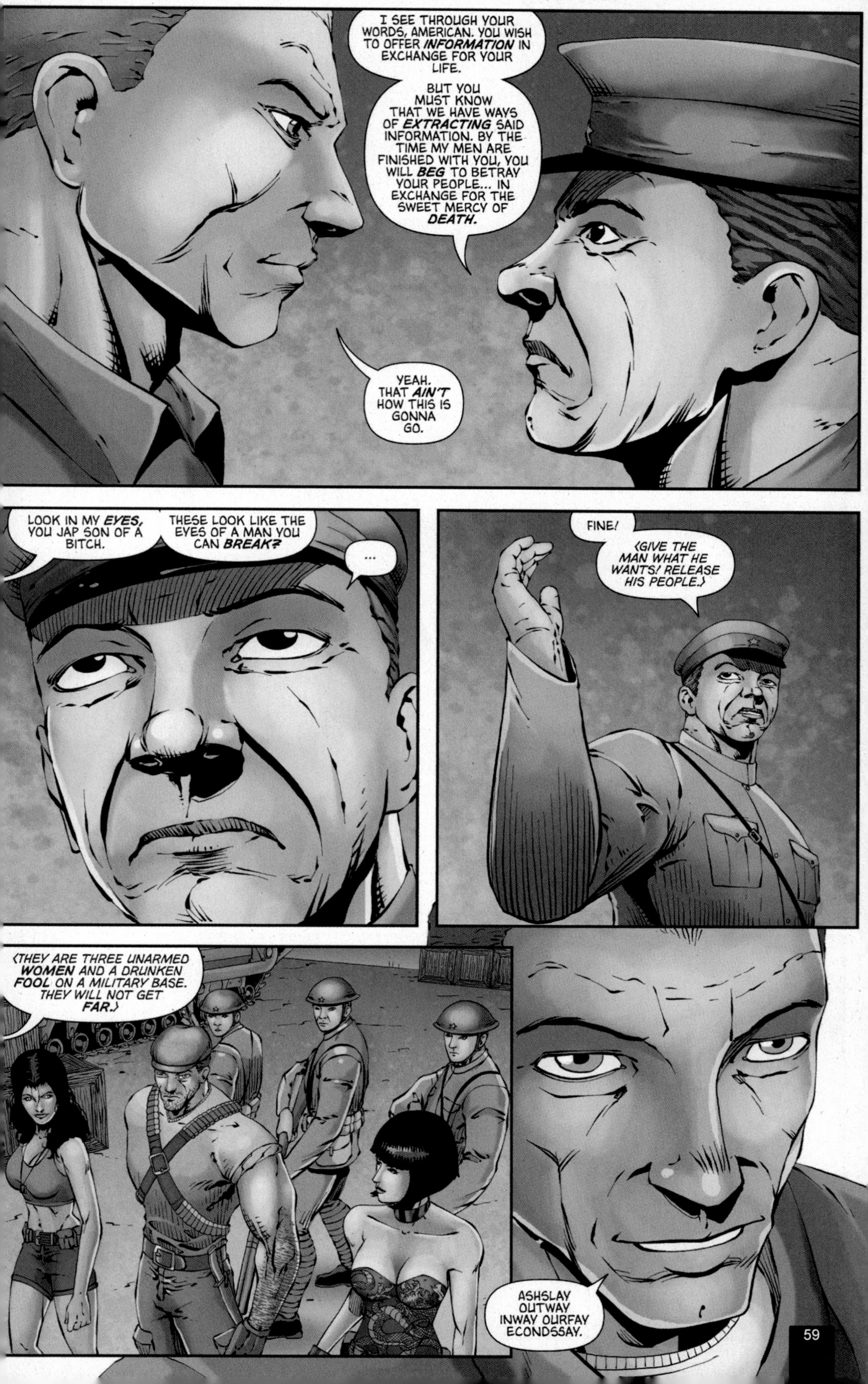
I SEE THROUGH YOUR WORDS, AMERICAN. YOU WISH TO OFFER INFORMATION IN EXCHANGE FOR YOUR LIFE.
BUT YOU MUST KNOW THAT WE HAVE WAYS OF EXTRACTING SAID INFORMATION. BY THE TIME MY MEN ARE FINISHED WITH YOU, YOU WILL BEG TO BETRAY YOUR PEOPLE... IN EXCHANGE FOR THE SWEET MERCY OF DEATH.
YEAH. THAT AIN'T HOW THIS IS GONNA GO.
LOOK IN MY EYES, YOU JAP SON OF A BITCH.
THESE LOOK LIKE THE EYES OF A MAN YOU CAN BREAK?
...
FINE!
‹GIVE THE MAN WHAT HE WANTS! RELEASE HIS PEOPLE.›
‹THEY ARE THREE UNARMED WOMEN AND A DRUNKEN FOOL ON A MILITARY BASE. THEY WILL NOT GET FAR.›
ASHSLAY OUTWAY INWAY OURFAY ECONDSSAY.

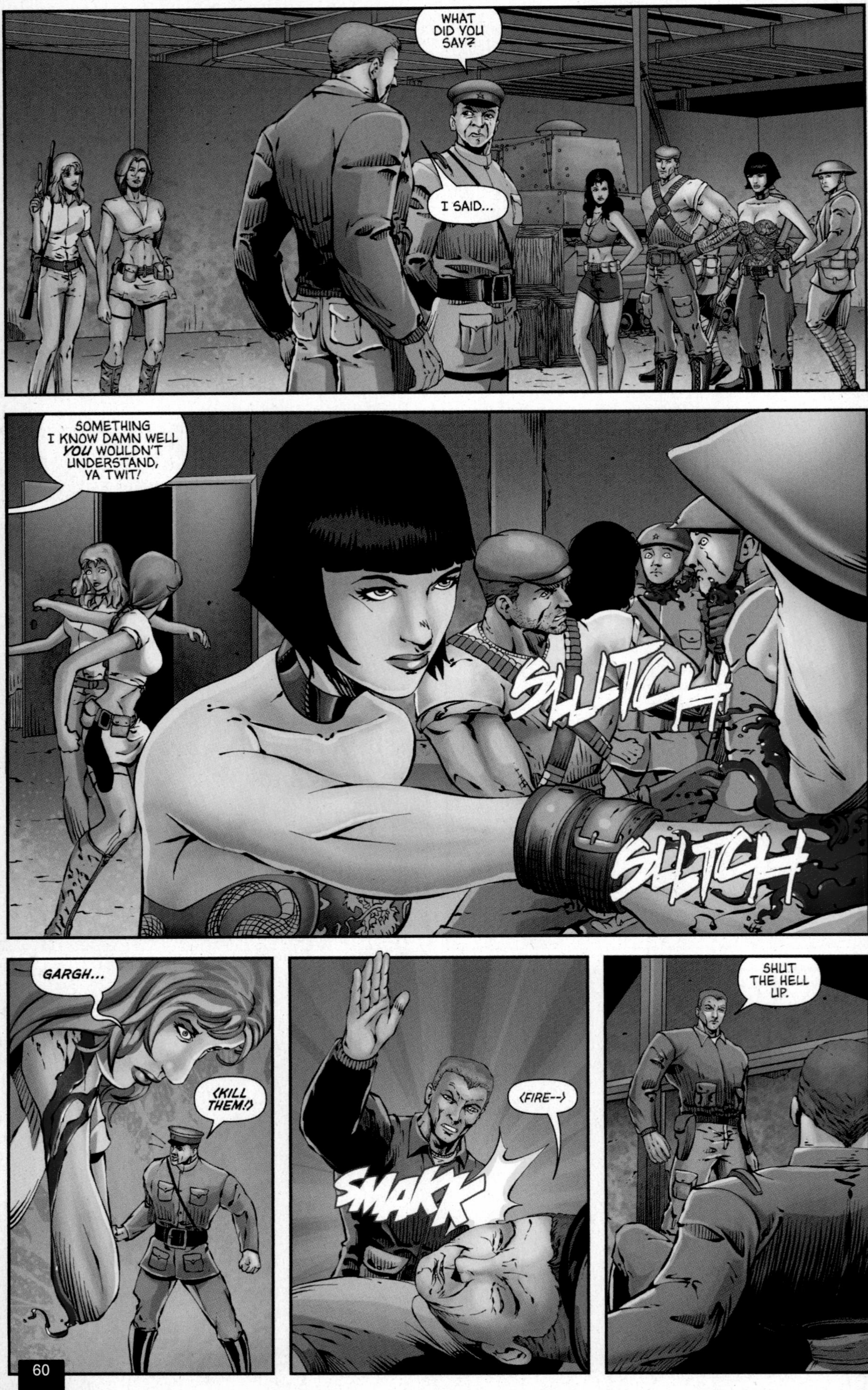
WHAT DID YOU SAY?
I SAID...
SOMETHING I KNOW DAMN WELL YOU WOULDN'T UNDERSTAND, YA TWIT!
SLLTCH
SLLTCH
GARGH...
‹KILL THEM!›
‹FIRE--›
SMAKK
SHUT THE HELL UP.

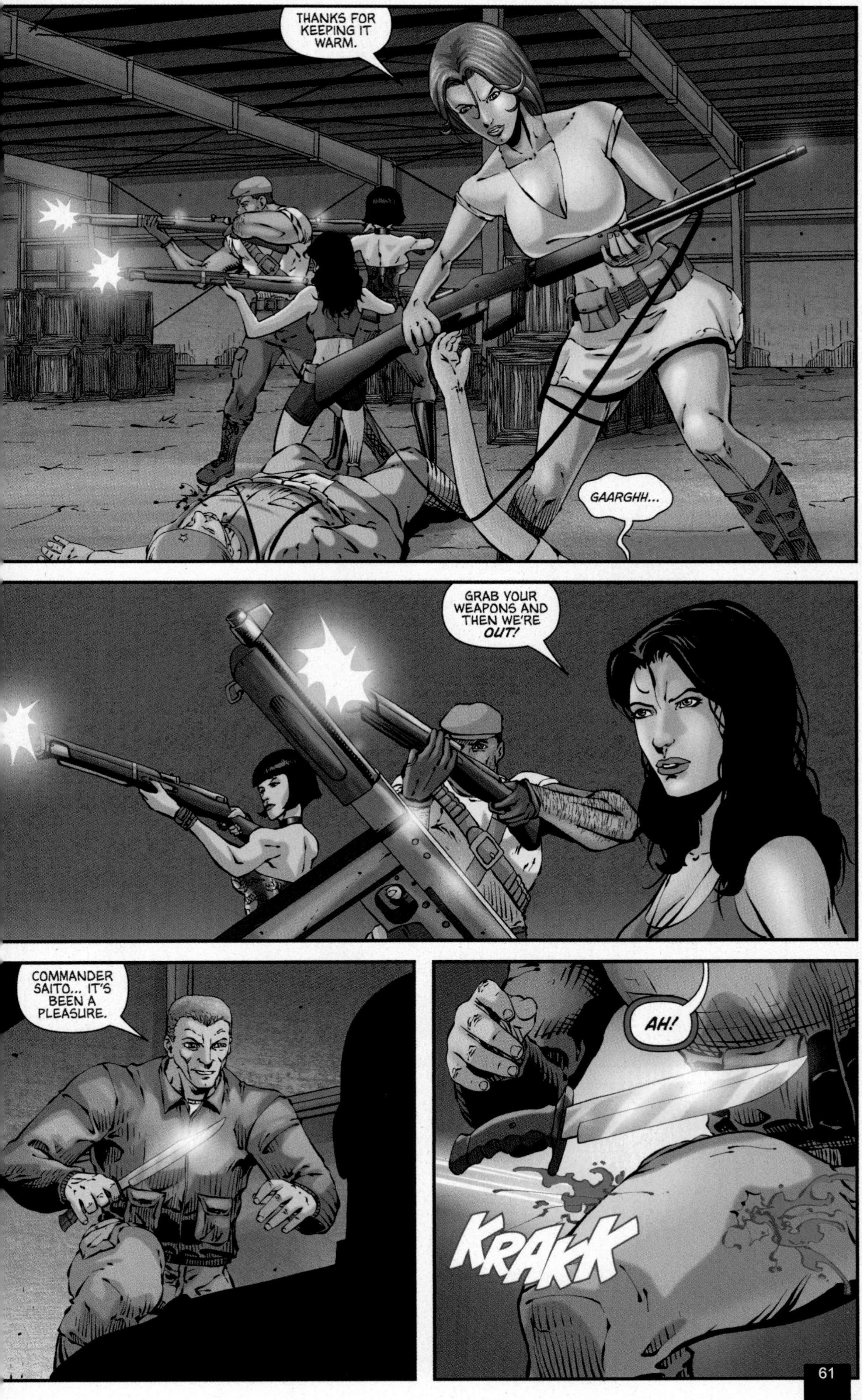
THANKS FOR KEEPING IT WARM.
GAARGHH...
GRAB YOUR WEAPONS AND THEN WE'RE OUT!
COMMANDER SAITO... IT'S BEEN A PLEASURE.
AH!
KRAKK

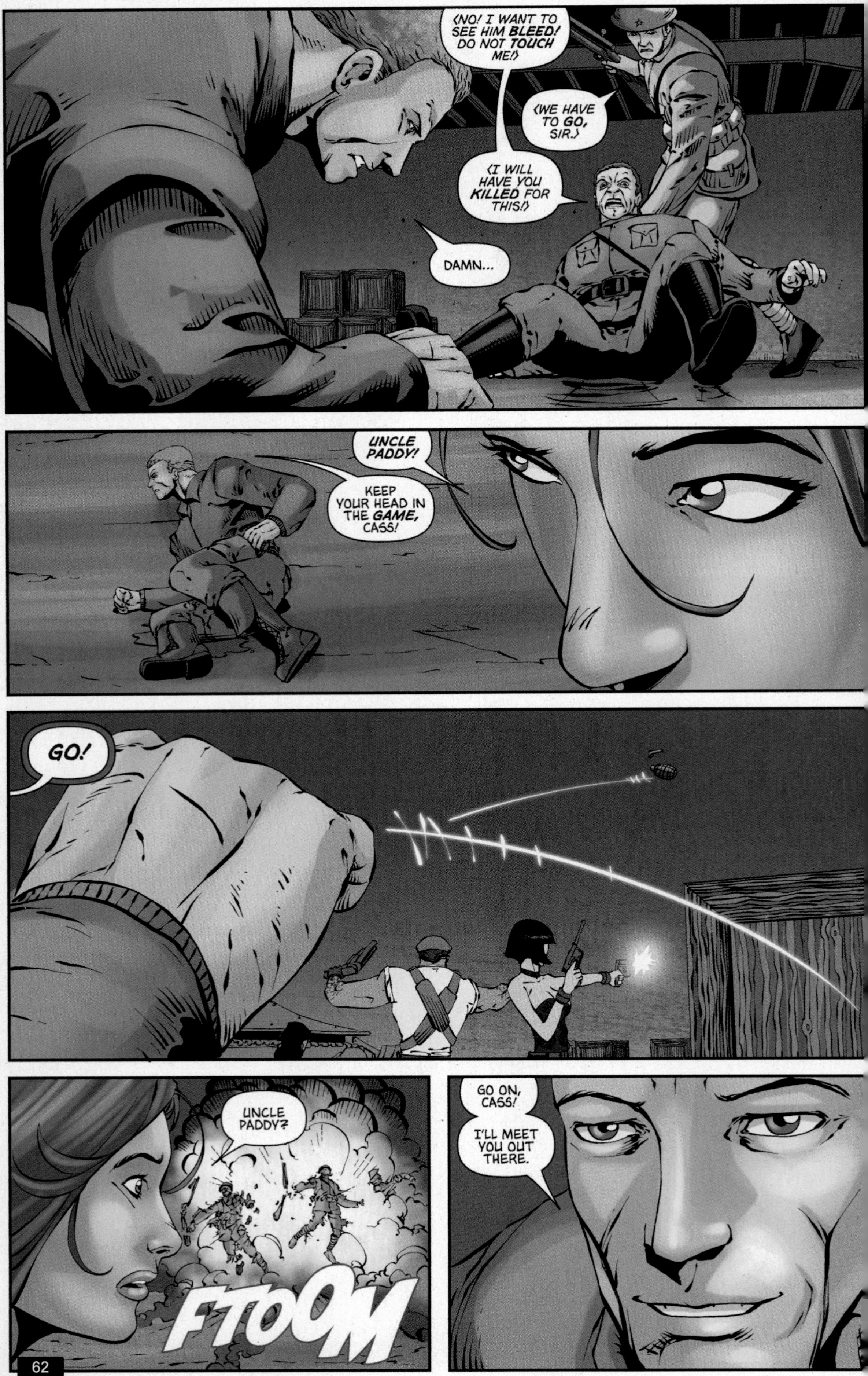

‹NO! I WANT TO SEE HIM BLEED! DO NOT TOUCH ME!›
‹WE HAVE TO GO, SIR.›
‹I WILL HAVE YOU KILLED FOR THIS!›
DAMN...
UNCLE PADDY!
KEEP YOUR HEAD IN THE GAME, CASS!
GO!
UNCLE PADDY?
FTOOM
GO ON, CASS!
I'LL MEET YOU OUT THERE.

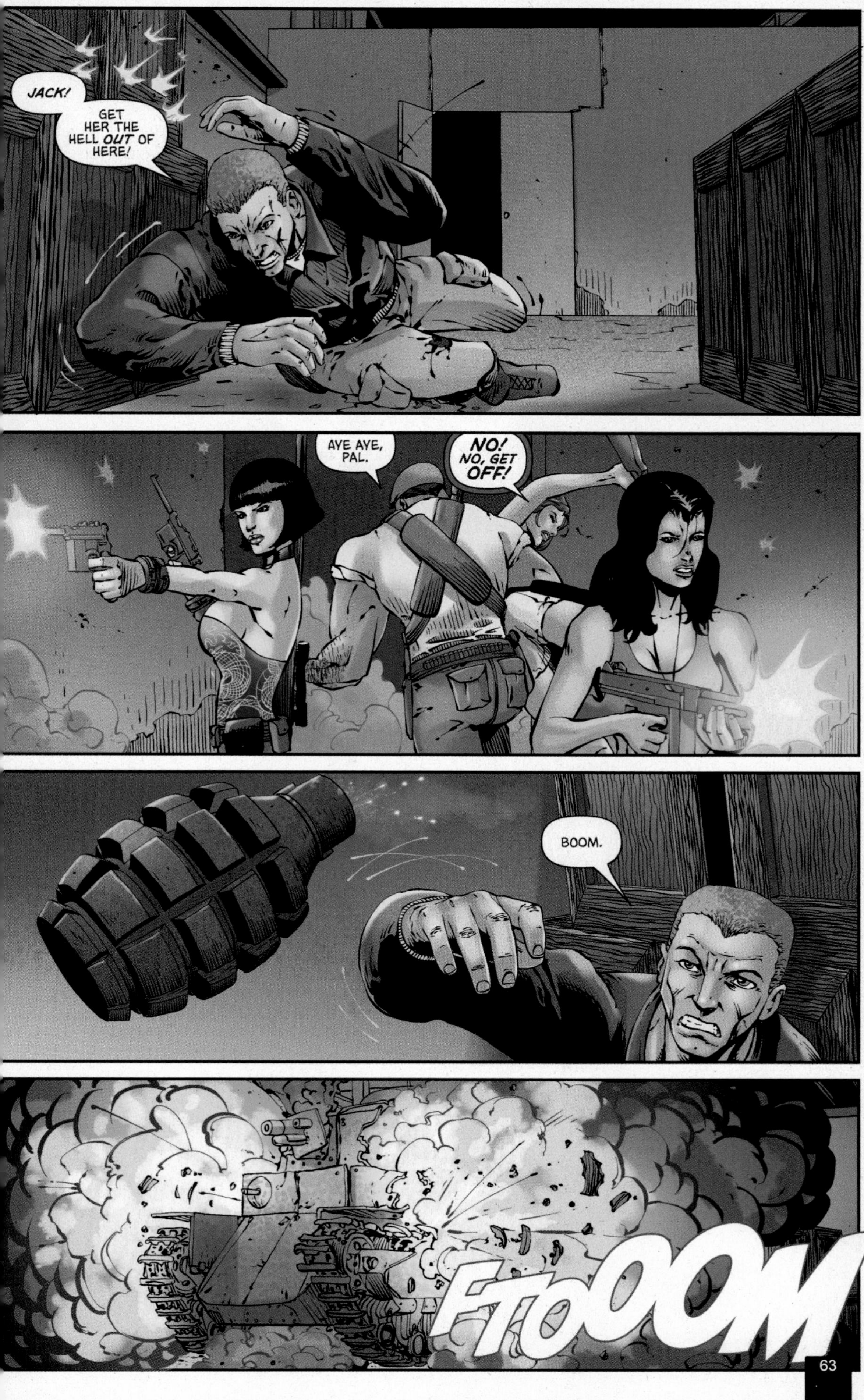
JACK!
GET HER THE HELL OUT OF HERE!
AYE AYE, PAL.
NO! NO, GET OFF!
BOOM.
FTOOOM

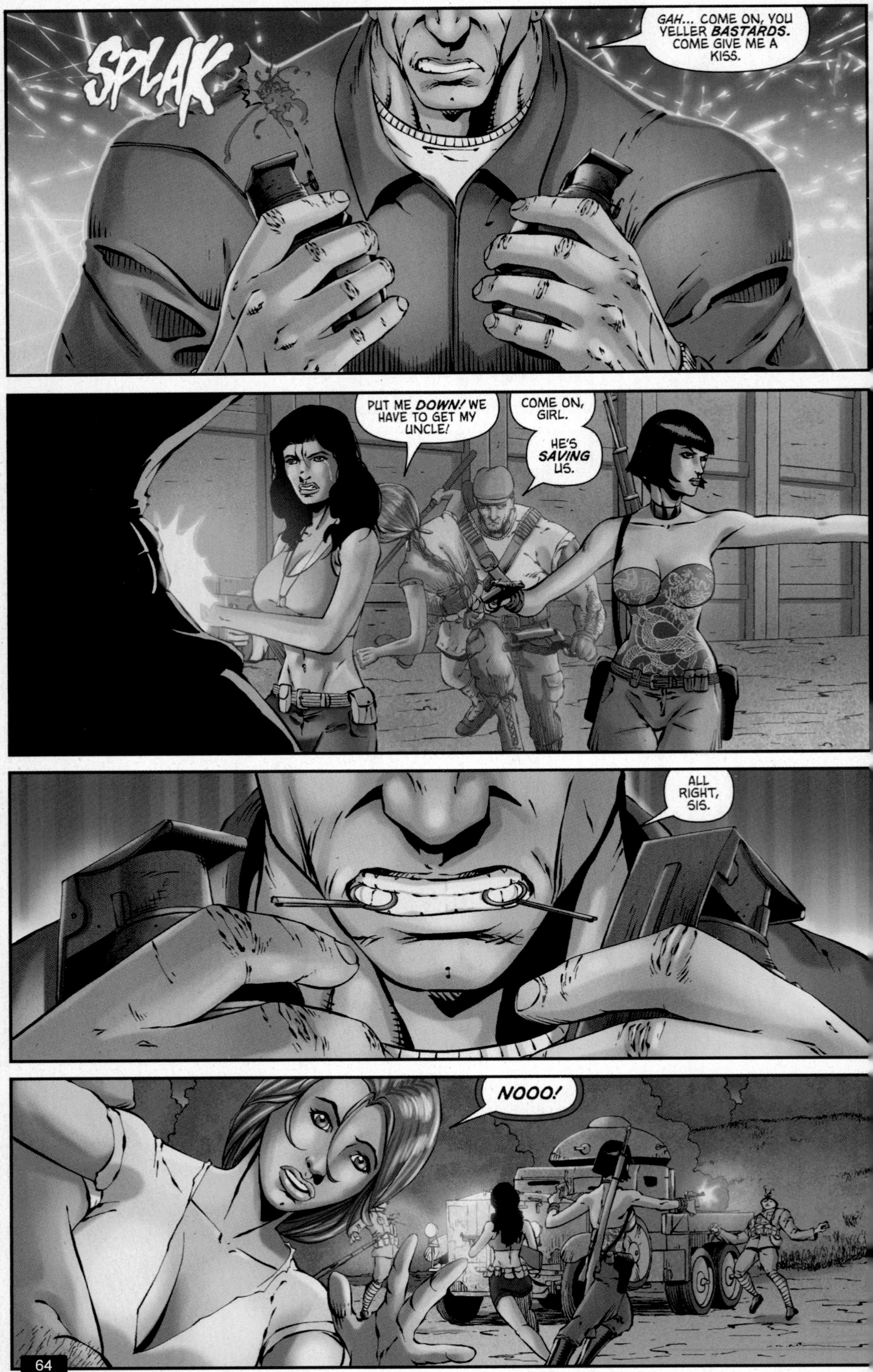
SPLAK
GAH... COME ON, YOU YELLER BASTARDS. COME GIVE ME A KISS.
PUT ME DOWN! WE HAVE TO GET MY UNCLE!
COME ON, GIRL.
HE'S SAVING US.
ALL RIGHT, SIS.
NOOO!

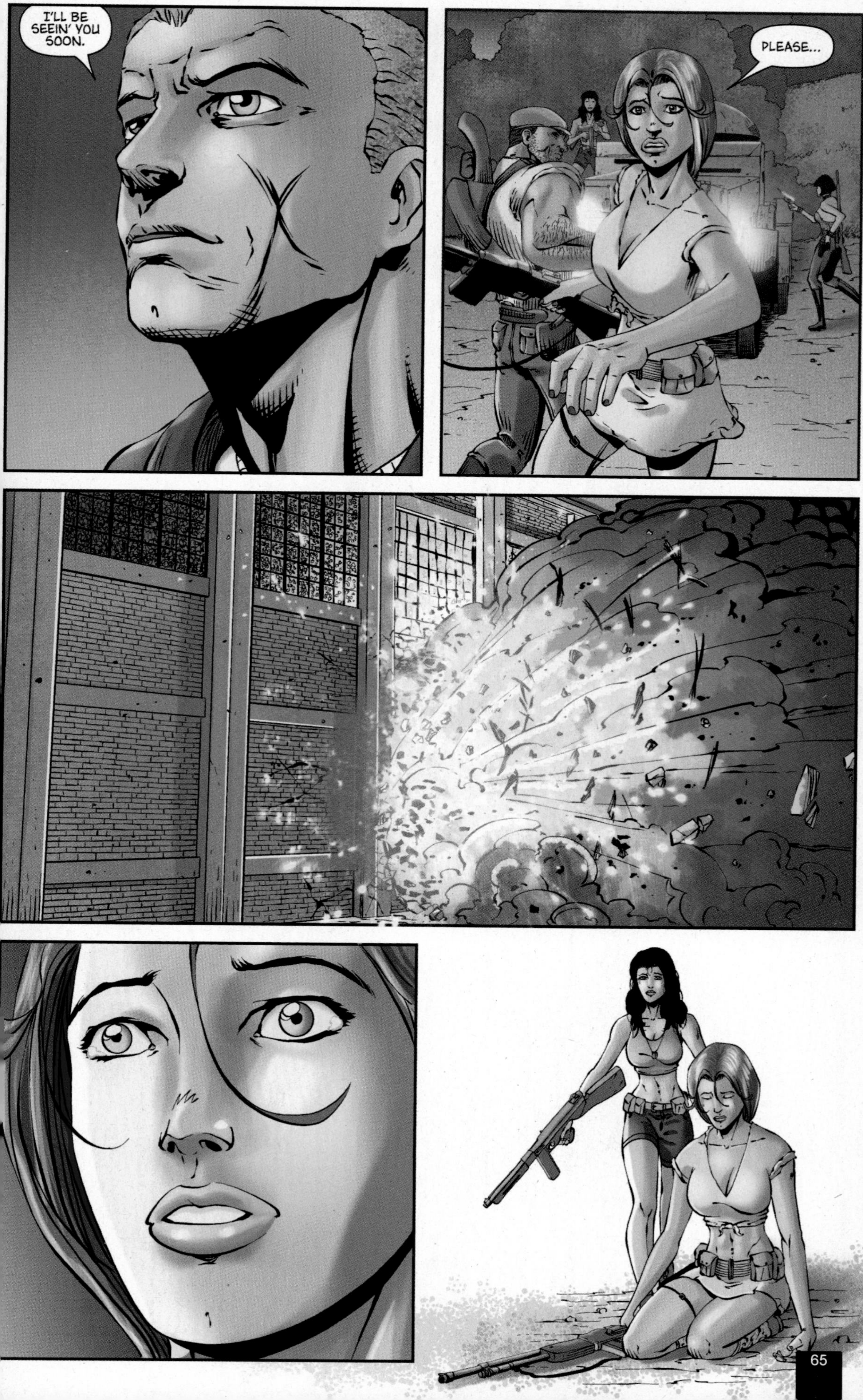
I'LL BE SEEIN' YOU SOON.
PLEASE...

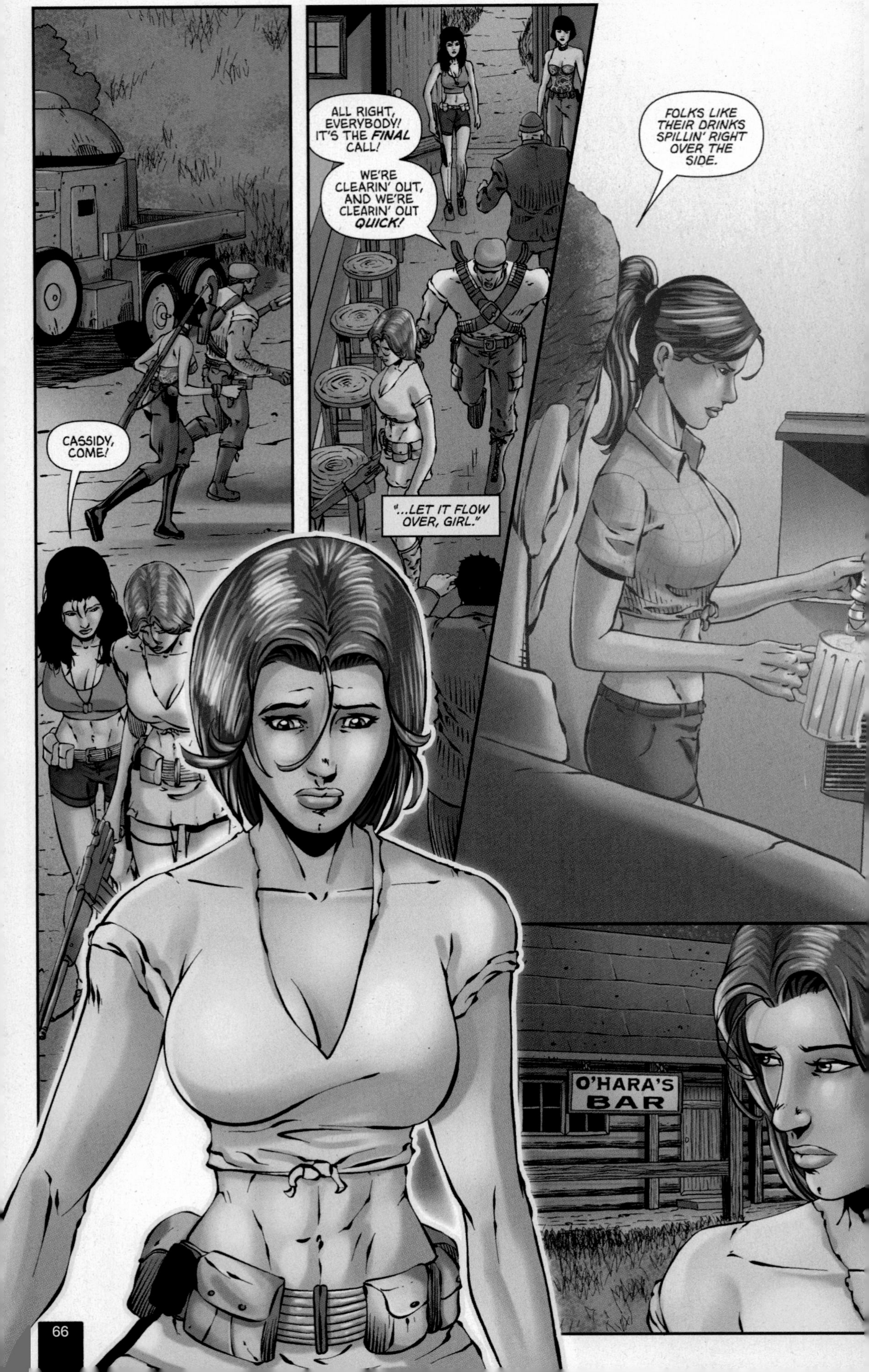
ALL RIGHT, EVERYBODY! IT'S THE FINAL CALL!
WE'RE CLEARIN' OUT, AND WE'RE CLEARIN' OUT QUICK!
FOLKS LIKE THEIR DRINKS SPILLIN' RIGHT OVER THE SIDE.
CASSIDY, COME!
"...LET IT FLOW OVER, GIRL."
O'HARA'S BAR

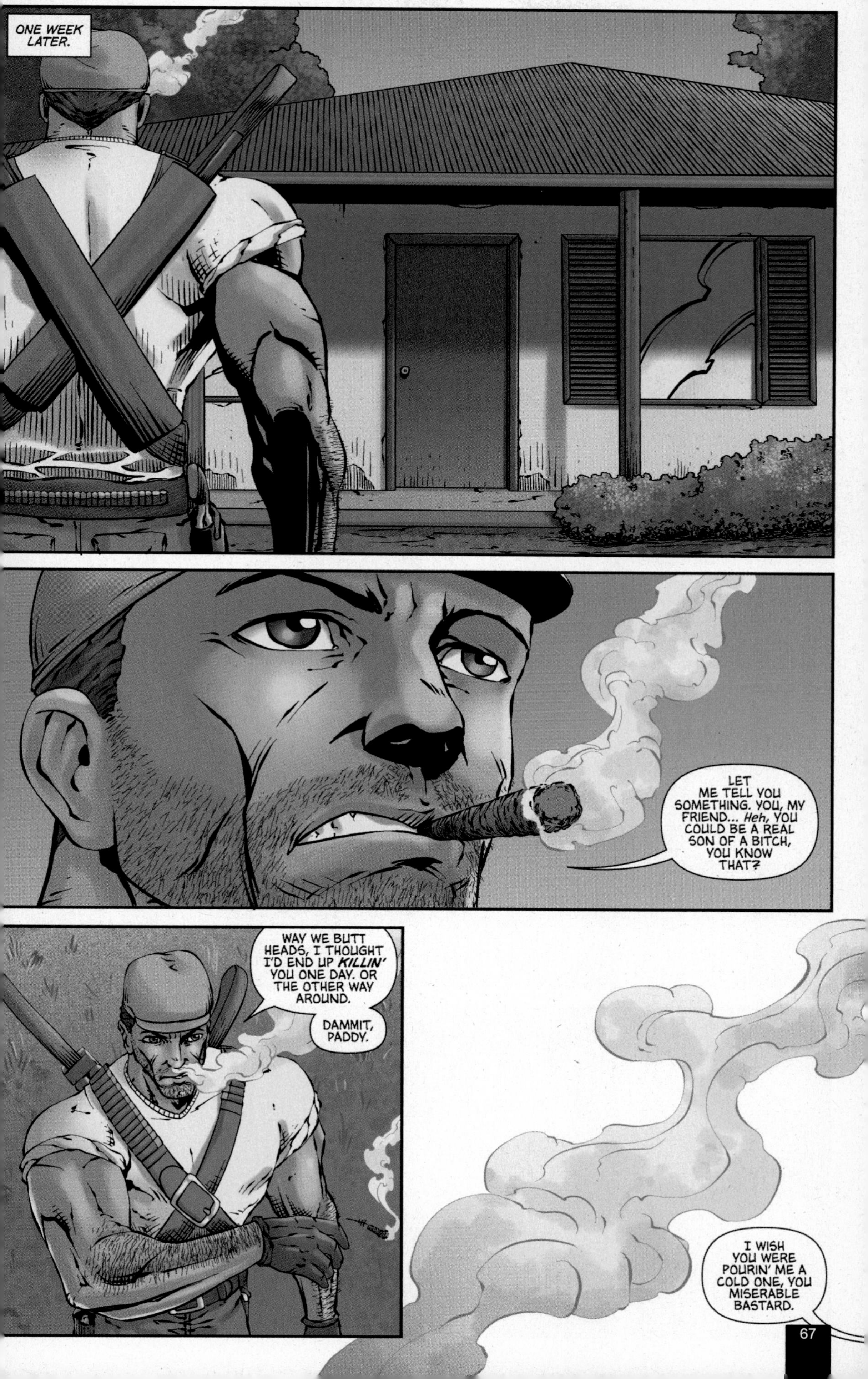
ONE WEEK LATER.
LET ME TELL YOU SOMETHING. YOU, MY FRIEND... *Heh,* YOU COULD BE A REAL SON OF A BITCH, YOU KNOW THAT?
WAY WE BUTT HEADS, I THOUGHT I'D END UP *KILLIN'* YOU ONE DAY. OR THE OTHER WAY AROUND.
DAMMIT, PADDY.
I WISH YOU WERE POURIN' ME A COLD ONE, YOU MISERABLE BASTARD.

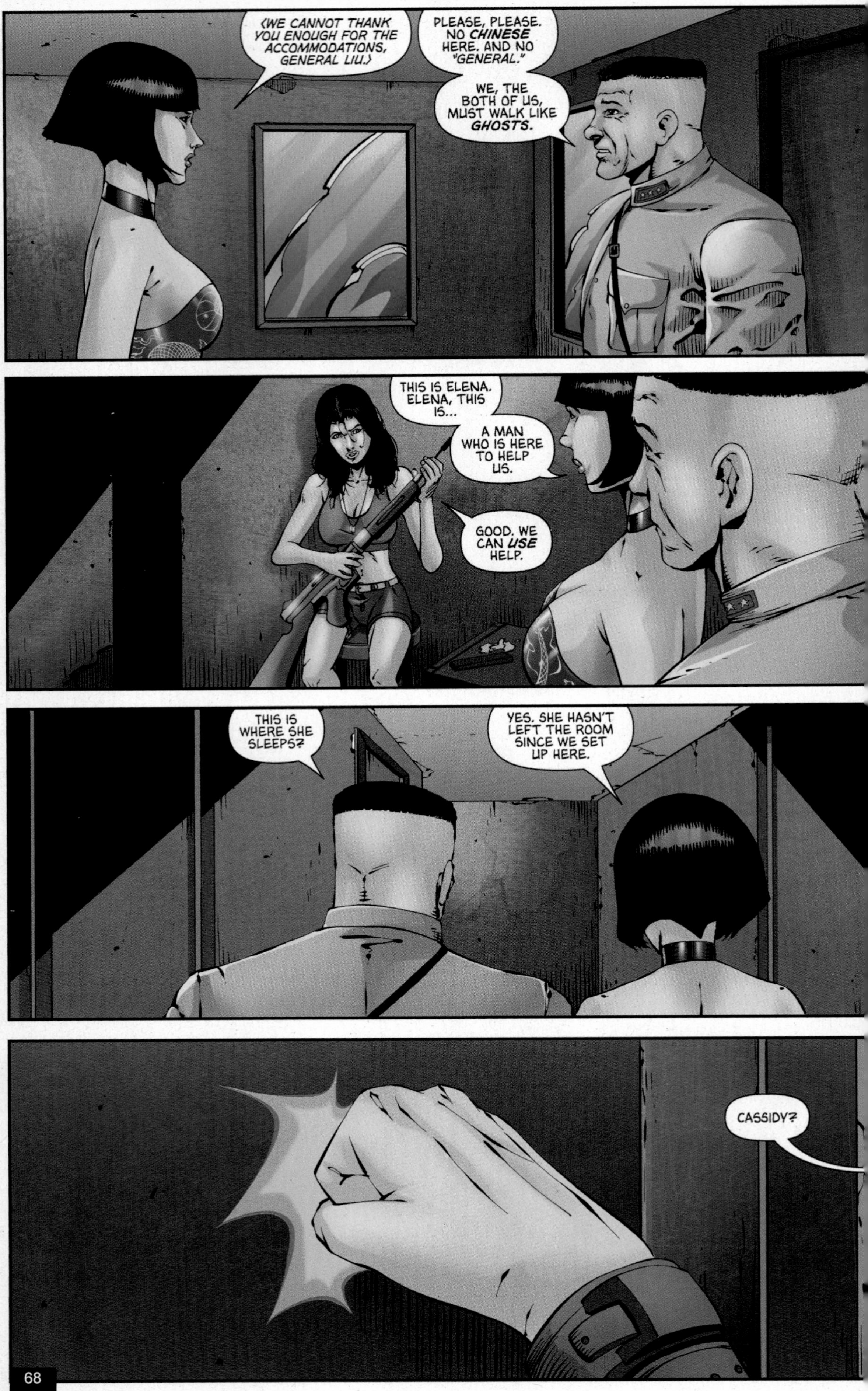
‹WE CANNOT THANK YOU ENOUGH FOR THE ACCOMMODATIONS, GENERAL LIU.›
PLEASE, PLEASE. NO CHINESE HERE. AND NO "GENERAL."
WE, THE BOTH OF US, MUST WALK LIKE GHOSTS.
THIS IS ELENA. ELENA, THIS IS...
A MAN WHO IS HERE TO HELP US.
GOOD. WE CAN USE HELP.
THIS IS WHERE SHE SLEEPS?
YES. SHE HASN'T LEFT THE ROOM SINCE WE SET UP HERE.
CASSIDY?

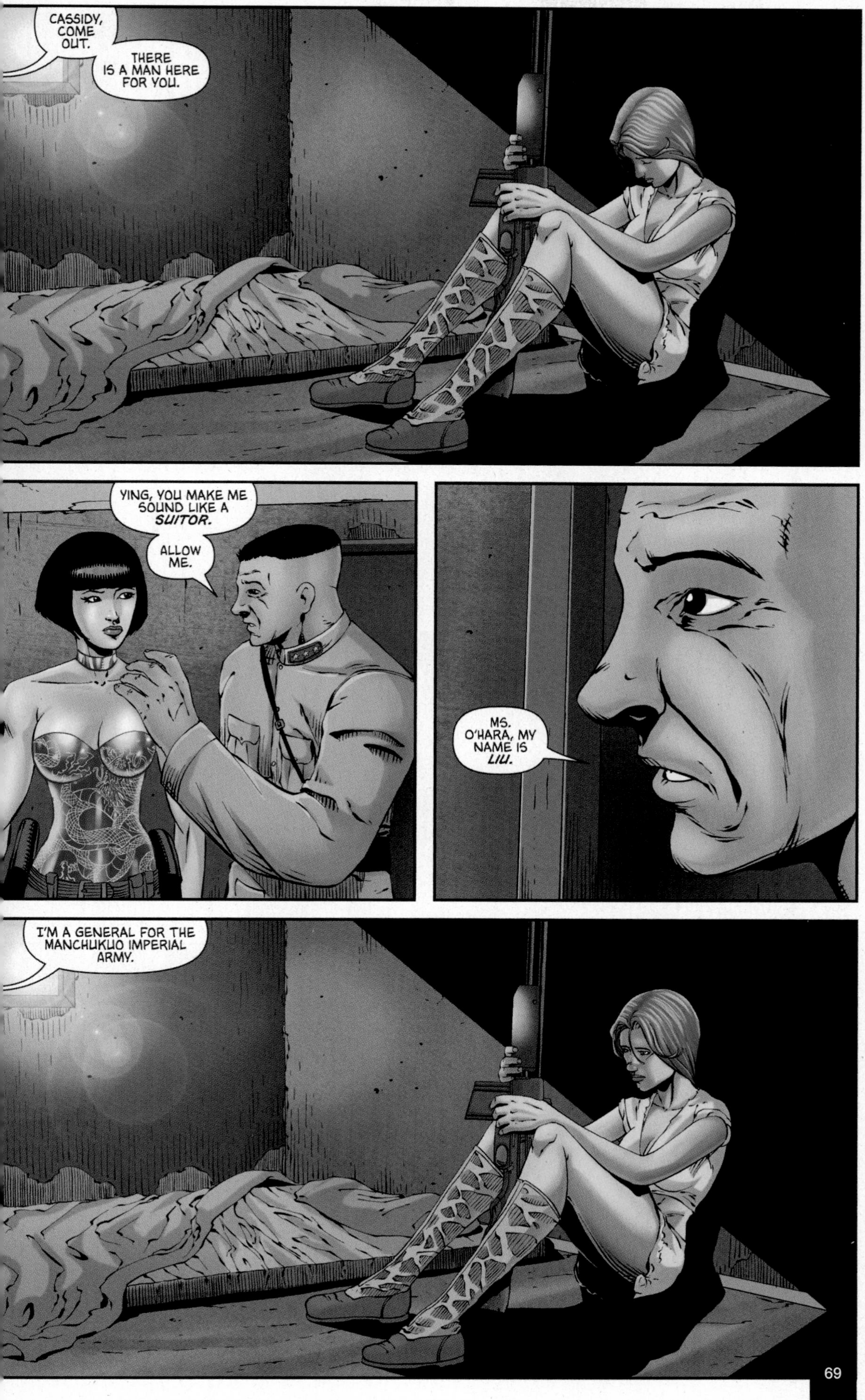
CASSIDY, COME OUT.
THERE IS A MAN HERE FOR YOU.
YING, YOU MAKE ME SOUND LIKE A SUITOR.
ALLOW ME.
MS. O'HARA, MY NAME IS LIU.
I'M A GENERAL FOR THE MANCHUKUO IMPERIAL ARMY.

DO NOT BE ALARMED. I HAVE BEEN *CLOSE* WITH *YING LEE* FOR SOME TIME.

SHE IS *FAMILY.*

I WANTED TO LET YOU KNOW... NOT *ALL* OF THE CHINESE ARE *COOPERATING* WITH THE JAPANESE INVADERS.

THERE ARE THOSE OUTWARDLY FIGHTING... AND THEN THERE ARE THOSE WHO ARE *INSIDE* THIS DARK MACHINE, OILING THE COGS... PREPARING TO *STRIKE* AT ITS WEAKEST POINT.

TAKE YOUR TIME TO *MOURN,* MS. O'HARA. WHEN YOU ARE *READY,* WE WILL HAVE WORDS.

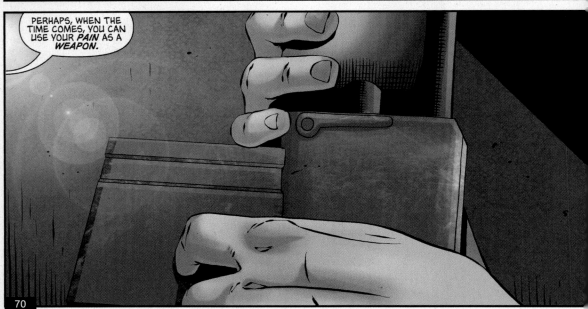

PERHAPS, WHEN THE TIME COMES, YOU CAN USE YOUR *PAIN* AS A *WEAPON.*

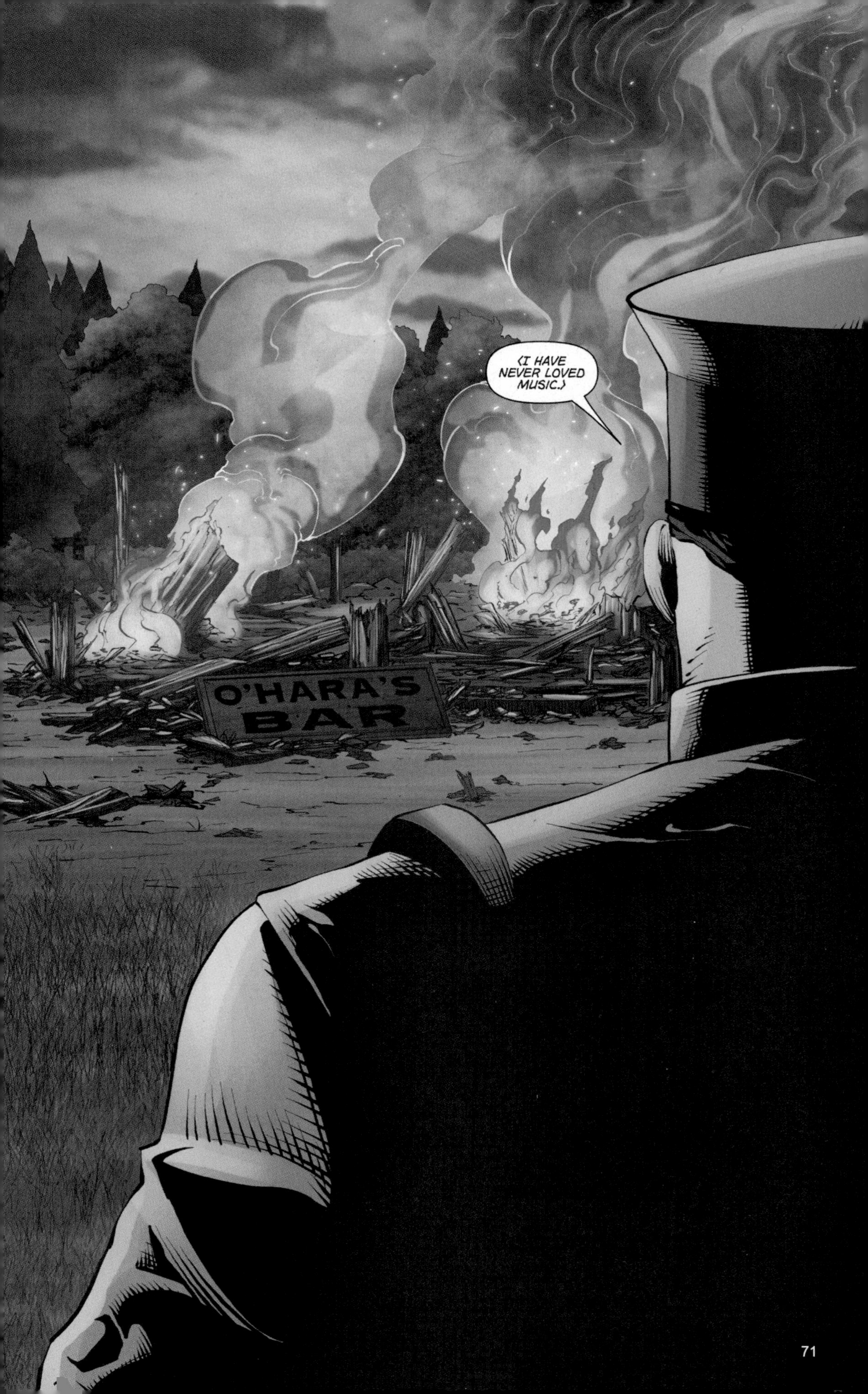

‹I HAVE NEVER LOVED MUSIC.›
O'HARA'S BAR

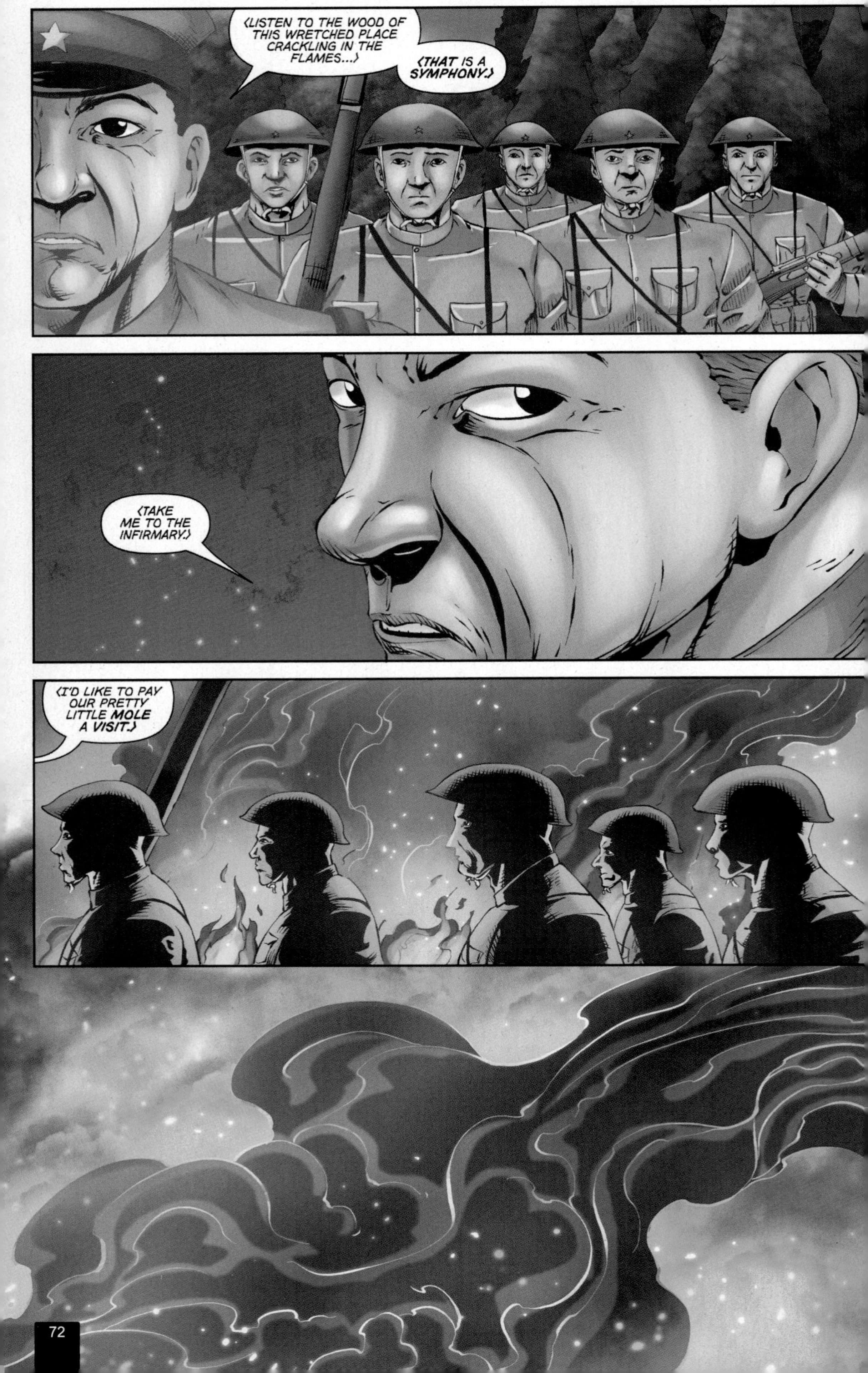
‹LISTEN TO THE WOOD OF THIS WRETCHED PLACE CRACKLING IN THE FLAMES...›
‹THAT IS A SYMPHONY.›
‹TAKE ME TO THE INFIRMARY.›
‹I'D LIKE TO PAY OUR PRETTY LITTLE MOLE A VISIT.›

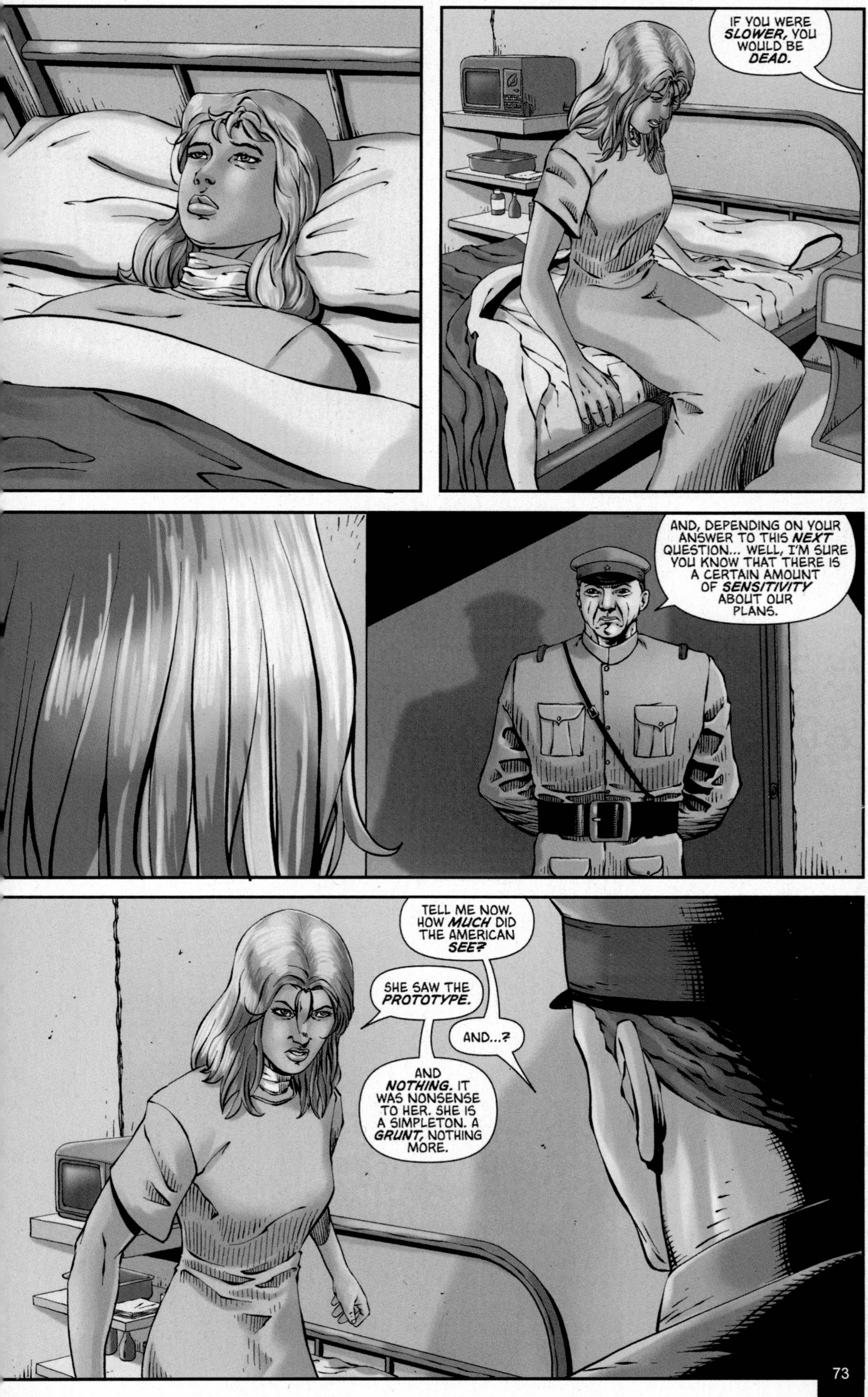
IF YOU WERE SLOWER, YOU WOULD BE DEAD.
AND, DEPENDING ON YOUR ANSWER TO THIS NEXT QUESTION... WELL, I'M SURE YOU KNOW THAT THERE IS A CERTAIN AMOUNT OF SENSITIVITY ABOUT OUR PLANS.
TELL ME NOW. HOW MUCH DID THE AMERICAN SEE?
SHE SAW THE PROTOTYPE.
AND...?
AND NOTHING. IT WAS NONSENSE TO HER. SHE IS A SIMPLETON. A GRUNT, NOTHING MORE.

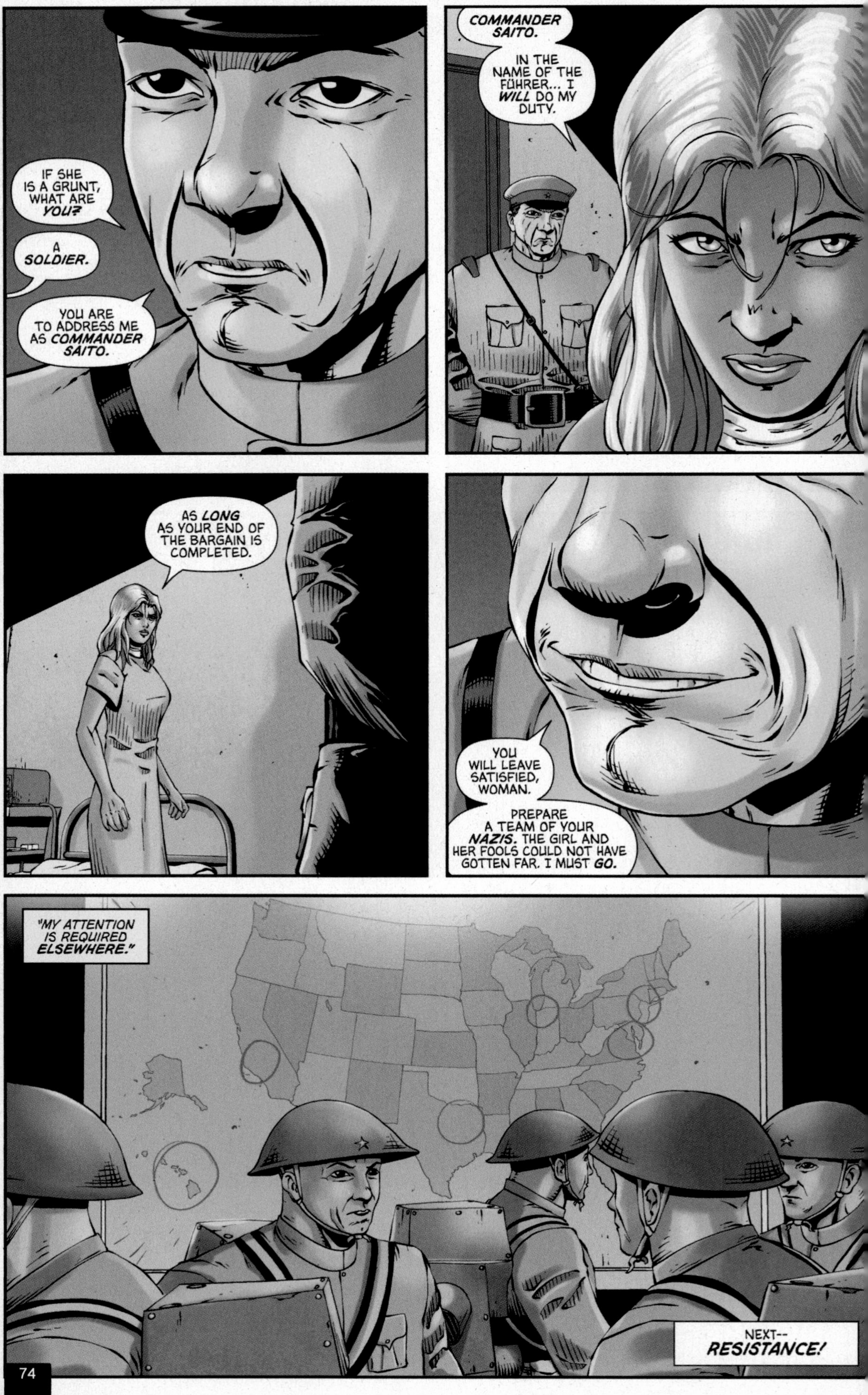
IF SHE IS A GRUNT, WHAT ARE YOU?
A SOLDIER.
YOU ARE TO ADDRESS ME AS COMMANDER SAITO.
COMMANDER SAITO.
IN THE NAME OF THE FÜHRER... I WILL DO MY DUTY.
AS LONG AS YOUR END OF THE BARGAIN IS COMPLETED.
YOU WILL LEAVE SATISFIED, WOMAN.
PREPARE A TEAM OF YOUR NAZIS. THE GIRL AND HER FOOLS COULD NOT HAVE GOTTEN FAR. I MUST GO.
"MY ATTENTION IS REQUIRED ELSEWHERE."
NEXT-- RESISTANCE!

B·A·R Maid

RESISTANCE

WRITER PAT SHAND ARTWORK JACOB BEAR
COLORS JOSE EXPOSITO & ROHVEL YUMUL LETTERS JIM CAMPBELL

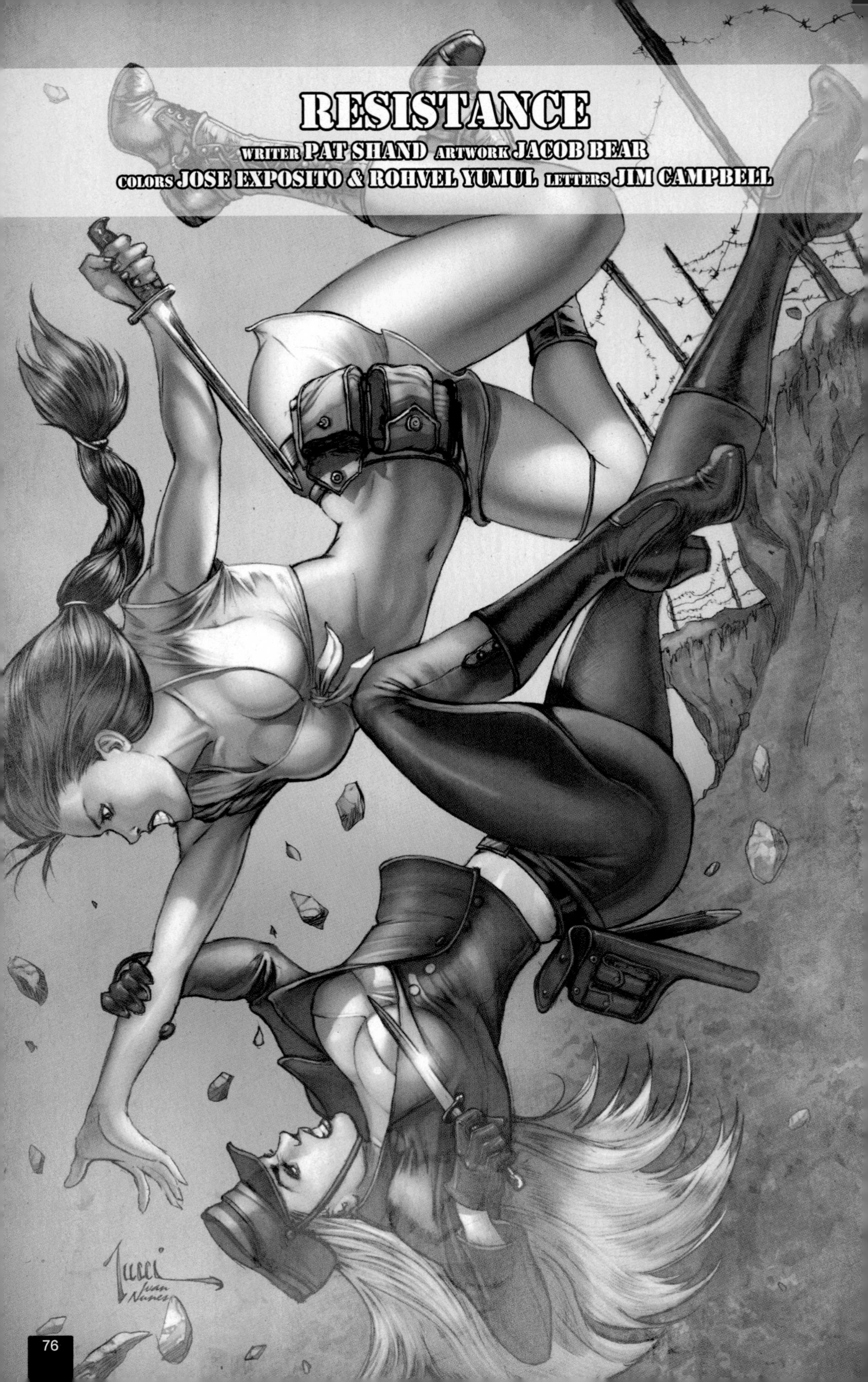

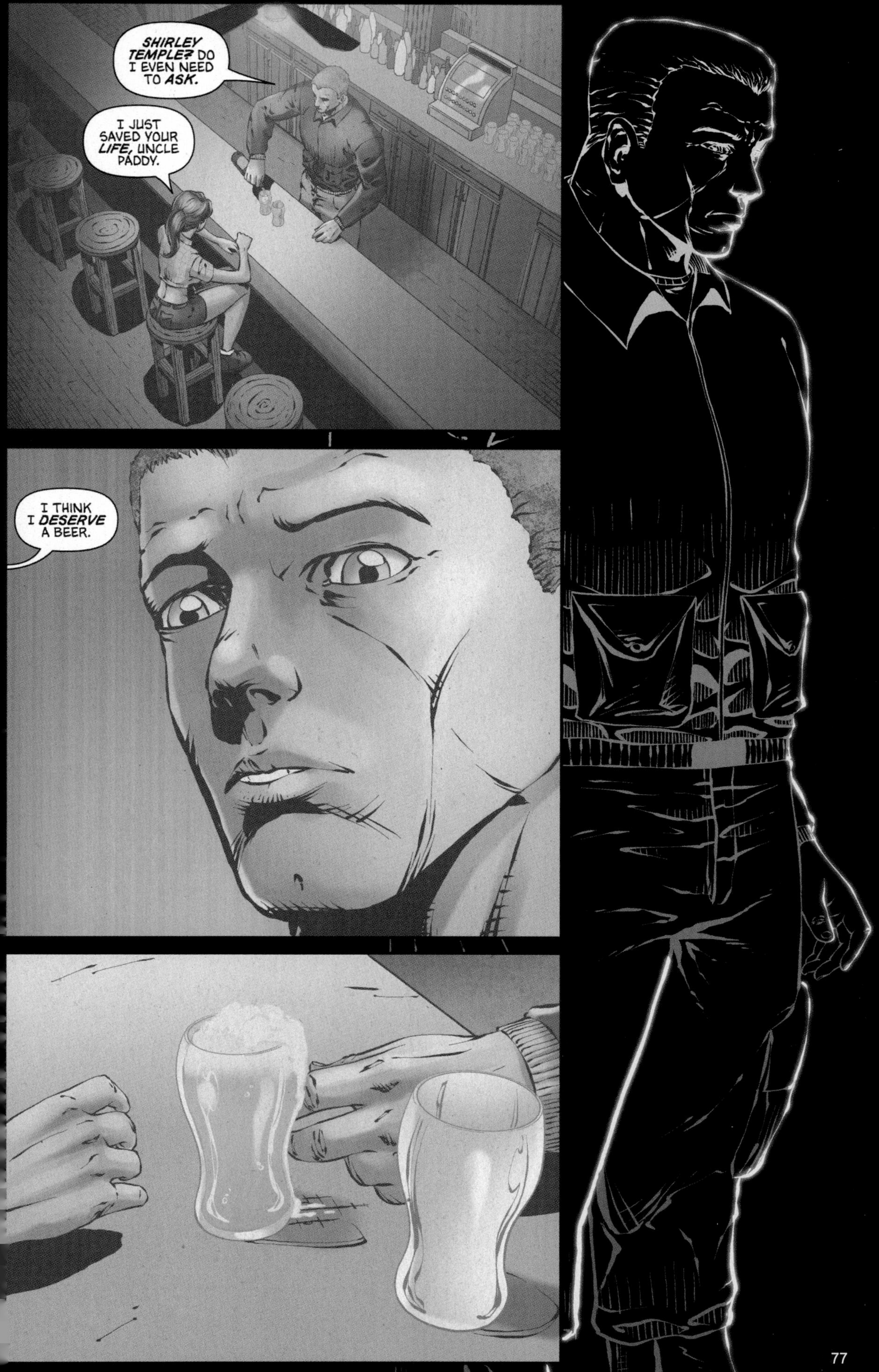
SHIRLEY TEMPLE? DO I EVEN NEED TO ASK.
I JUST SAVED YOUR LIFE, UNCLE PADDY.
I THINK I DESERVE A BEER.

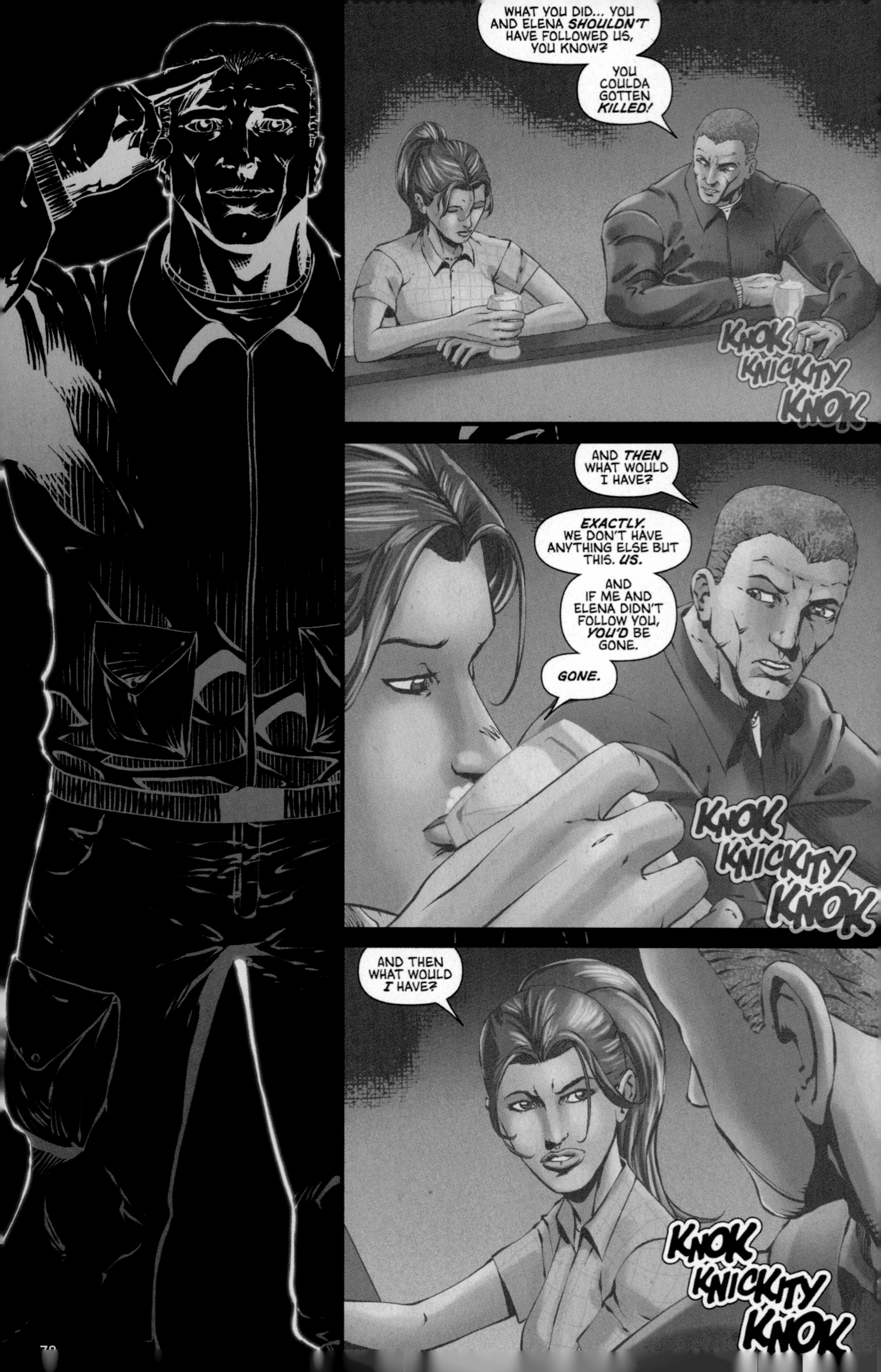
WHAT YOU DID... YOU AND ELENA SHOULDN'T HAVE FOLLOWED US, YOU KNOW?
YOU COULDA GOTTEN KILLED!
KNOK KNICKITY KNOK
AND THEN WHAT WOULD I HAVE?
EXACTLY. WE DON'T HAVE ANYTHING ELSE BUT THIS. US.
AND IF ME AND ELENA DIDN'T FOLLOW YOU, YOU'D BE GONE.
GONE.
KNOK KNICKITY KNOK
AND THEN WHAT WOULD I HAVE?
KNOK KNICKITY KNOK

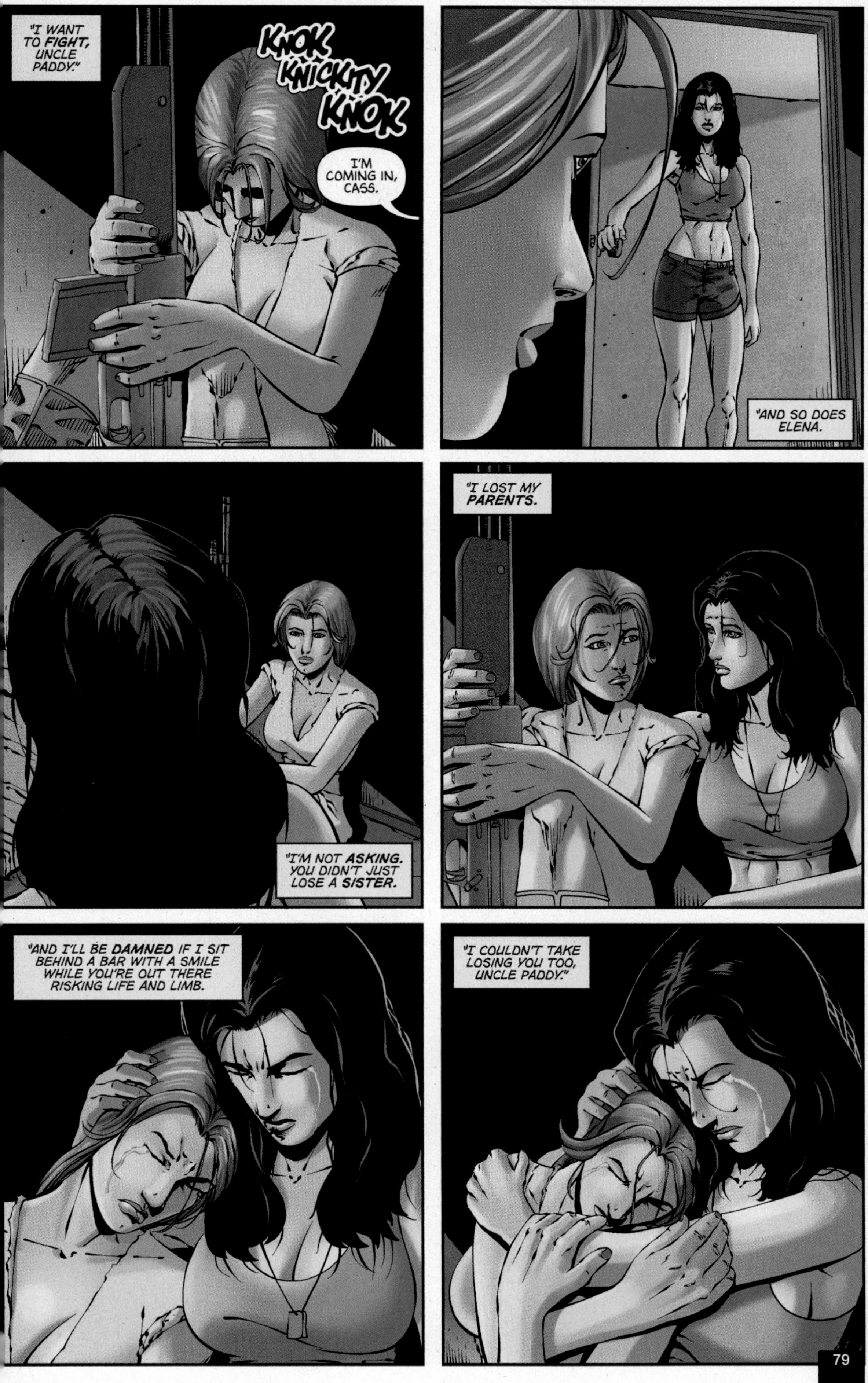
"I WANT TO FIGHT, UNCLE PADDY."
KNOK KNICKITY KNOK
I'M COMING IN, CASS.
"AND SO DOES ELENA.
"I'M NOT ASKING. YOU DIDN'T JUST LOSE A SISTER.
"I LOST MY PARENTS.
"AND I'LL BE DAMNED IF I SIT BEHIND A BAR WITH A SMILE WHILE YOU'RE OUT THERE RISKING LIFE AND LIMB.
"I COULDN'T TAKE LOSING YOU TOO, UNCLE PADDY."

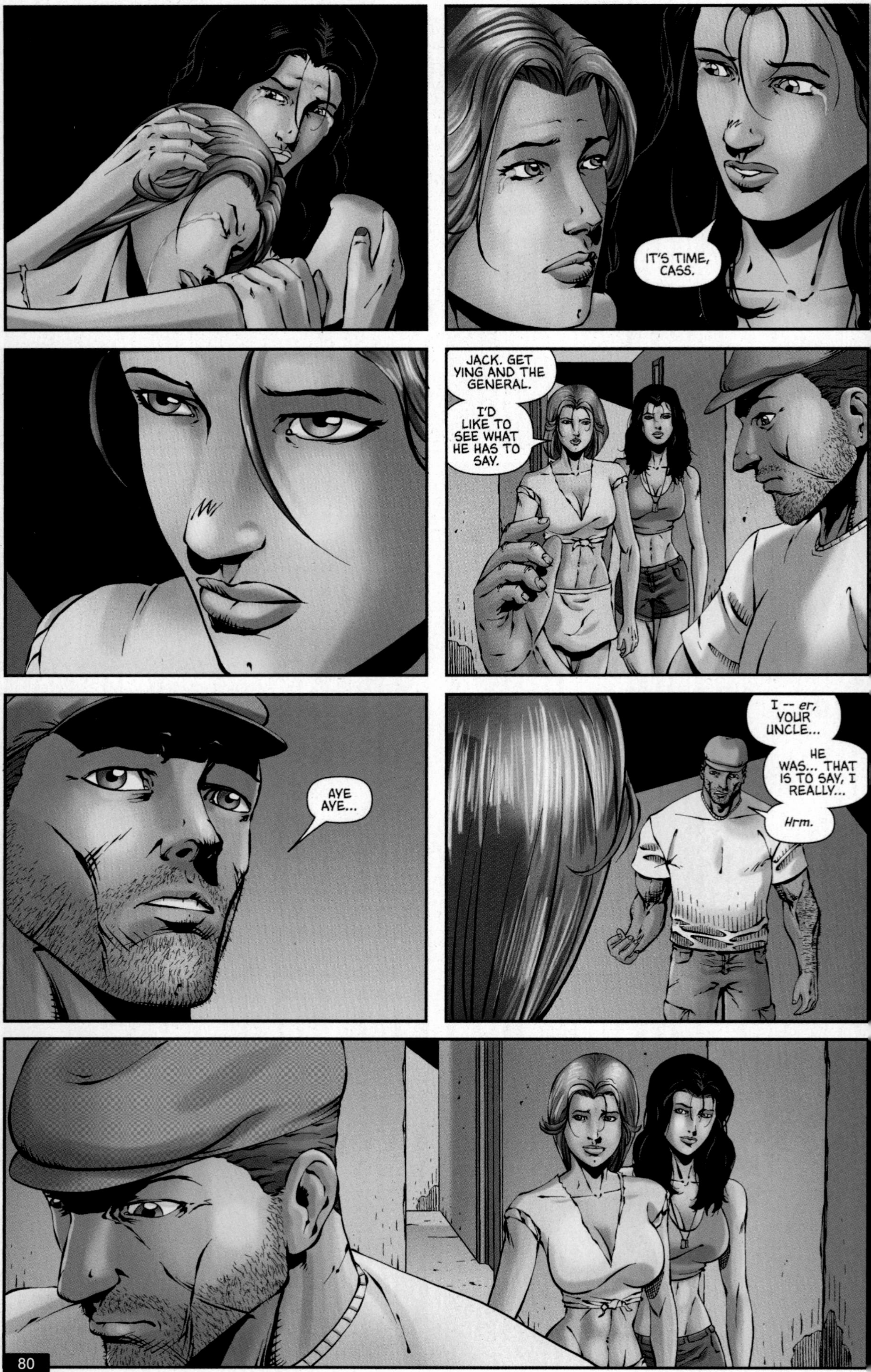

IT'S TIME, CASS.
JACK. GET YING AND THE GENERAL.
I'D LIKE TO SEE WHAT HE HAS TO SAY.
AYE AYE...
I -- *er*, YOUR UNCLE...
HE WAS... THAT IS TO SAY, I REALLY...
Hrm.

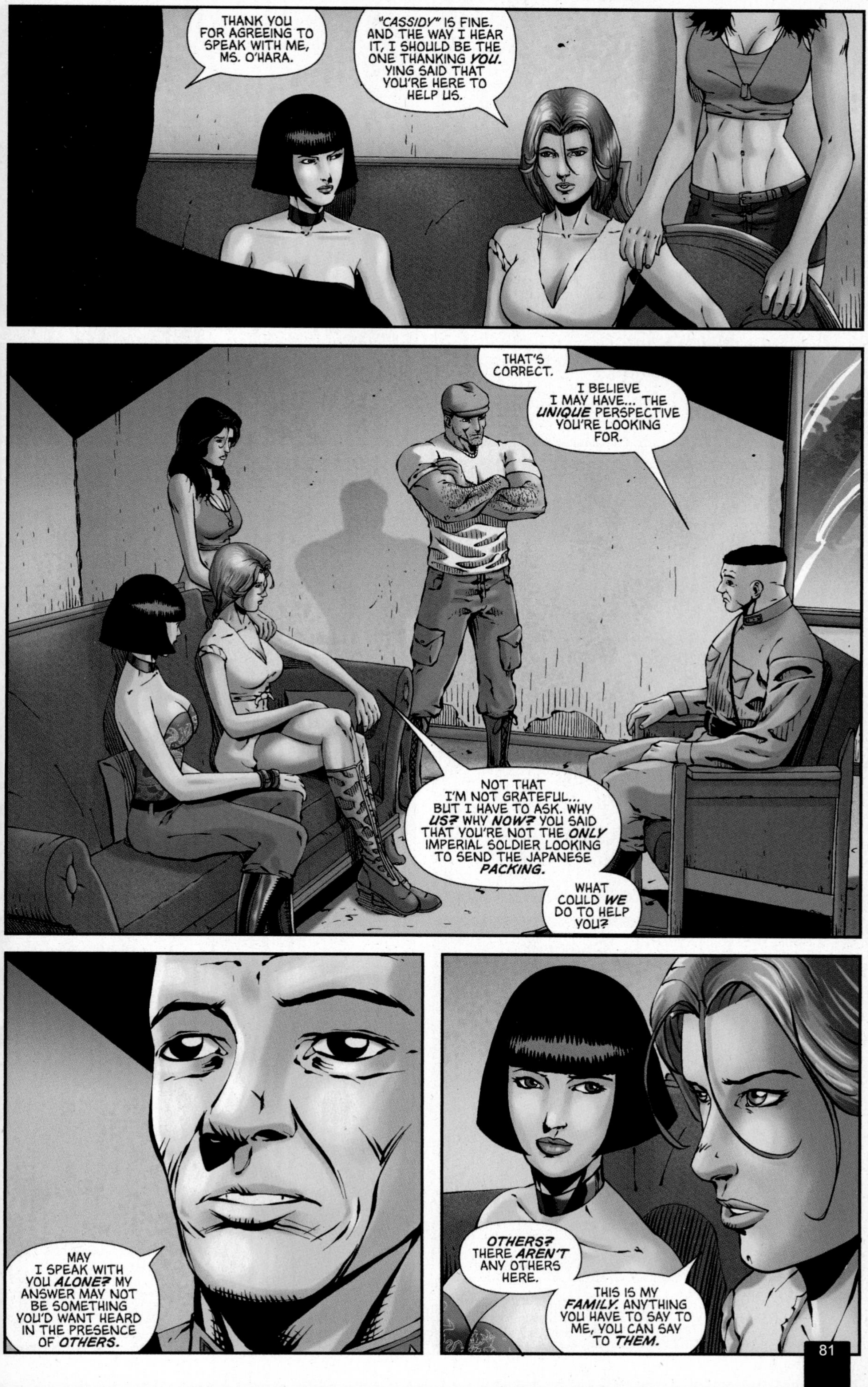
THANK YOU FOR AGREEING TO SPEAK WITH ME, MS. O'HARA.
"CASSIDY" IS FINE. AND THE WAY I HEAR IT, I SHOULD BE THE ONE THANKING *YOU*. YING SAID THAT YOU'RE HERE TO HELP US.
THAT'S CORRECT.
I BELIEVE I MAY HAVE... THE *UNIQUE* PERSPECTIVE YOU'RE LOOKING FOR.
NOT THAT I'M NOT GRATEFUL... BUT I HAVE TO ASK. WHY *US?* WHY *NOW?* YOU SAID THAT YOU'RE NOT THE *ONLY* IMPERIAL SOLDIER LOOKING TO SEND THE JAPANESE *PACKING.*
WHAT COULD *WE* DO TO HELP YOU?
MAY I SPEAK WITH YOU *ALONE?* MY ANSWER MAY NOT BE SOMETHING YOU'D WANT HEARD IN THE PRESENCE OF *OTHERS.*
OTHERS? THERE *AREN'T* ANY OTHERS HERE.
THIS IS MY *FAMILY.* ANYTHING YOU HAVE TO SAY TO ME, YOU CAN SAY TO *THEM.*

Ah. VERY WELL.

So *much* like your mother...

WHAT DID YOU SAY?

"THIS IS WHY I WANTED TO SPEAK WITH YOU *ALONE*, CASSIDY."

"THIS ISN'T THE *FIRST* TIME WE MET.

"I KNOW THIS IS A *SENSITIVE* TOPIC, SO FORGIVE ME... BUT THERE IS *MUCH* THAT YOUR UNCLE PADDY, AS WELL AS YOUR PARENTS, *KEPT* FROM YOU.

"YOUR PARENTS WERE *NOT* MISSIONARIES. THEY POSED AS SUCH BUT, TRULY, THEY WERE *SPIES* FOR THE UNITED STATES GOVERNMENT.

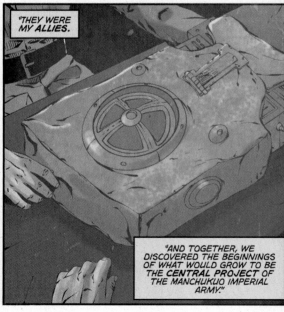

"THEY WERE MY *ALLIES*.

"AND TOGETHER, WE DISCOVERED THE BEGINNINGS OF WHAT WOULD GROW TO BE THE *CENTRAL PROJECT* OF THE MANCHUKUO IMPERIAL ARMY."

"THEY WERE *DISCOVERED* AND *KILLED.*

"IT IS BY THE GRACE OF GOD THAT THE MEN WHO WOULD SOMEDAY LEAD THIS ARMY BELIEVED THAT THEY WERE ACTING *ALONE* -- AND THAT THOSE UNITED WITH THEM, MYSELF INCLUDED, LIVED TO *CONTINUE* THEIR WORK."

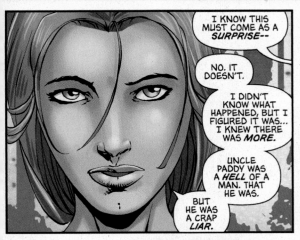

I KNOW THIS MUST COME AS A *SURPRISE*--

NO. IT DOESN'T.

I DIDN'T KNOW WHAT HAPPENED, BUT I FIGURED IT WAS... I KNEW THERE WAS *MORE.*

UNCLE PADDY WAS A *HELL* OF A MAN. THAT HE WAS.

BUT HE WAS A CRAP *LIAR.*

I TAKE IT YING TOLD YOU ABOUT THE *BLUEPRINT* I DISCOVERED.

SHE DID.

AND YOU THINK IT'S CONNECTED TO THIS "*CENTRAL PROJECT.*"

I DO.

I'M STILL NOT *FOLLOWING.* I SAW THE BLUEPRINTS, BUT I'M NOT A TECHNICIAN. IT LOOKED LIKE *GOBBLEDYGOOK* TO ME. WHAT *IS* IT?

CLEARLY YOU *KNOW* SOMETHING. IF YOU WANT TO HELP US, TELL ME WHAT IT IS--

EASY.

...IT'S A *TIME MACHINE.*

...WAIT, *WHAT?*

⟨I DO NOT UNDERSTAND THE INNER WORKINGS OF YOUR *BRAIN*, SAITO.⟩

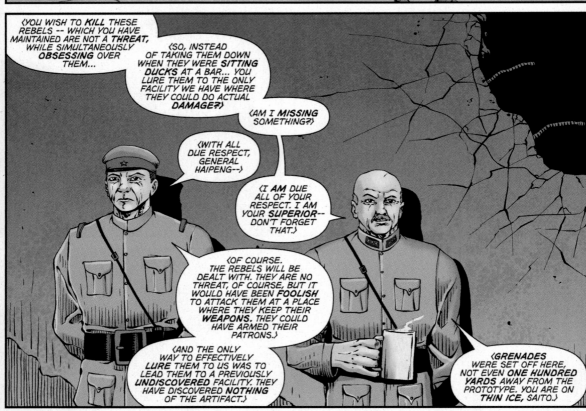

⟨YOU WISH TO *KILL* THESE REBELS -- WHICH YOU HAVE MAINTAINED ARE NOT A *THREAT*, WHILE SIMULTANEOUSLY *OBSESSING* OVER THEM...⟩

⟨SO, INSTEAD OF TAKING THEM DOWN WHEN THEY WERE *SITTING DUCKS* AT A BAR... YOU LURE THEM TO THE ONLY FACILITY WE HAVE WHERE THEY COULD DO ACTUAL *DAMAGE?*⟩

⟨AM I *MISSING* SOMETHING?⟩

⟨WITH ALL DUE RESPECT, GENERAL HAIPENG--⟩

⟨I AM DUE ALL OF YOUR RESPECT. I AM YOUR *SUPERIOR*-- DON'T FORGET THAT.⟩

⟨OF COURSE. THE REBELS WILL BE DEALT WITH. THEY ARE NO THREAT, OF COURSE, BUT IT WOULD HAVE BEEN *FOOLISH* TO ATTACK THEM AT A PLACE WHERE THEY KEEP THEIR *WEAPONS*. THEY COULD HAVE ARMED THEIR *PATRONS*.⟩

⟨AND THE ONLY WAY TO EFFECTIVELY *LURE* THEM TO US WAS TO LEAD THEM TO A PREVIOUSLY *UNDISCOVERED* FACILITY. THEY HAVE DISCOVERED *NOTHING* OF THE ARTIFACT.⟩

⟨*GRENADES* WERE SET OFF HERE, NOT EVEN *ONE HUNDRED YARDS* AWAY FROM THE PROTOTYPE. YOU ARE ON *THIN ICE*, SAITO.⟩

⟨THIS HAD BETTER *IMPRESS* ME IF YOU WISH TO SAVE FACE.⟩

⟨I BELIEVE IT WILL.⟩

⟨I HAVE PLACED AN AMERICAN FLAG *FIVE MILES* FROM THIS LOCATION. I BELIEVE THAT WILL SERVE AS AN ACCURATE DEMONSTRATION OF HOW *FAR* OUR ARTIFACT HAS COME.⟩

⟨*ENOUGH TALK. SHOW* ME.⟩

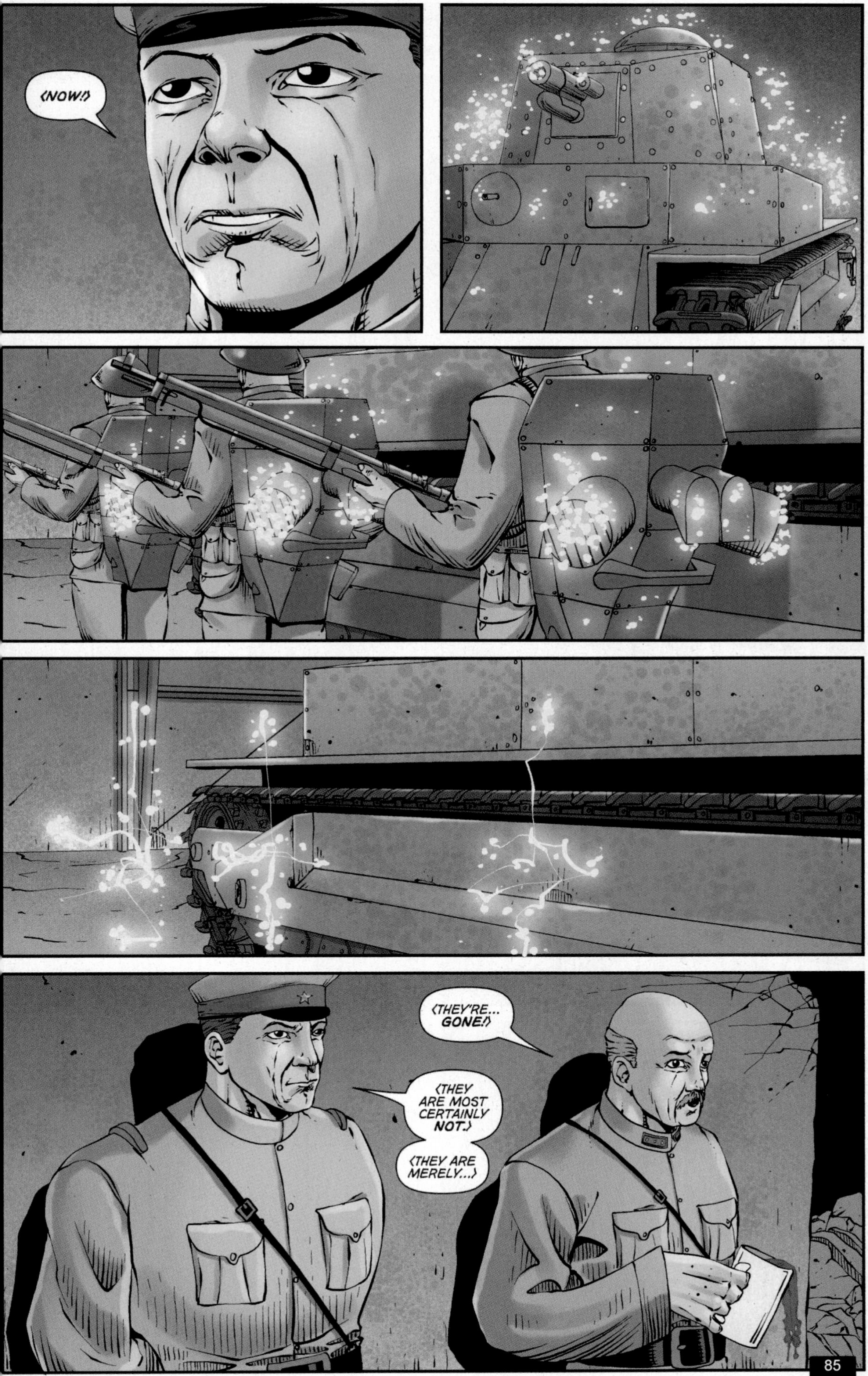
‹NOW!›
‹THEY'RE... GONE!›
‹THEY ARE MOST CERTAINLY NOT.›
‹THEY ARE MERELY...›

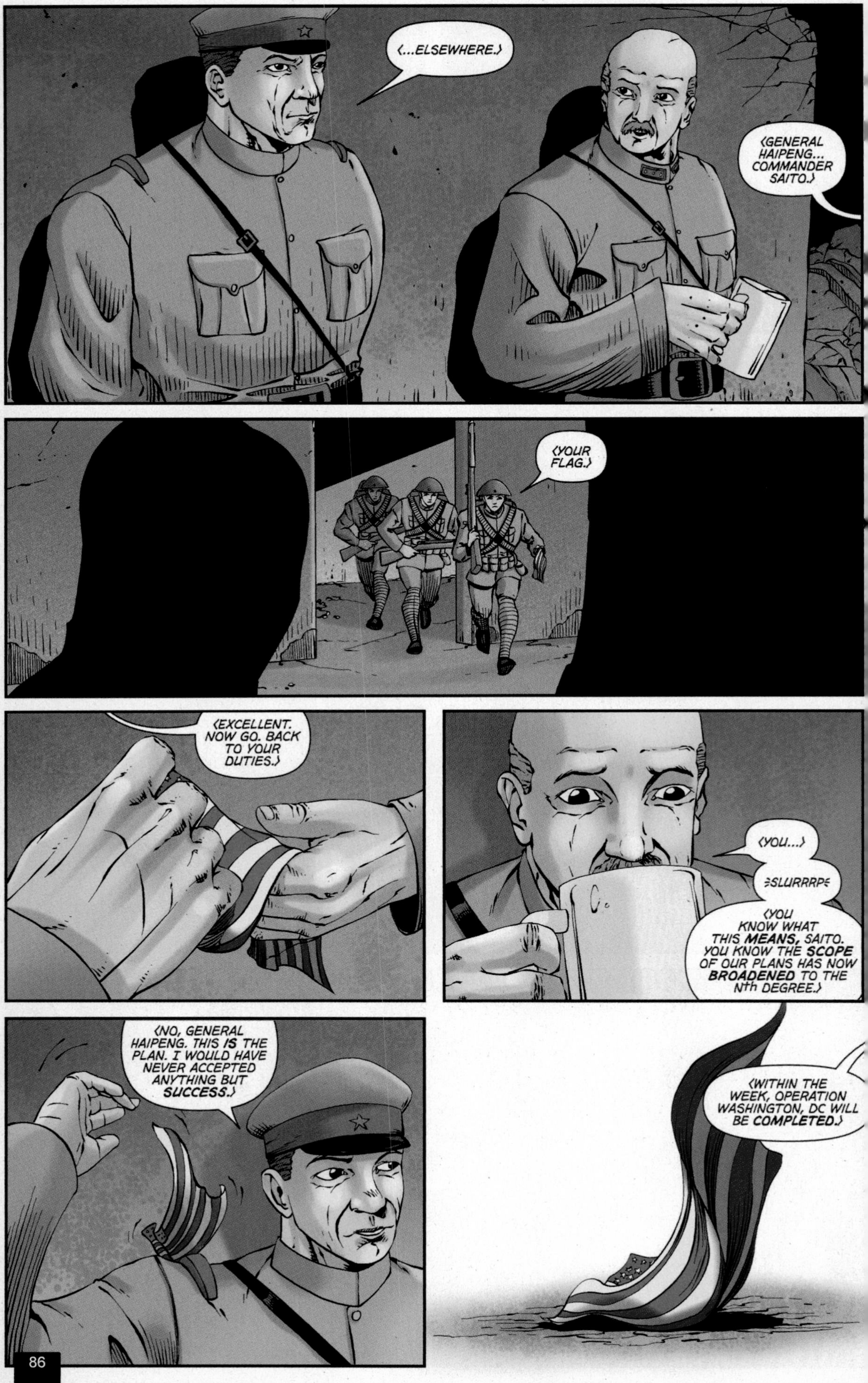

<...ELSEWHERE.>
<GENERAL HAIPENG... COMMANDER SAITO.>
<YOUR FLAG.>
<EXCELLENT. NOW GO. BACK TO YOUR DUTIES.>
<YOU...>
SLURRRP
<YOU KNOW WHAT THIS MEANS, SAITO. YOU KNOW THE SCOPE OF OUR PLANS HAS NOW BROADENED TO THE Nth DEGREE.>
<NO, GENERAL HAIPENG. THIS IS THE PLAN. I WOULD HAVE NEVER ACCEPTED ANYTHING BUT SUCCESS.>
<WITHIN THE WEEK, OPERATION WASHINGTON, DC WILL BE COMPLETED.>

"⟨AND THE REBELS...⟩"

"⟨THEY HAVE NOT SEEN MUCH...⟩"

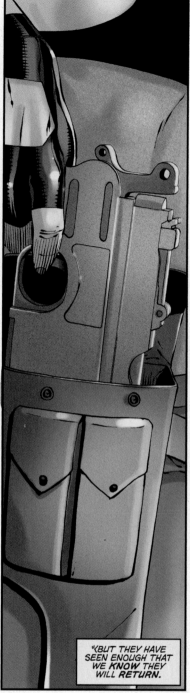

"⟨BUT THEY HAVE SEEN ENOUGH THAT WE KNOW THEY WILL RETURN.⟩"

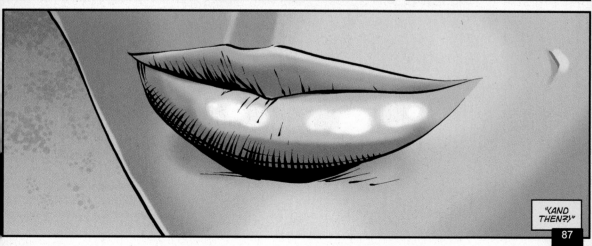

"⟨AND THEN?⟩"

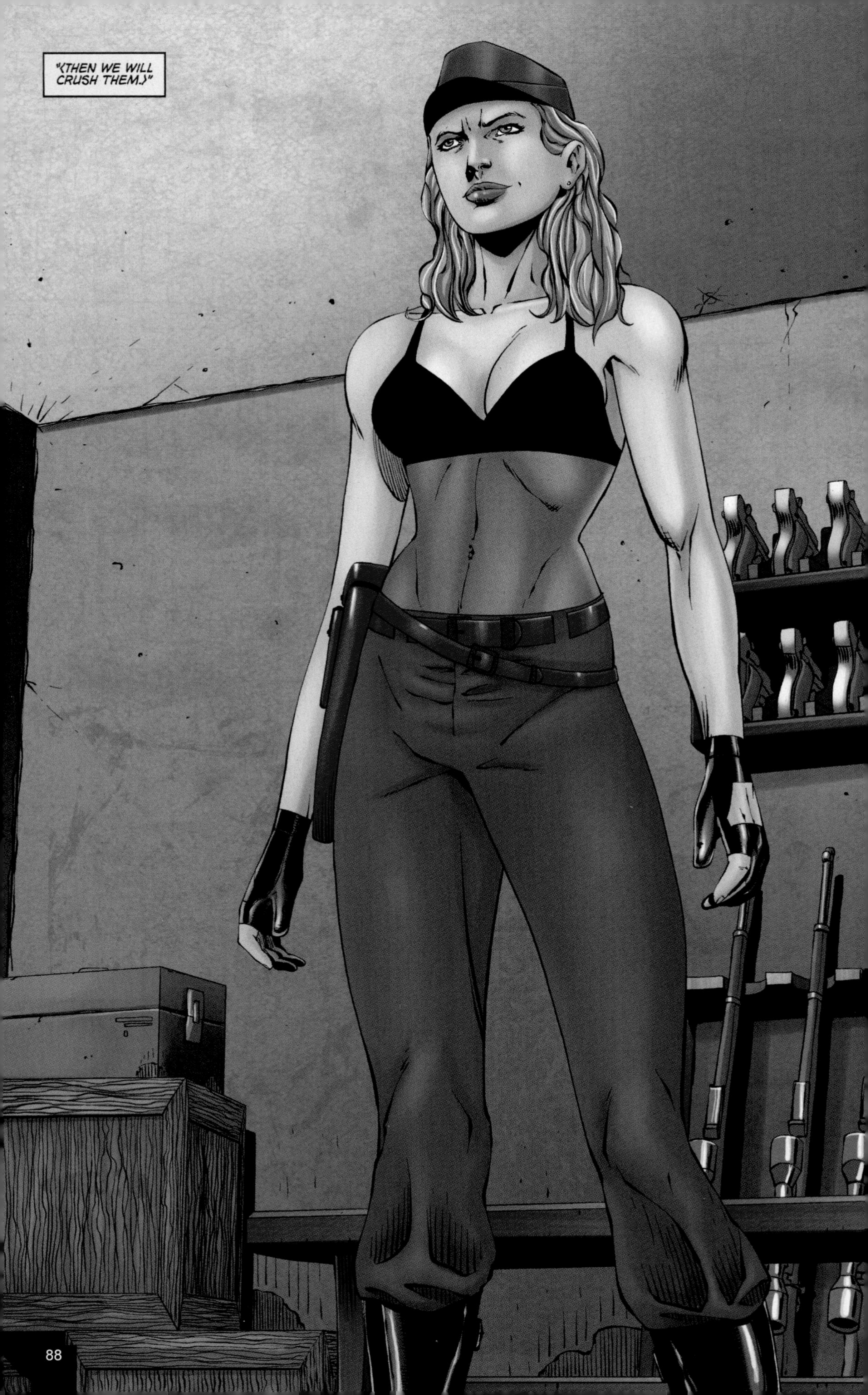
"‹THEN WE WILL CRUSH THEM.›"

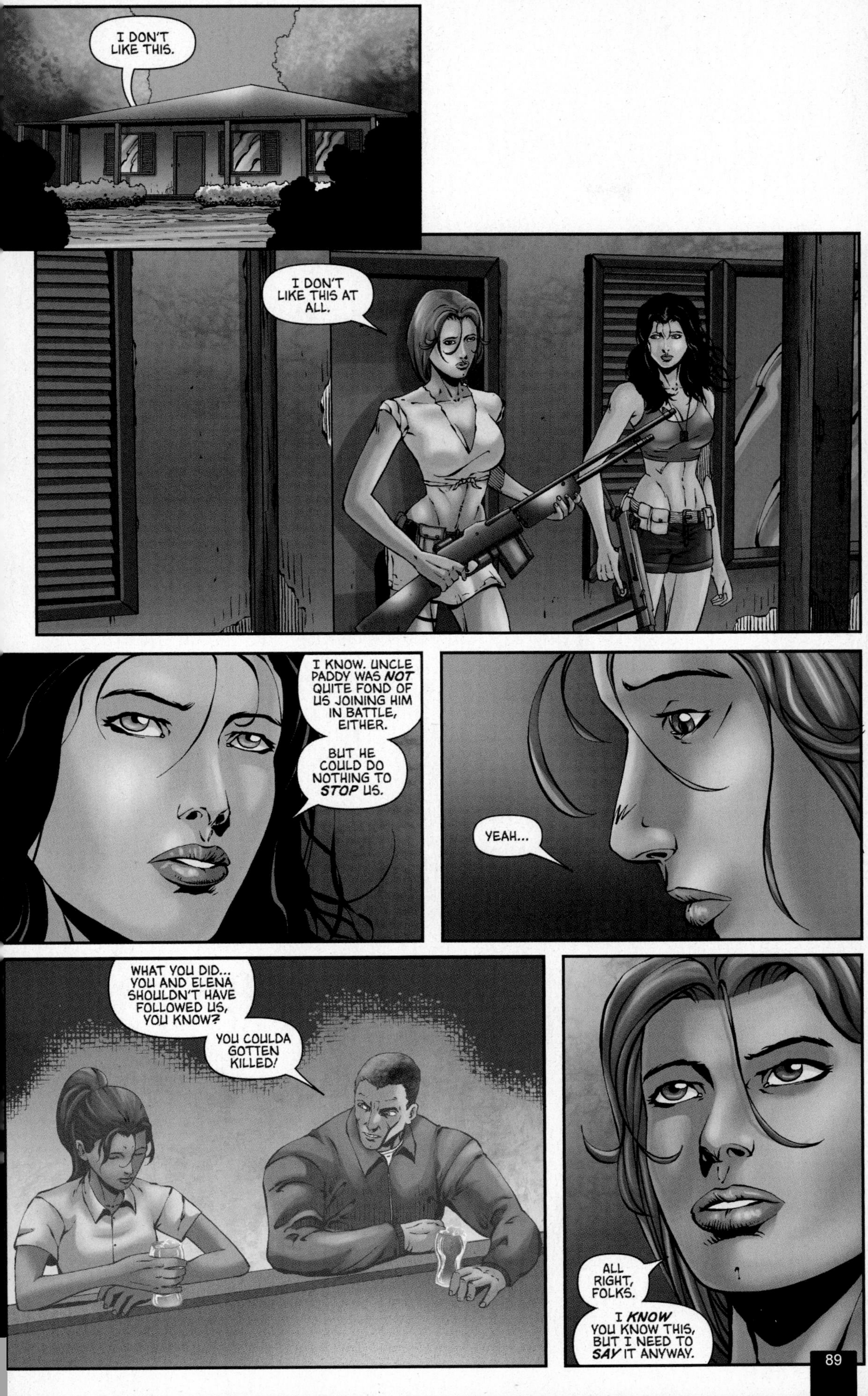
I DON'T LIKE THIS.
I DON'T LIKE THIS AT ALL.
I KNOW. UNCLE PADDY WAS *NOT* QUITE FOND OF US JOINING HIM IN BATTLE, EITHER.
BUT HE COULD DO NOTHING TO *STOP* US.
YEAH...
WHAT YOU DID... YOU AND ELENA SHOULDN'T HAVE FOLLOWED US, YOU KNOW?
YOU COULDA GOTTEN KILLED!
ALL RIGHT, FOLKS.
I *KNOW* YOU KNOW THIS, BUT I NEED TO *SAY* IT ANYWAY.

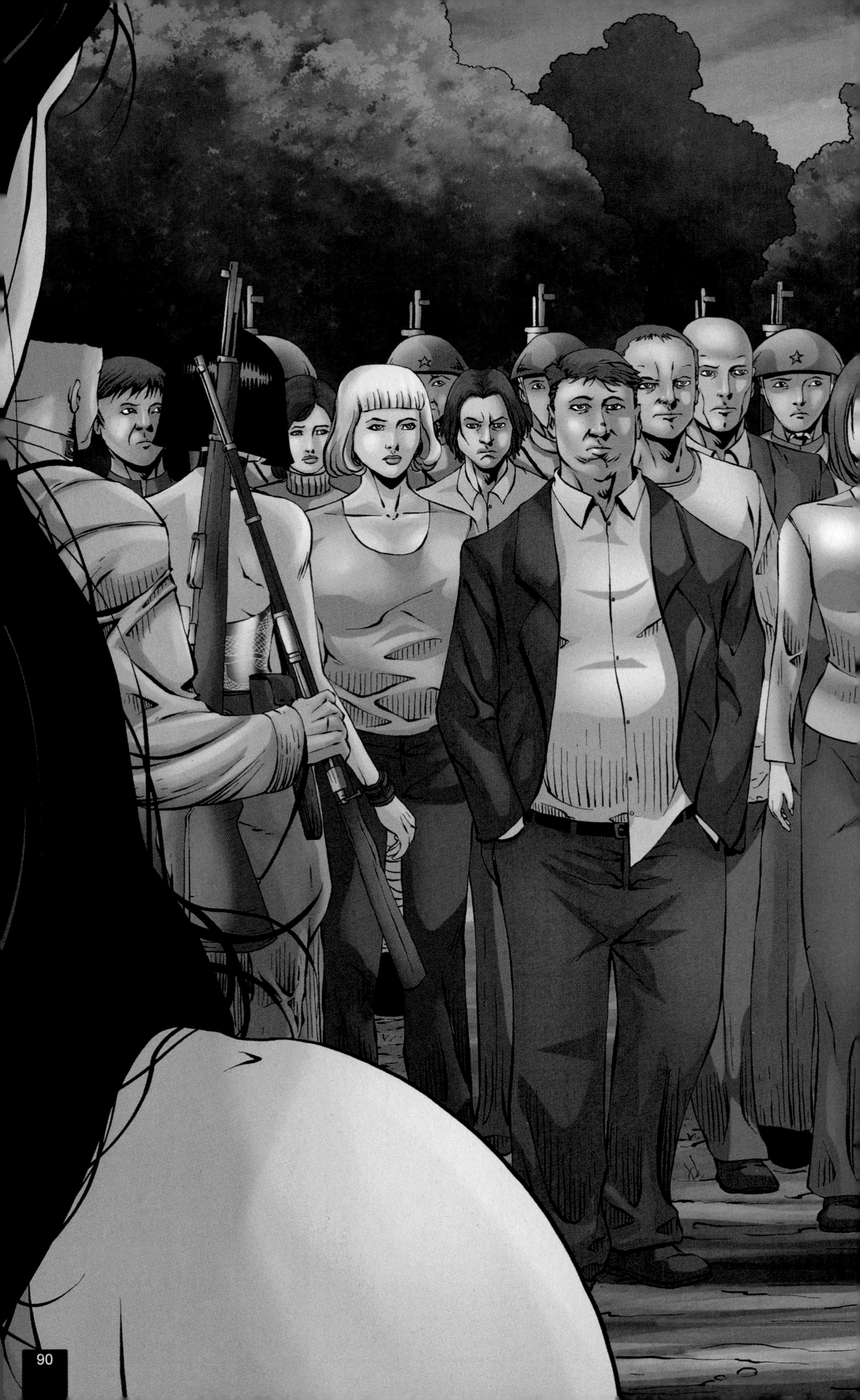

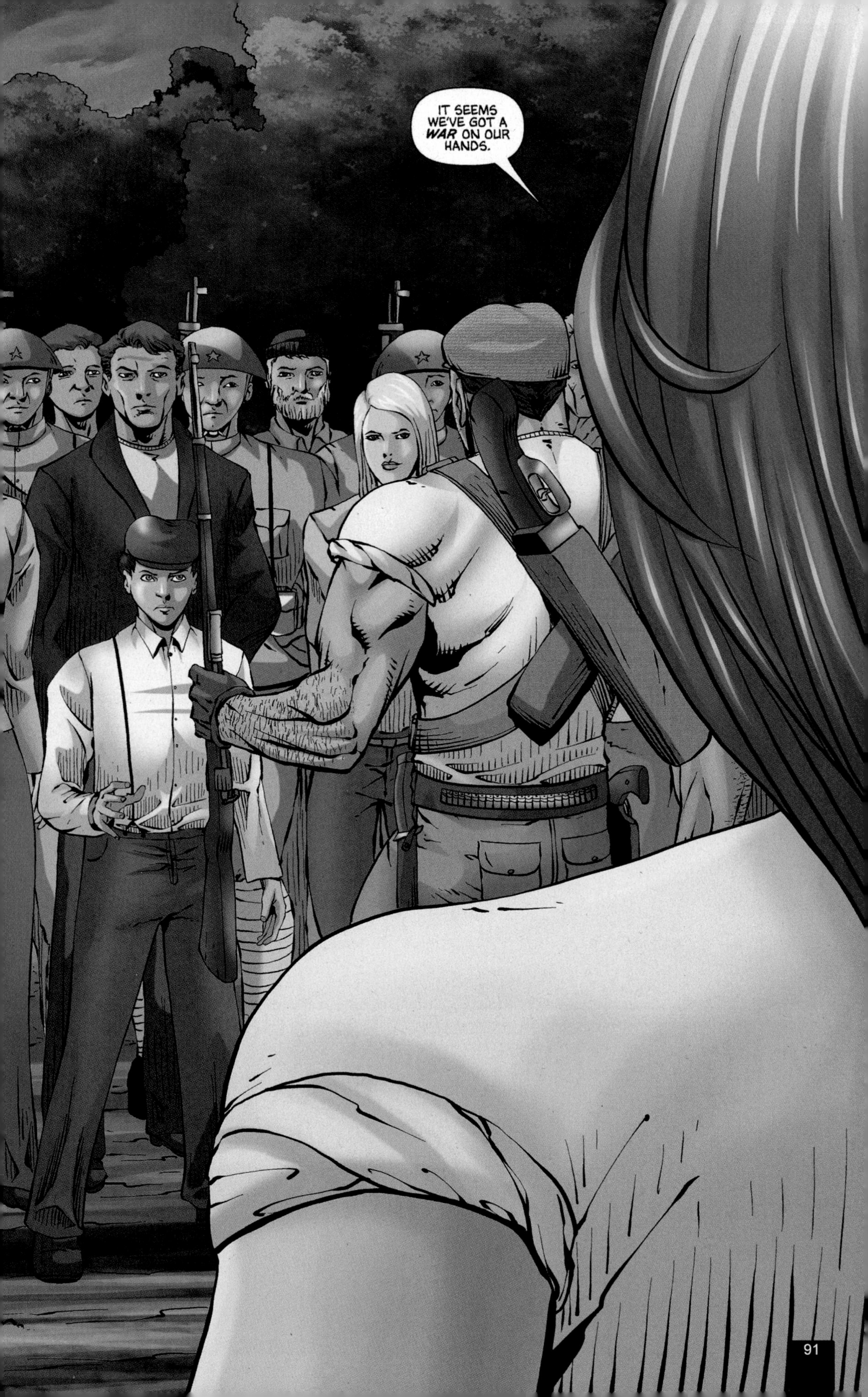
IT SEEMS WE'VE GOT A **WAR** ON OUR HANDS.

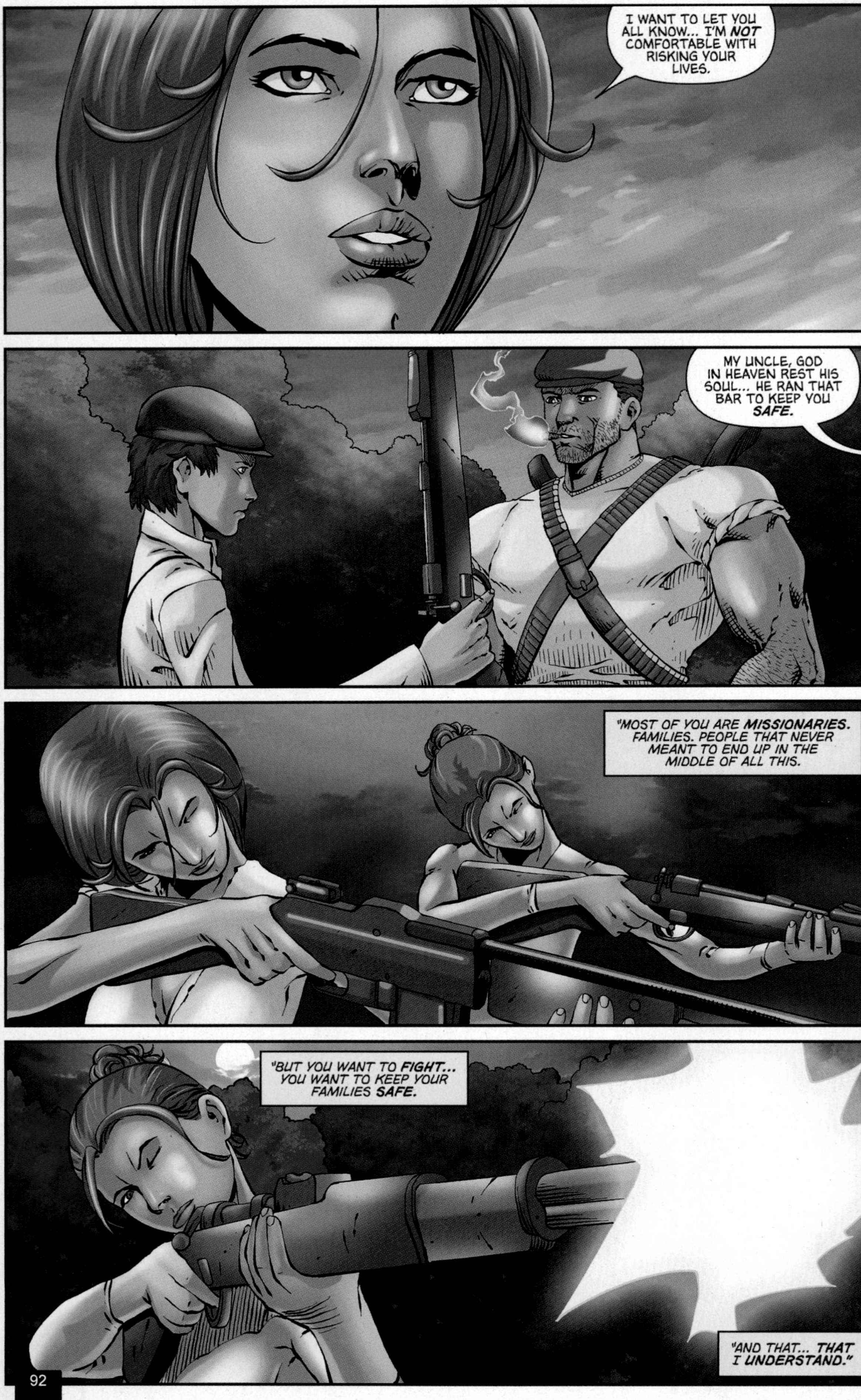
I WANT TO LET YOU ALL KNOW... I'M ***NOT*** COMFORTABLE WITH RISKING YOUR LIVES.
MY UNCLE, GOD IN HEAVEN REST HIS SOUL... HE RAN THAT BAR TO KEEP YOU ***SAFE.***
"MOST OF YOU ARE ***MISSIONARIES.*** FAMILIES. PEOPLE THAT NEVER MEANT TO END UP IN THE MIDDLE OF ALL THIS.
"BUT YOU WANT TO ***FIGHT...*** YOU WANT TO KEEP YOUR FAMILIES ***SAFE.***
"AND THAT... ***THAT*** I ***UNDERSTAND.***"

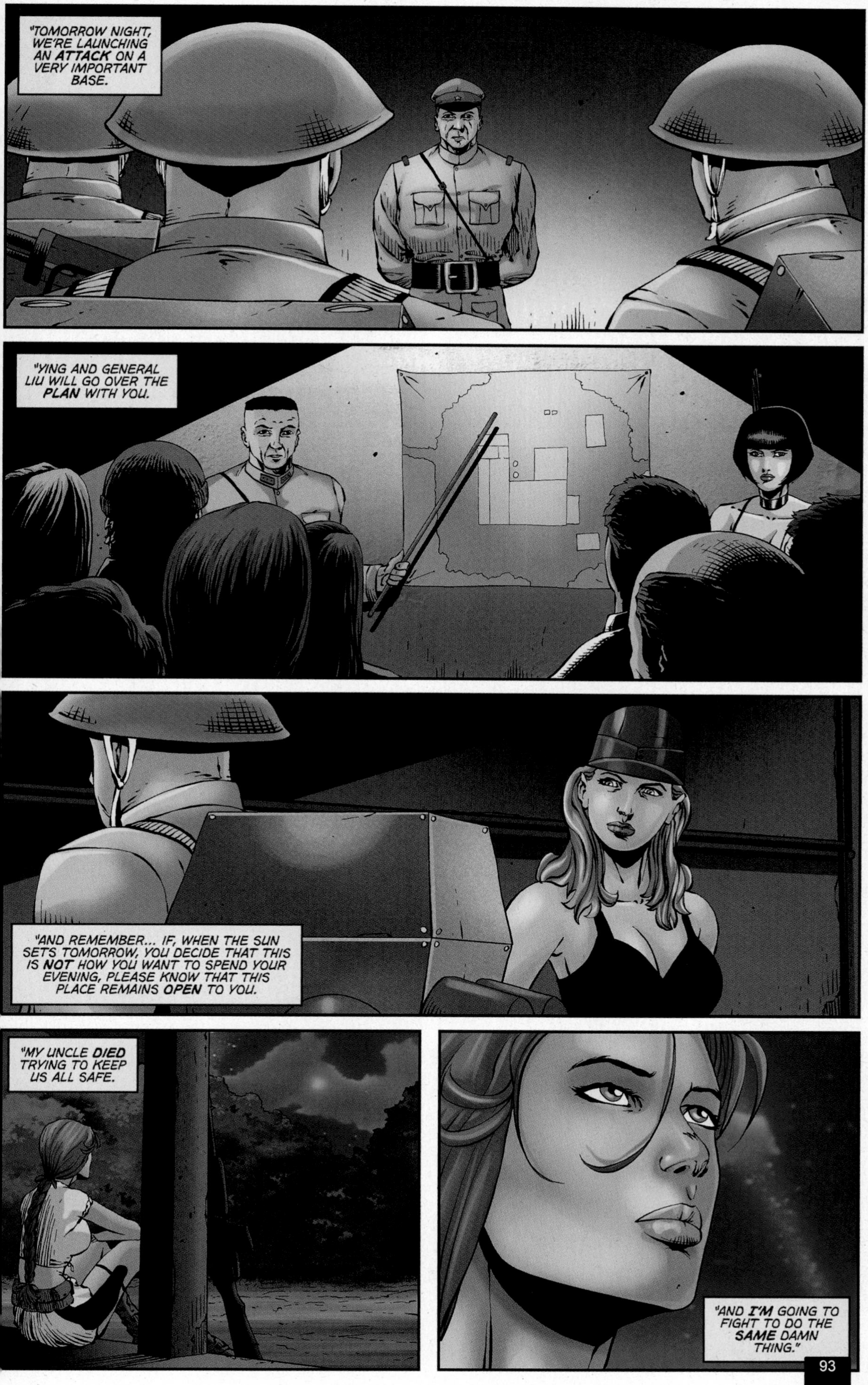
"TOMORROW NIGHT, WE'RE LAUNCHING AN ATTACK ON A VERY IMPORTANT BASE.
"YING AND GENERAL LIU WILL GO OVER THE PLAN WITH YOU.
"AND REMEMBER... IF, WHEN THE SUN SETS TOMORROW, YOU DECIDE THAT THIS IS NOT HOW YOU WANT TO SPEND YOUR EVENING, PLEASE KNOW THAT THIS PLACE REMAINS OPEN TO YOU.
"MY UNCLE DIED TRYING TO KEEP US ALL SAFE.
"AND I'M GOING TO FIGHT TO DO THE SAME DAMN THING."

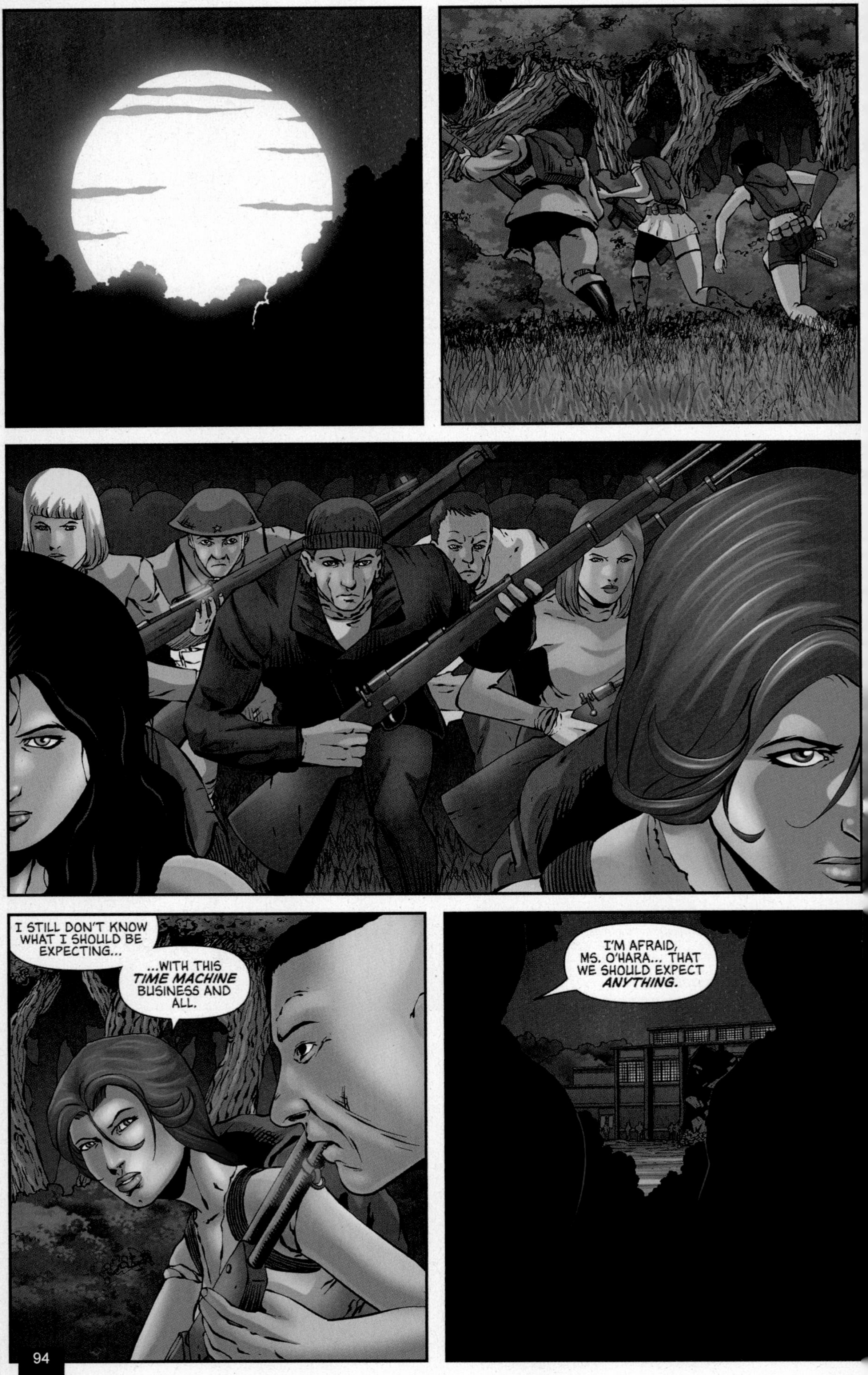
I STILL DON'T KNOW WHAT I SHOULD BE EXPECTING...
...WITH THIS *TIME MACHINE* BUSINESS AND ALL.
I'M AFRAID, MS. O'HARA... THAT WE SHOULD EXPECT *ANYTHING.*

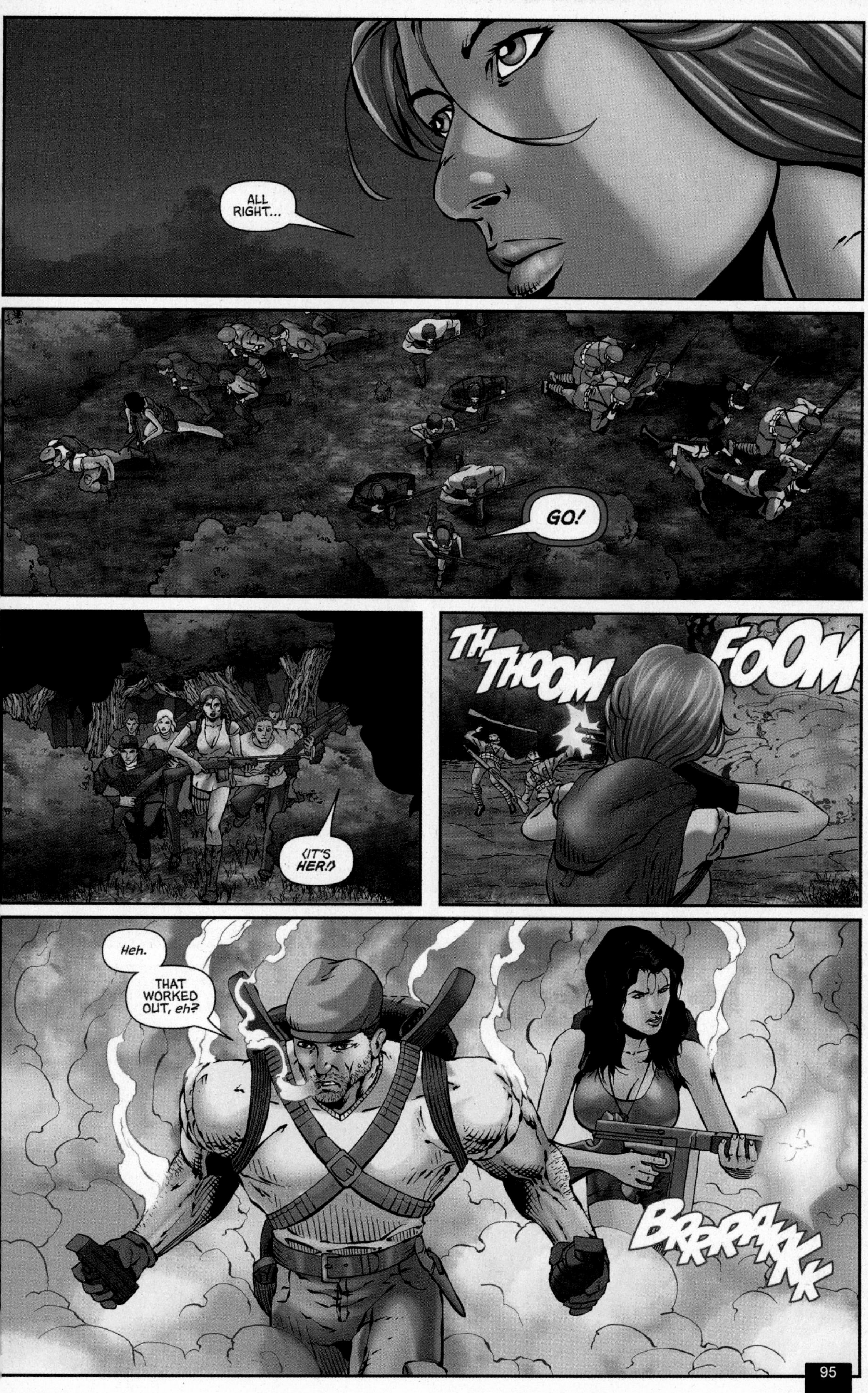
ALL RIGHT...
GO!
‹IT'S HER!›
TH THOOM
FOOM
Heh.
THAT WORKED OUT, *eh?*
BRRRAKKK

‹SAITO!›

‹SAITO, GET YOUR ASS IN HERE THIS INSTANT!›

‹DO TELL ME, SAITO, THAT YOUR REBELS -- THE ONES WHO ARE NOT A CONCERN OF OURS -- AREN'T ATTACKING OUR FACILITY WITH GENERAL LIU AND A SOME OF OUR MEN BY THEIR SIDE?›

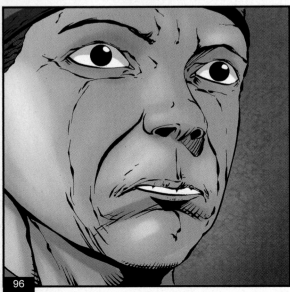

‹SAITO!›

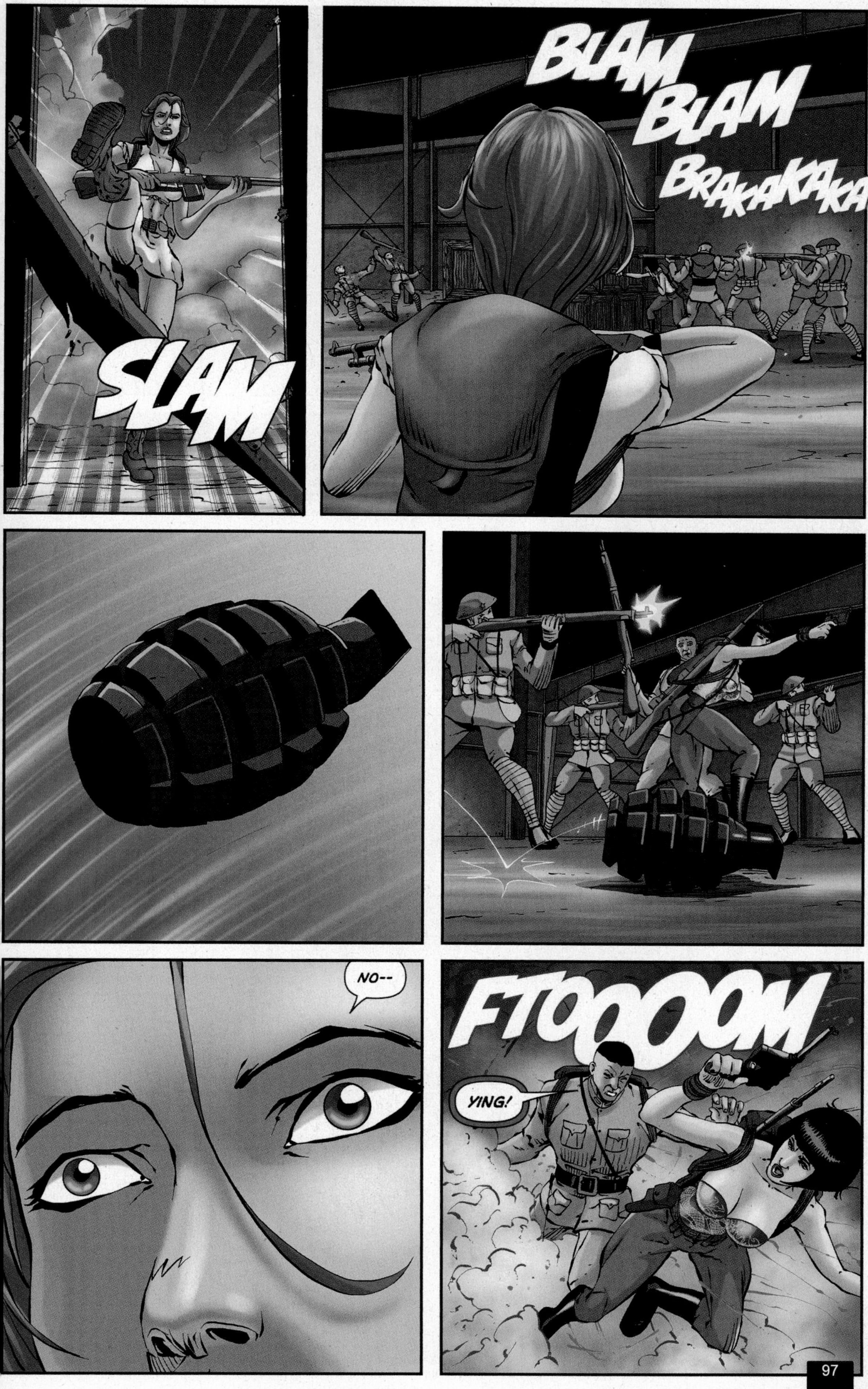
SLAM
BLAM
BLAM
BRAKAKAKA
NO--
FTOOOOM
YING!

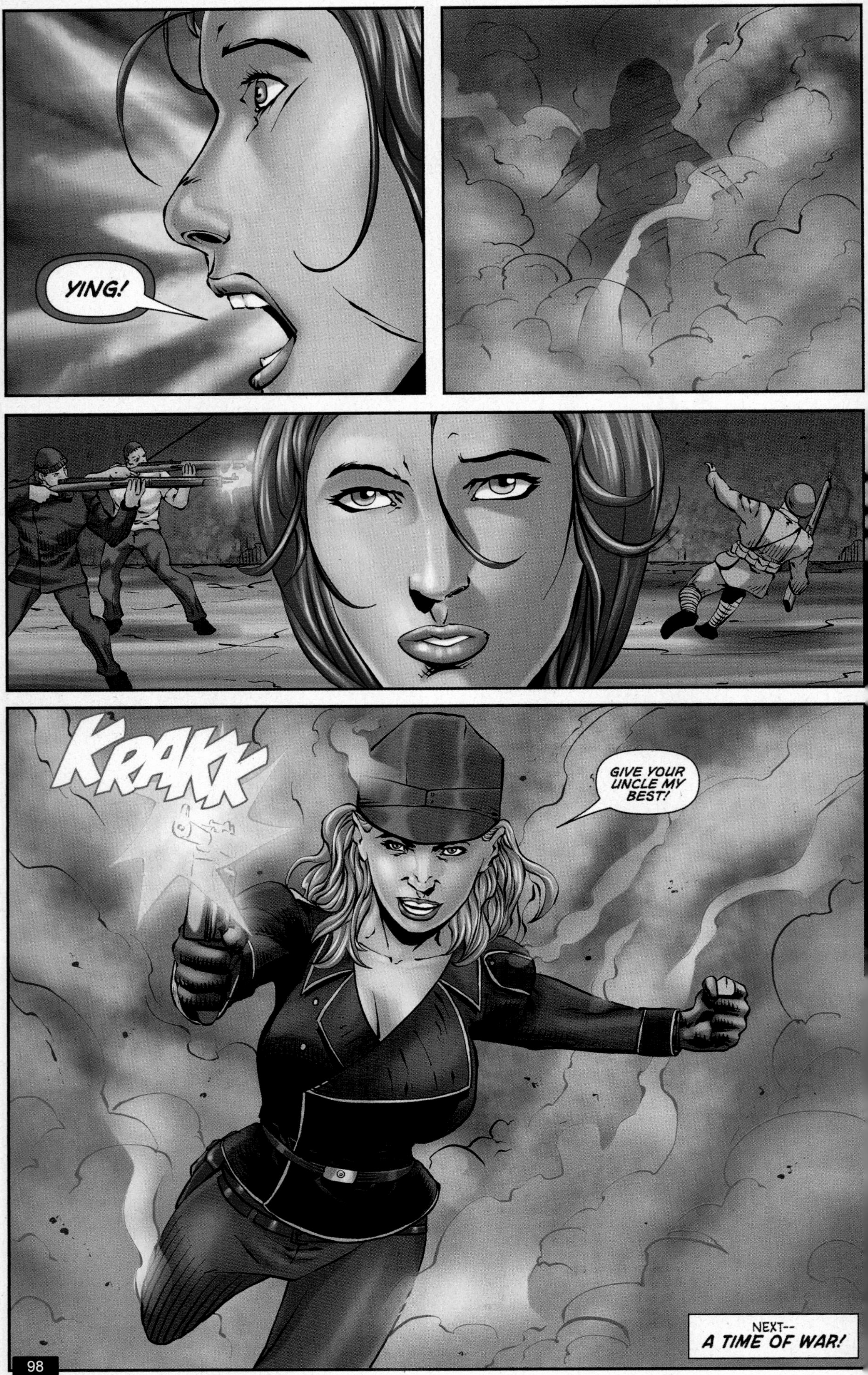
YING!
KRAKK
GIVE YOUR UNCLE MY BEST!
NEXT--
A TIME OF WAR!

BAR Maid

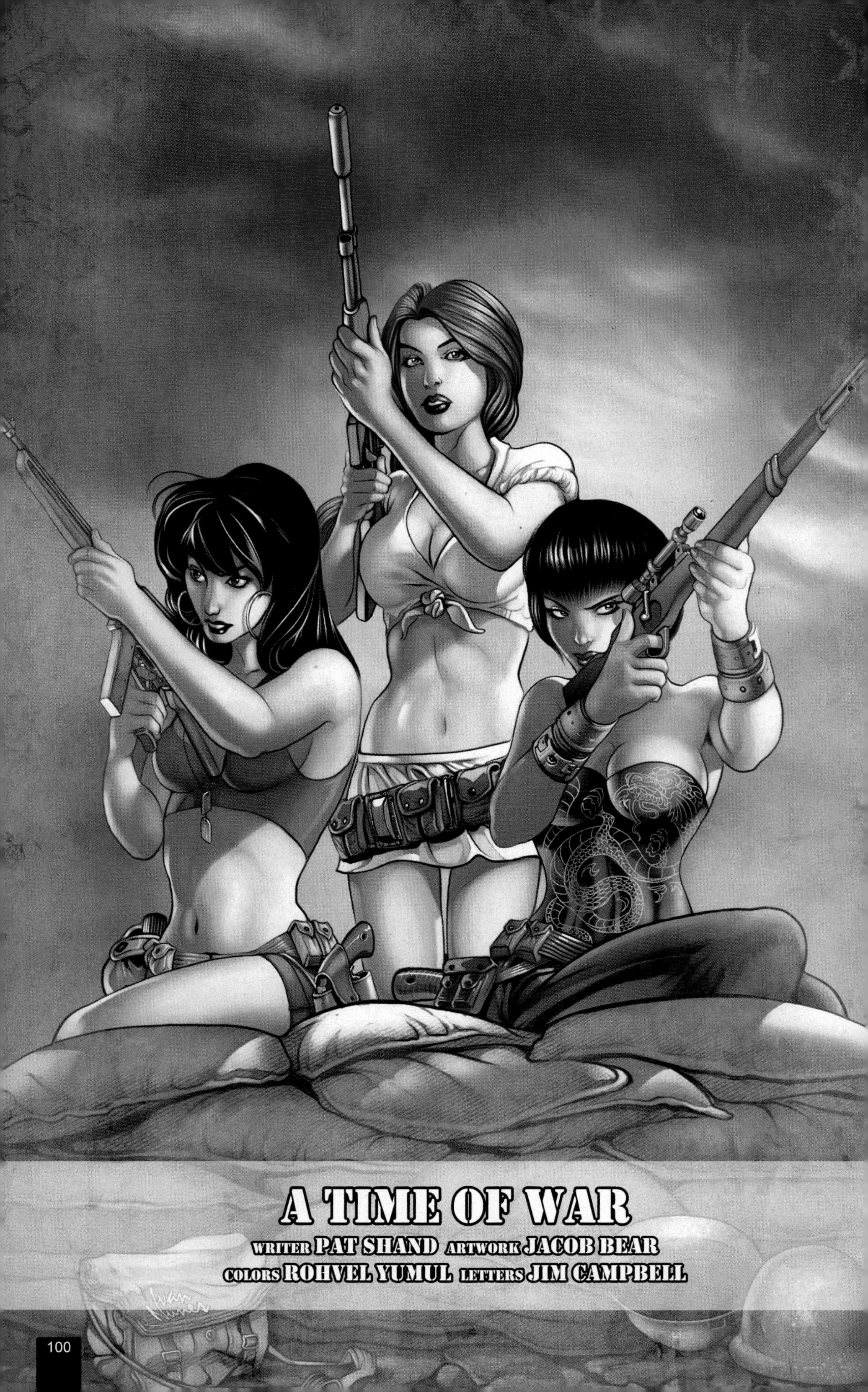

A TIME OF WAR

WRITER PAT SHAND ARTWORK JACOB BEAR
COLORS ROHVEL YUMUL LETTERS JIM CAMPBELL

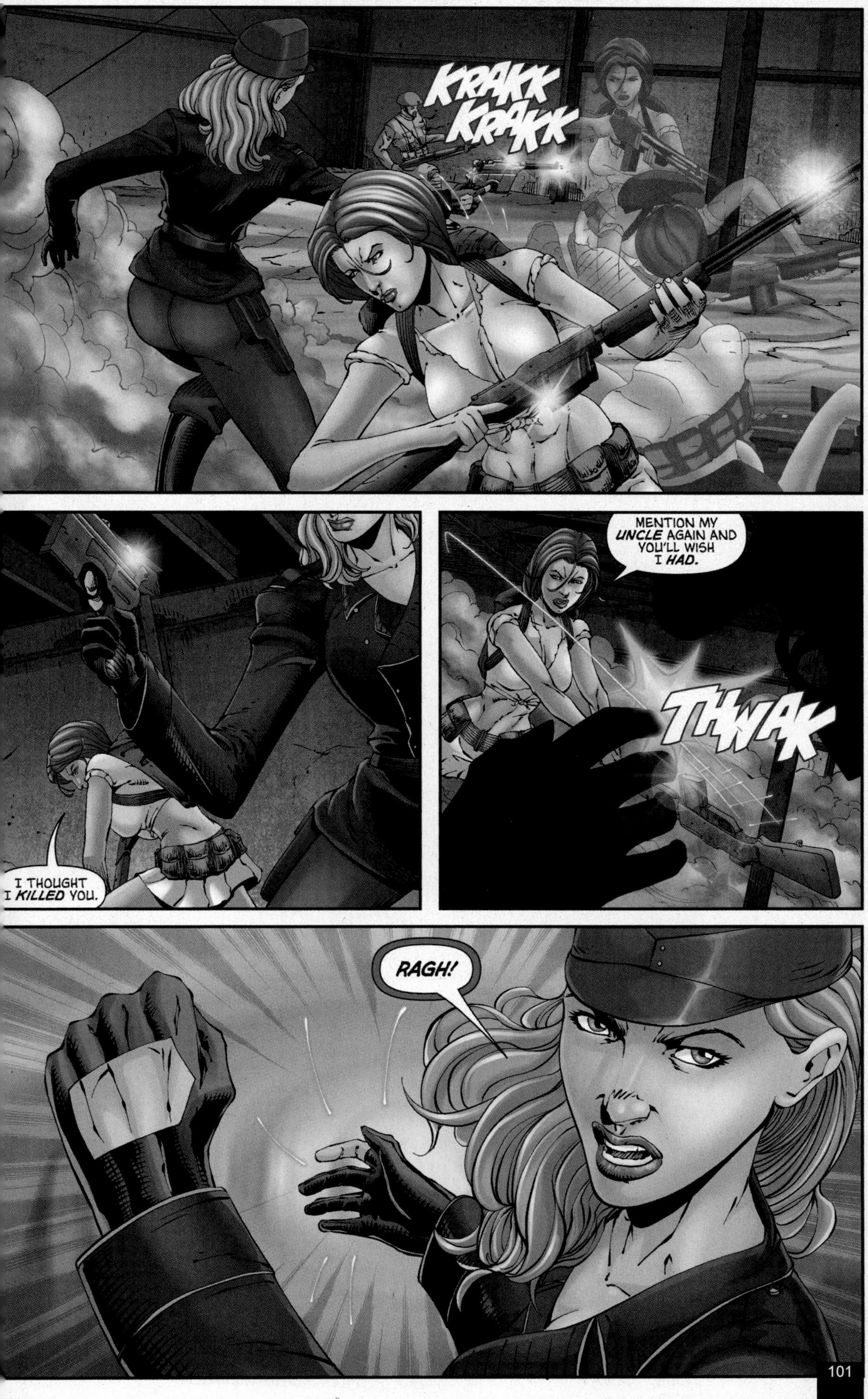
KRAKK
KRAKK
I THOUGHT I KILLED YOU.
MENTION MY UNCLE AGAIN AND YOU'LL WISH I HAD.
THWAK
RAGH!

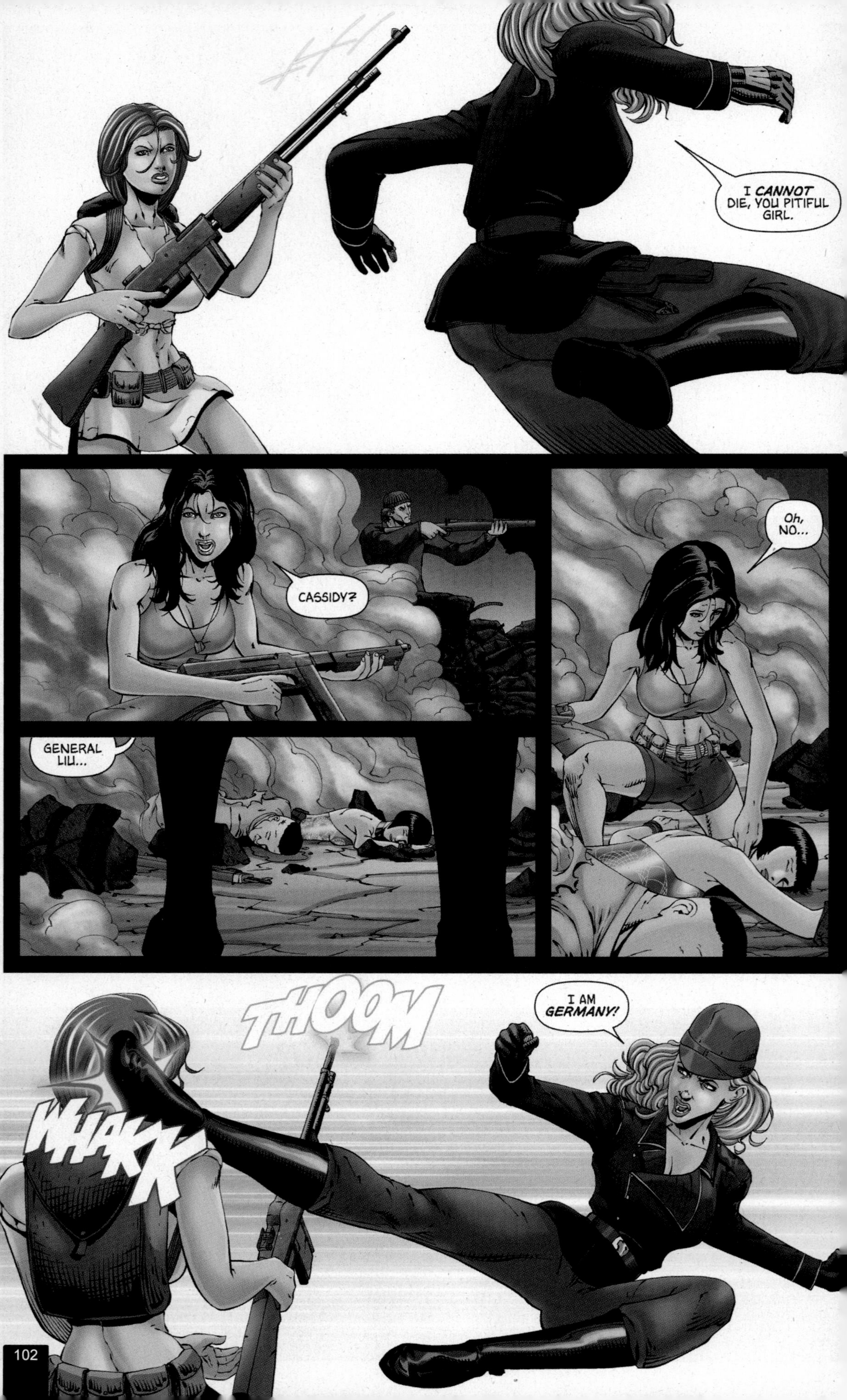
I CANNOT DIE, YOU PITIFUL GIRL.
CASSIDY?
Oh, NO...
GENERAL LIU...
THOOM
I AM GERMANY!
WHAKK

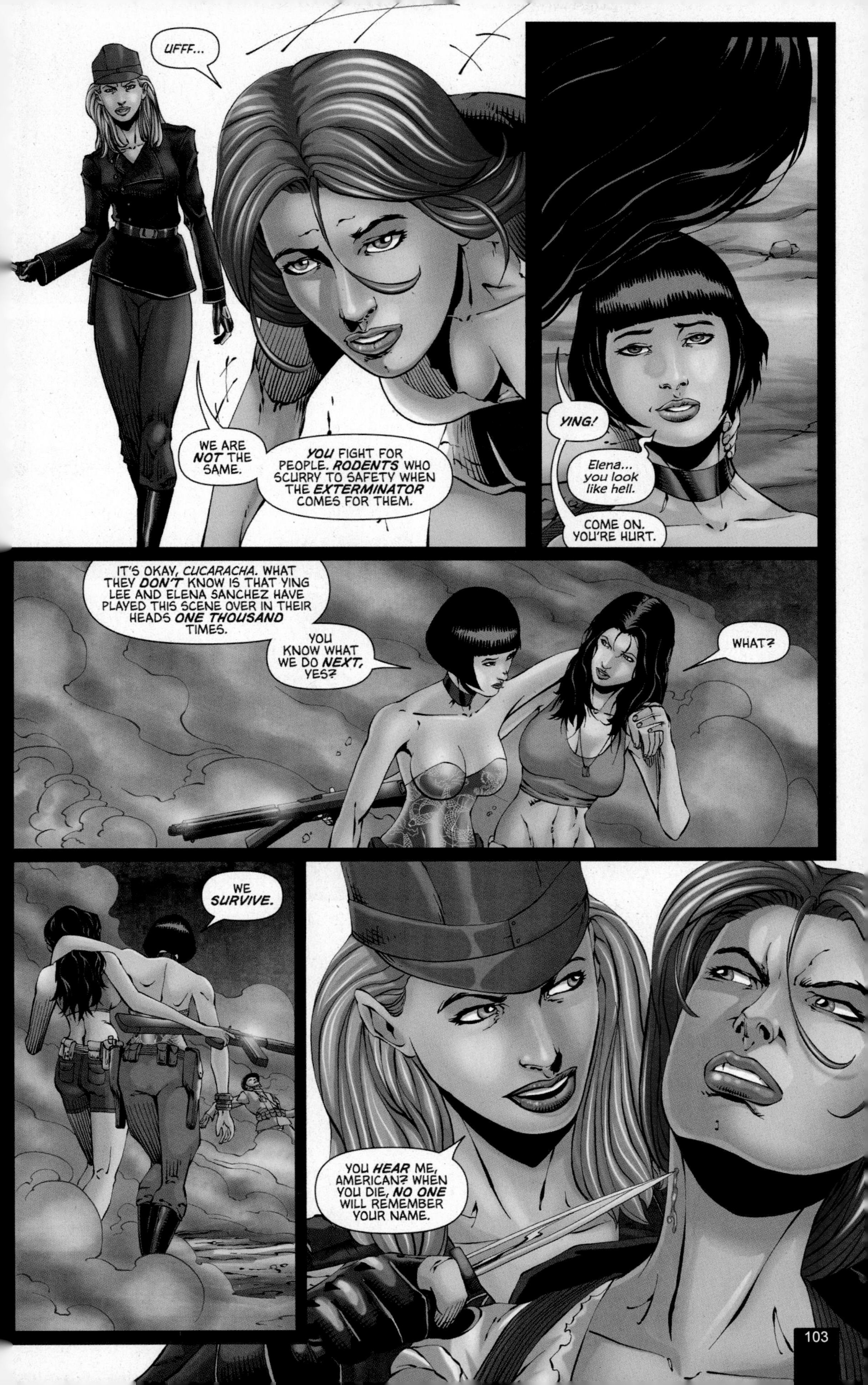
UFFF...
WE ARE NOT THE SAME.
YOU FIGHT FOR PEOPLE. RODENTS WHO SCURRY TO SAFETY WHEN THE EXTERMINATOR COMES FOR THEM.
YING!
Elena... you look like hell.
COME ON. YOU'RE HURT.
IT'S OKAY, CUCARACHA. WHAT THEY DON'T KNOW IS THAT YING LEE AND ELENA SANCHEZ HAVE PLAYED THIS SCENE OVER IN THEIR HEADS ONE THOUSAND TIMES.
YOU KNOW WHAT WE DO NEXT, YES?
WHAT?
WE SURVIVE.
YOU HEAR ME, AMERICAN? WHEN YOU DIE, NO ONE WILL REMEMBER YOUR NAME.

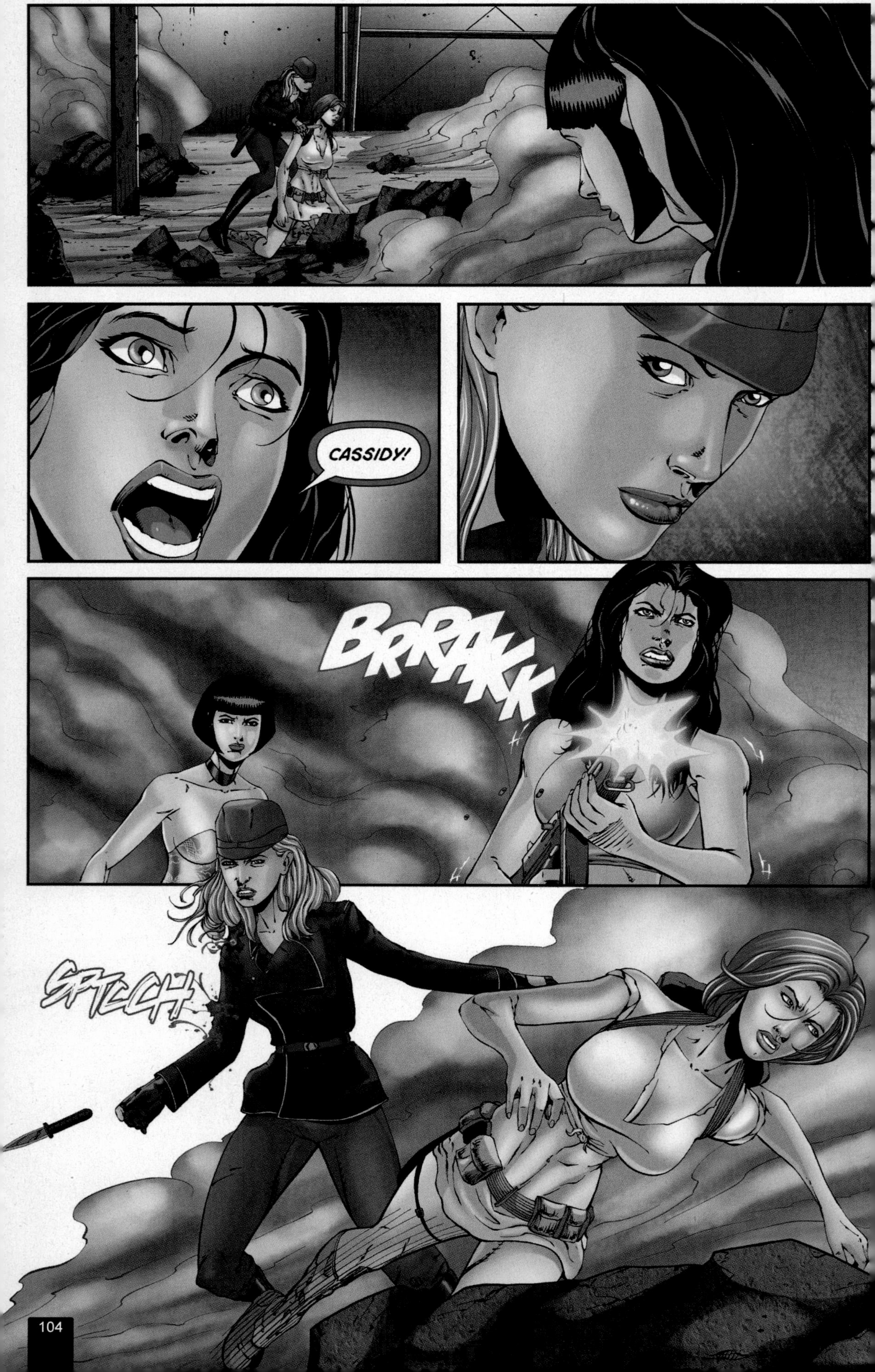
CASSIDY!
BRRAKK
SPTLCH

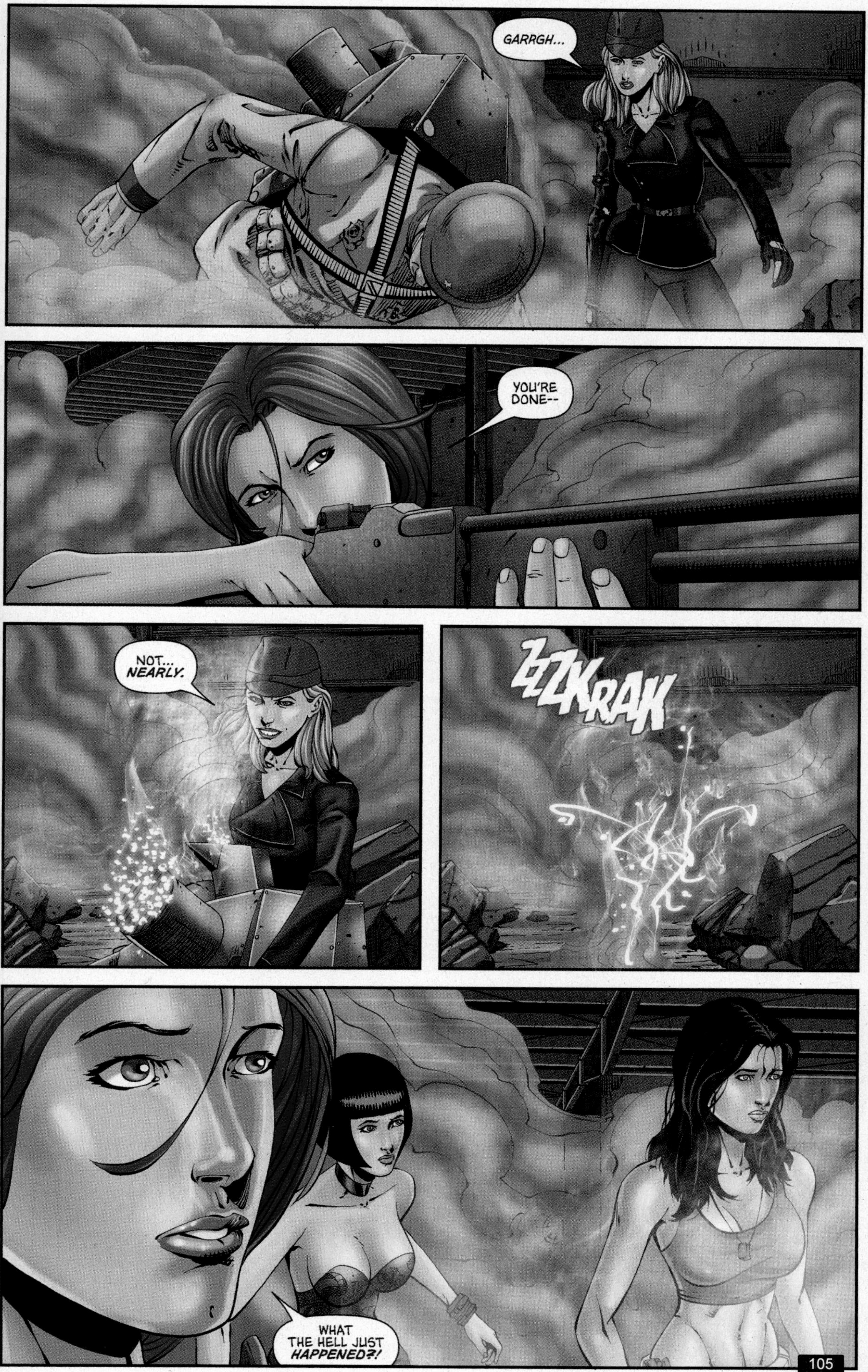
GARRGH...
YOU'RE DONE--
NOT... NEARLY.
ZZZKRAK
WHAT THE HELL JUST HAPPENED?!

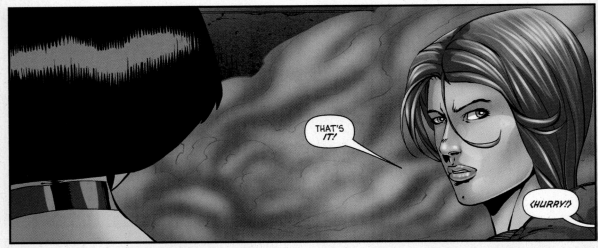

THAT'S IT!

⟨HURRY!⟩

⟨COVER ME, YOU IMBECILES! IF I AM EVEN GRAZED, I WILL HAVE YOUR HEADS MOUNTED ON MY WALL!⟩

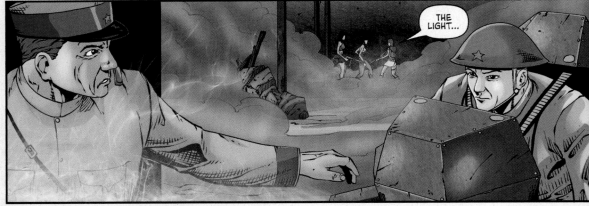

THE LIGHT...

THAT'S WHERE THAT TIME MACHINE THING IS!

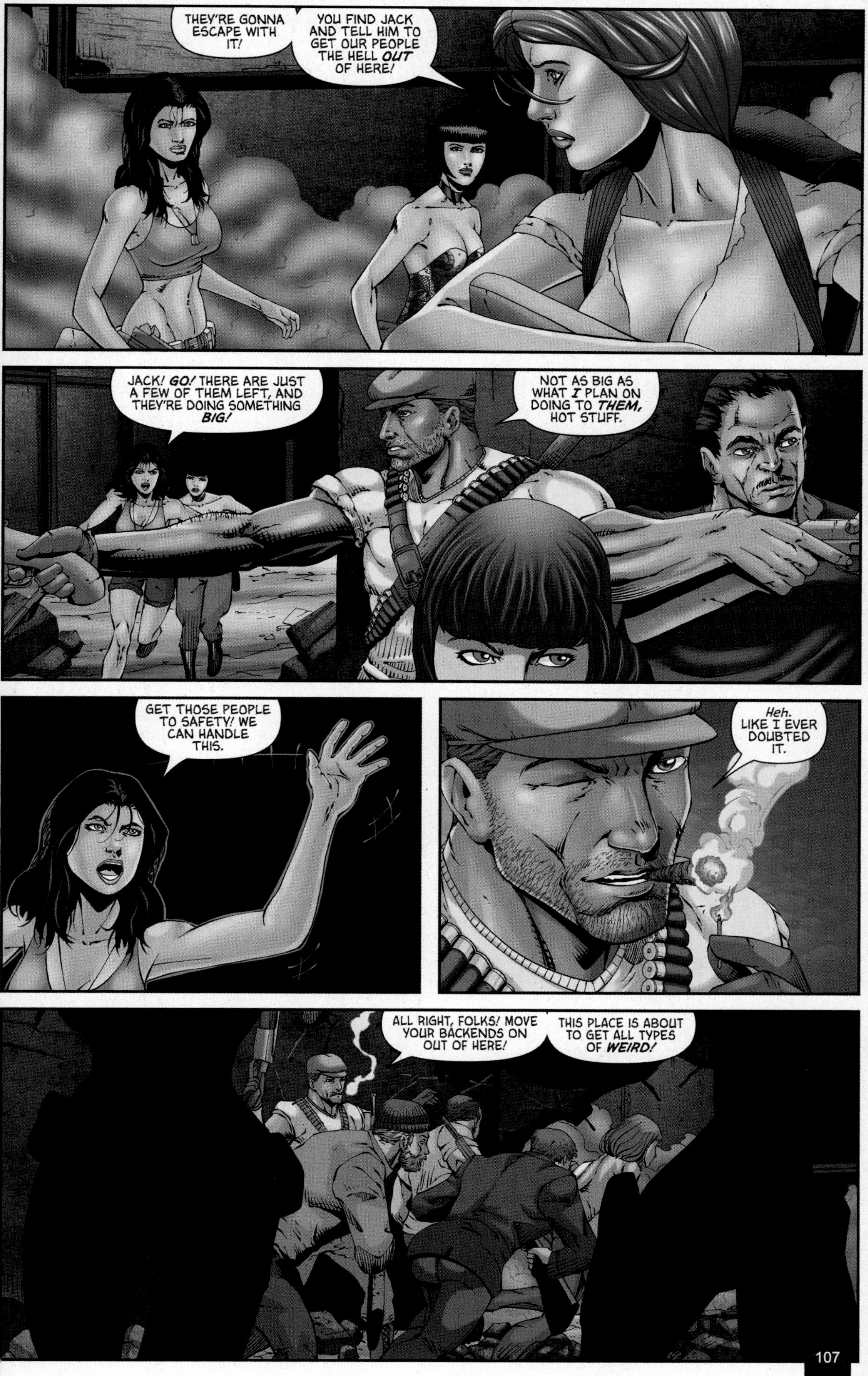
THEY'RE GONNA ESCAPE WITH IT!
YOU FIND JACK AND TELL HIM TO GET OUR PEOPLE THE HELL *OUT* OF HERE!
JACK! *GO!* THERE ARE JUST A FEW OF THEM LEFT, AND THEY'RE DOING SOMETHING *BIG!*
NOT AS BIG AS WHAT *I* PLAN ON DOING TO *THEM,* HOT STUFF.
GET THOSE PEOPLE TO SAFETY! WE CAN HANDLE THIS.
Heh. LIKE I EVER DOUBTED IT.
ALL RIGHT, FOLKS! MOVE YOUR BACKENDS ON OUT OF HERE!
THIS PLACE IS ABOUT TO GET ALL TYPES OF *WEIRD!*

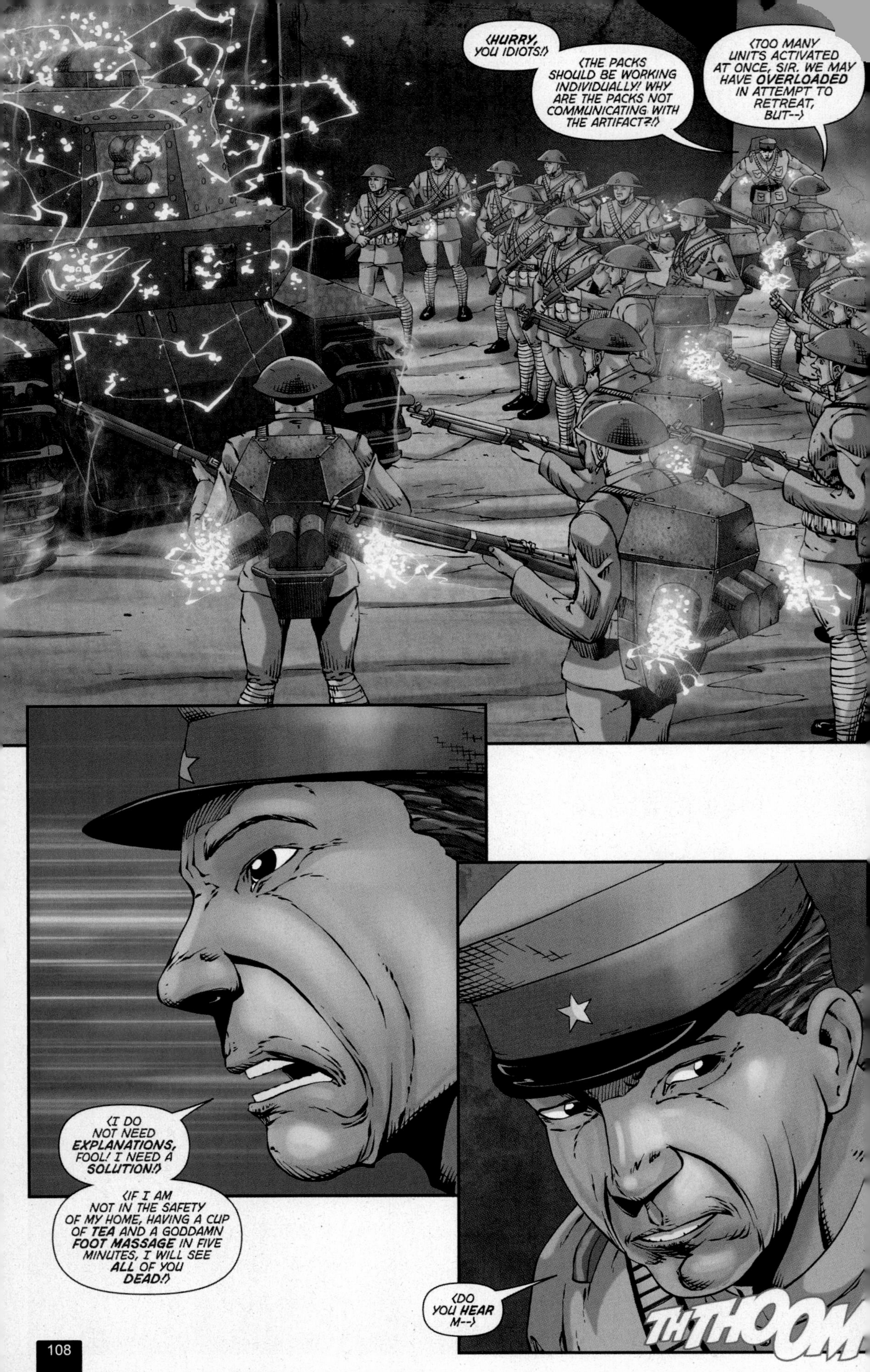
‹HURRY, YOU IDIOTS!›
‹THE PACKS SHOULD BE WORKING INDIVIDUALLY! WHY ARE THE PACKS NOT COMMUNICATING WITH THE ARTIFACT?!›
‹TOO MANY UNITS ACTIVATED AT ONCE, SIR. WE MAY HAVE OVERLOADED IN ATTEMPT TO RETREAT, BUT--›
‹I DO NOT NEED EXPLANATIONS, FOOL! I NEED A SOLUTION!›
‹IF I AM NOT IN THE SAFETY OF MY HOME, HAVING A CUP OF TEA AND A GODDAMN FOOT MASSAGE IN FIVE MINUTES, I WILL SEE ALL OF YOU DEAD!›
‹DO YOU HEAR M--›
THTHOOM

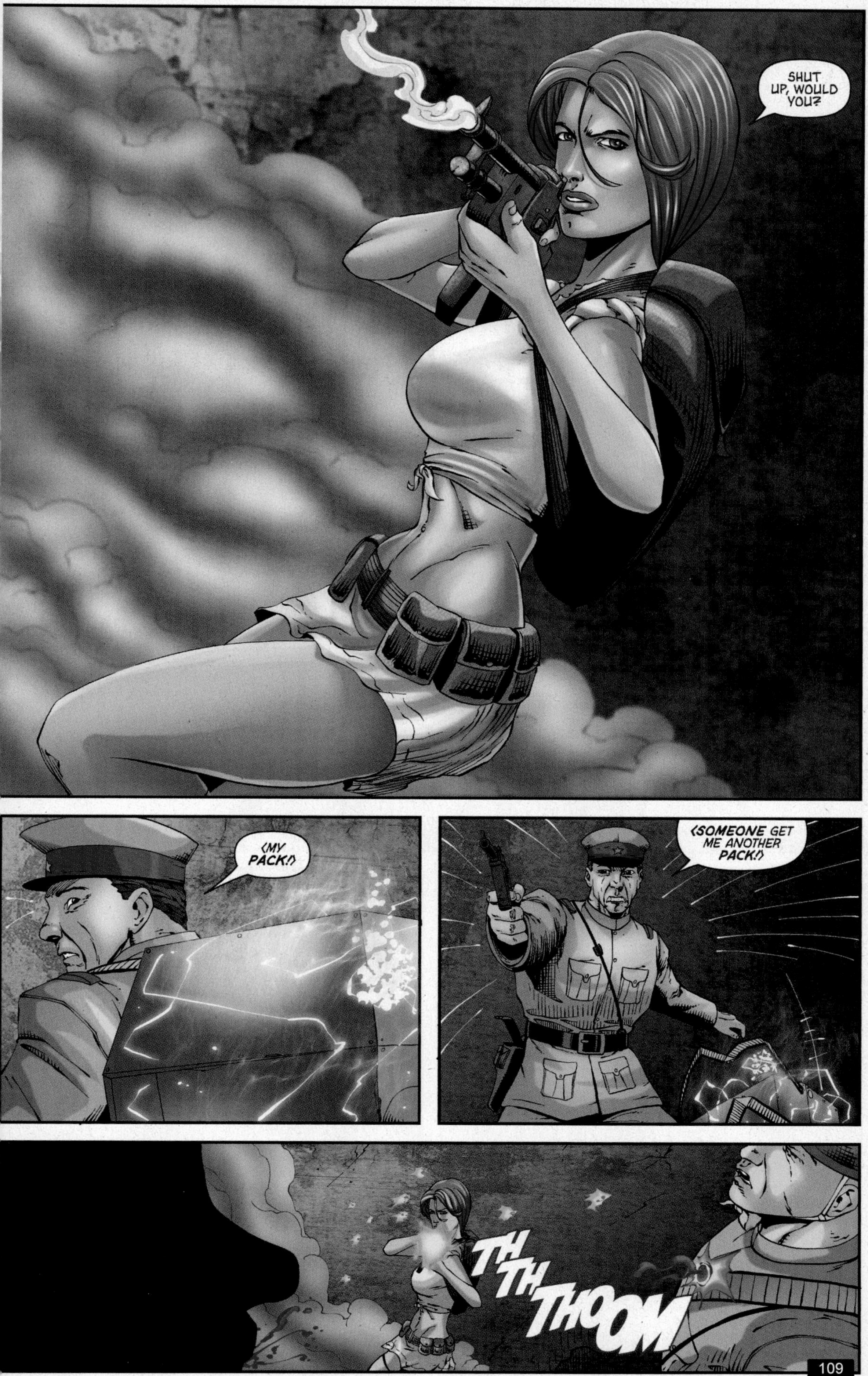
SHUT UP, WOULD YOU?
‹MY PACK!›
‹SOMEONE GET ME ANOTHER PACK!›
TH TH THOOM

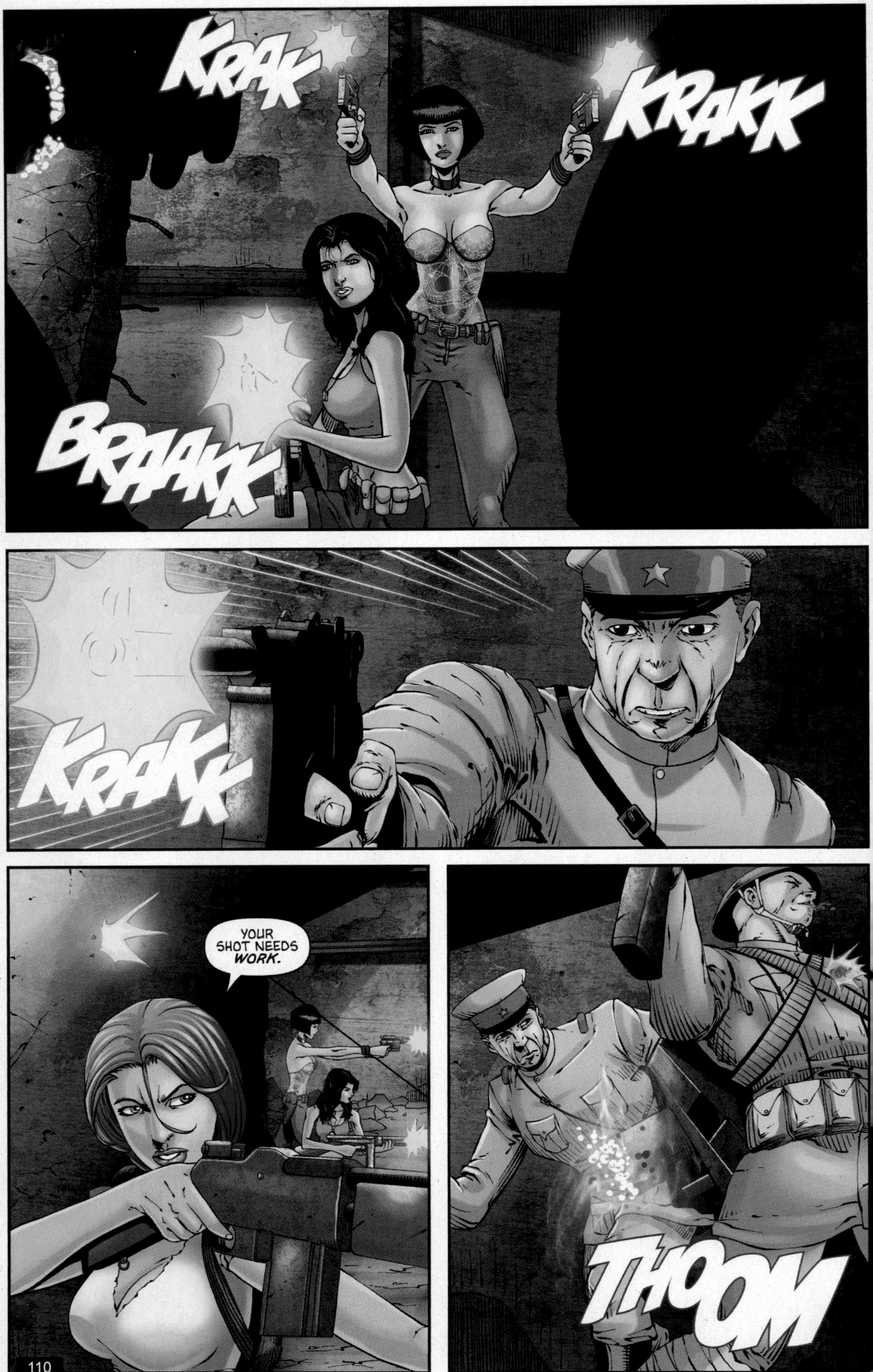
KRAK
KRAKK
BRAKK
KRAKK
YOUR SHOT NEEDS WORK.
THOOM

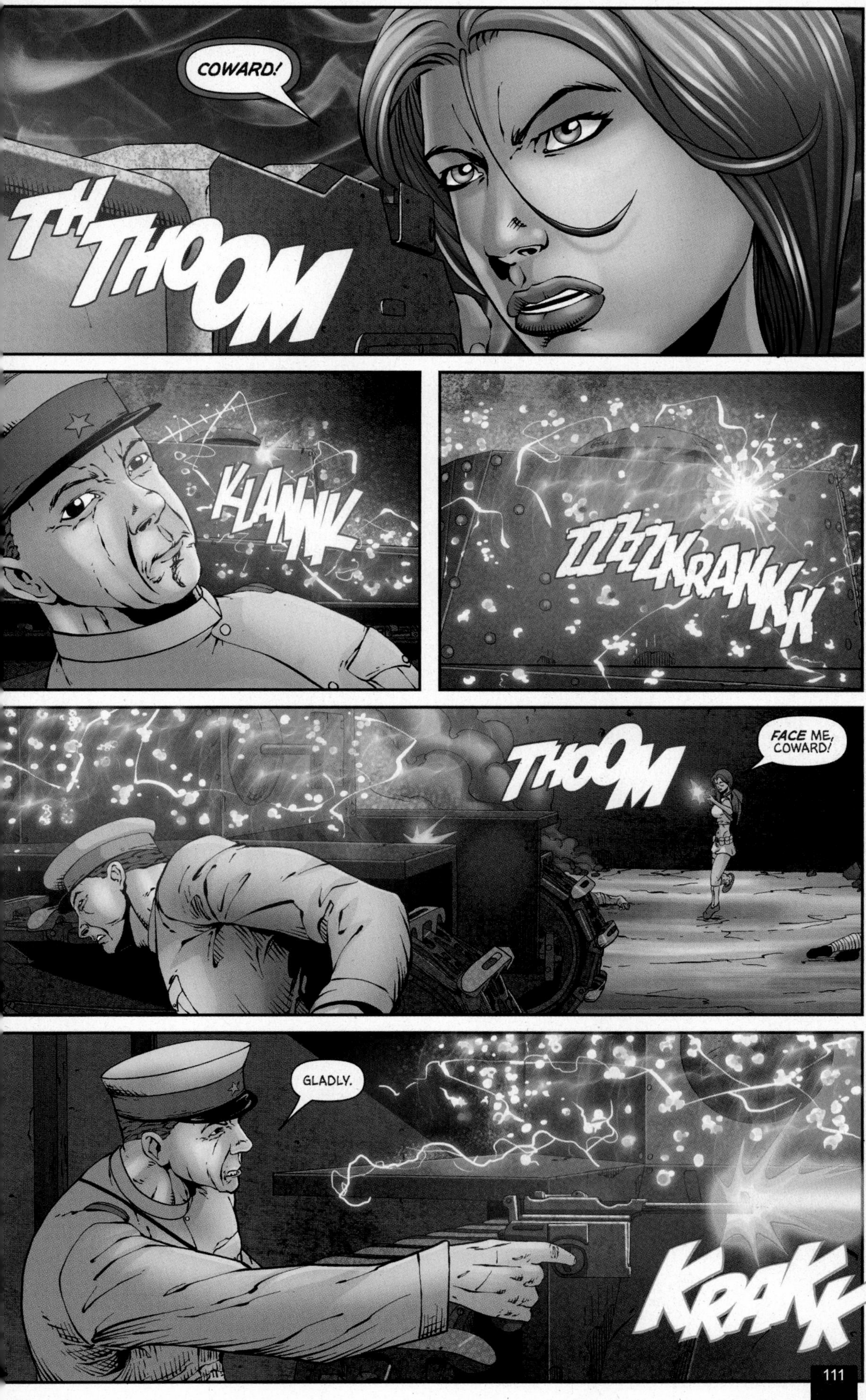
COWARD!
TH THOOM
KLANNK
ZZZZKRANKKK
THOOM
FACE ME, COWARD!
GLADLY.
KRAKK

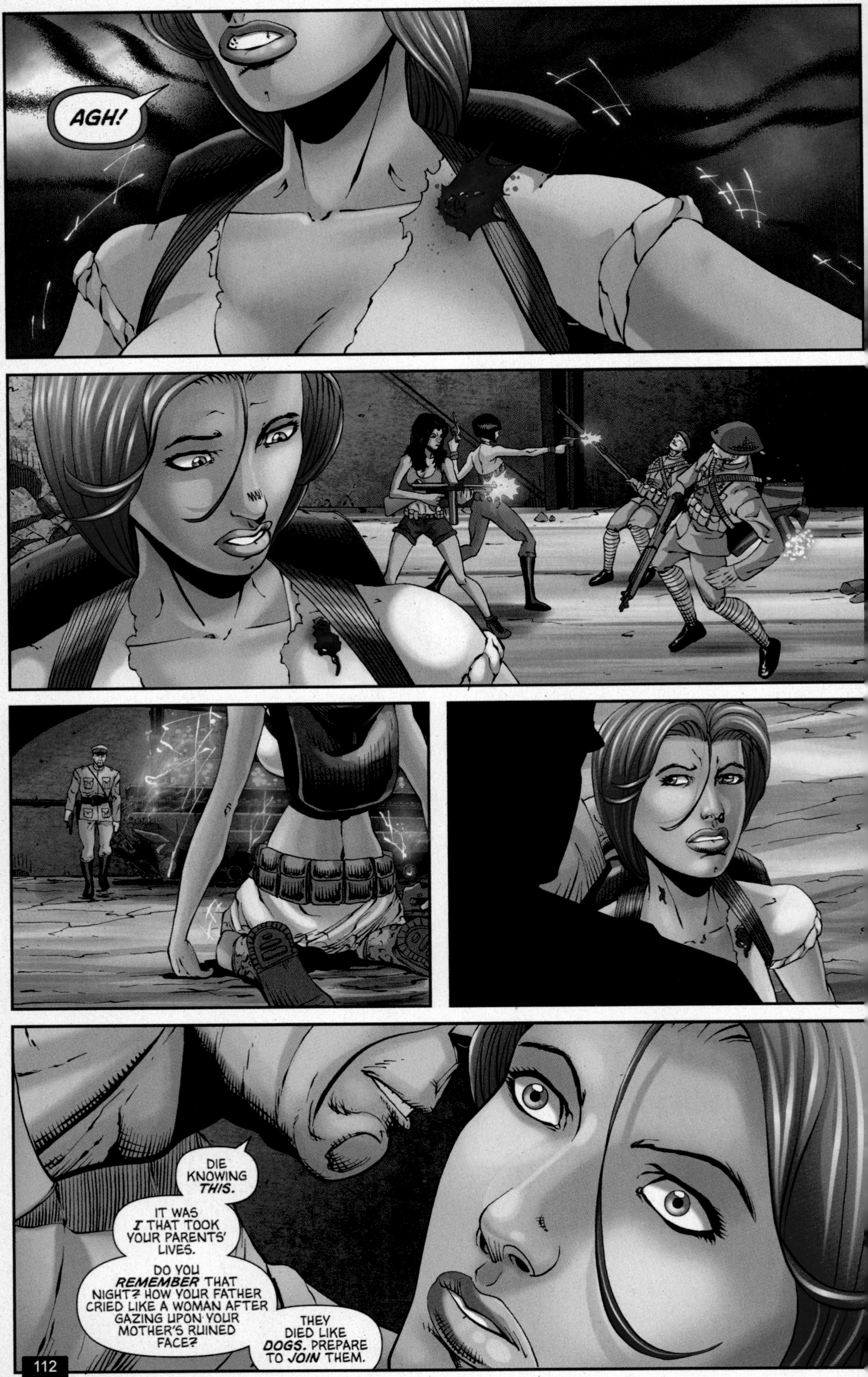
AGH!
DIE KNOWING THIS.
IT WAS I THAT TOOK YOUR PARENTS' LIVES.
DO YOU REMEMBER THAT NIGHT? HOW YOUR FATHER CRIED LIKE A WOMAN AFTER GAZING UPON YOUR MOTHER'S RUINED FACE?
THEY DIED LIKE DOGS. PREPARE TO JOIN THEM.

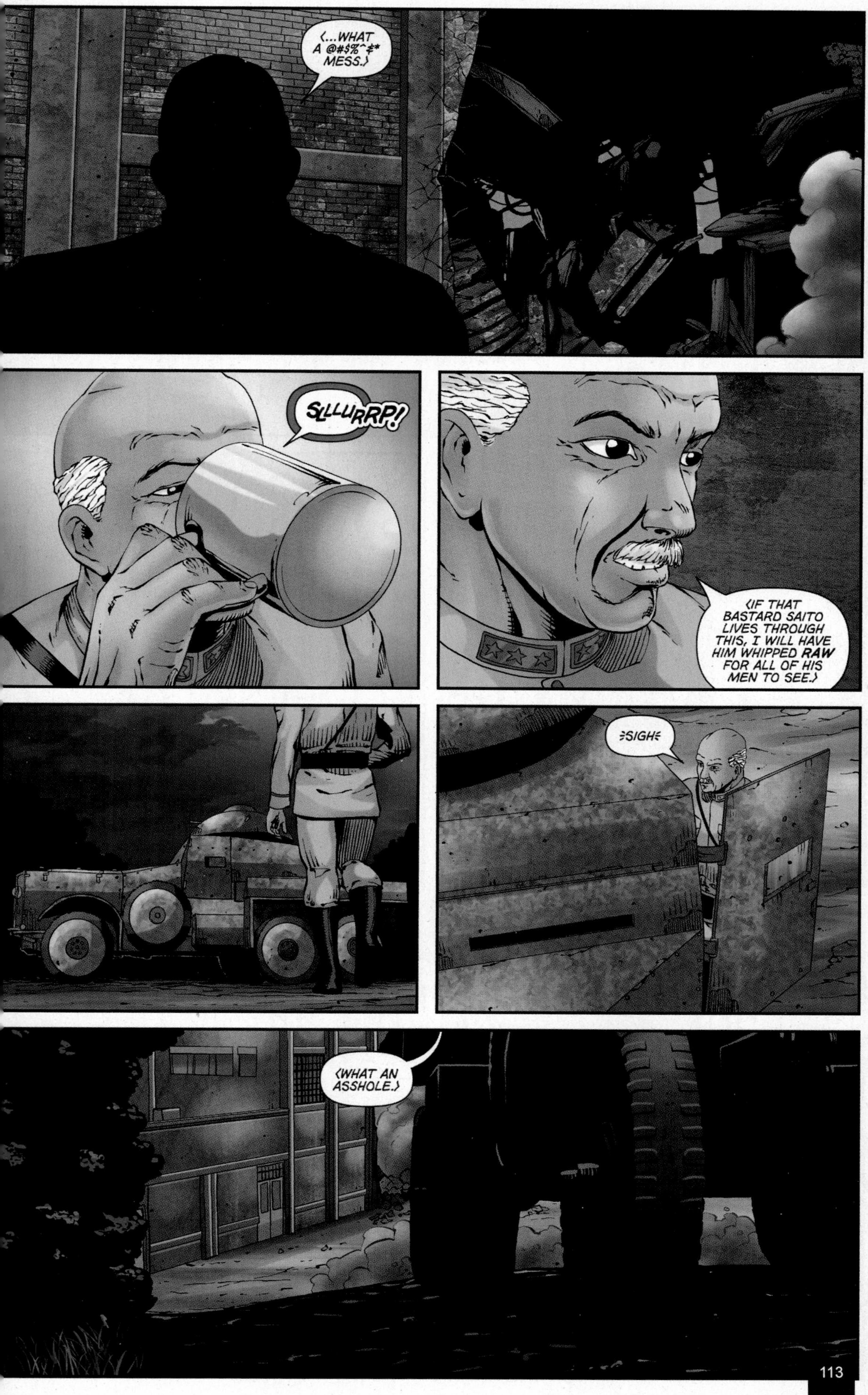
‹...WHAT A @#$%^&* MESS.›
SLLLURRP!
‹IF THAT BASTARD SAITO LIVES THROUGH THIS, I WILL HAVE HIM WHIPPED RAW FOR ALL OF HIS MEN TO SEE.›
SIGH
‹WHAT AN ASSHOLE.›

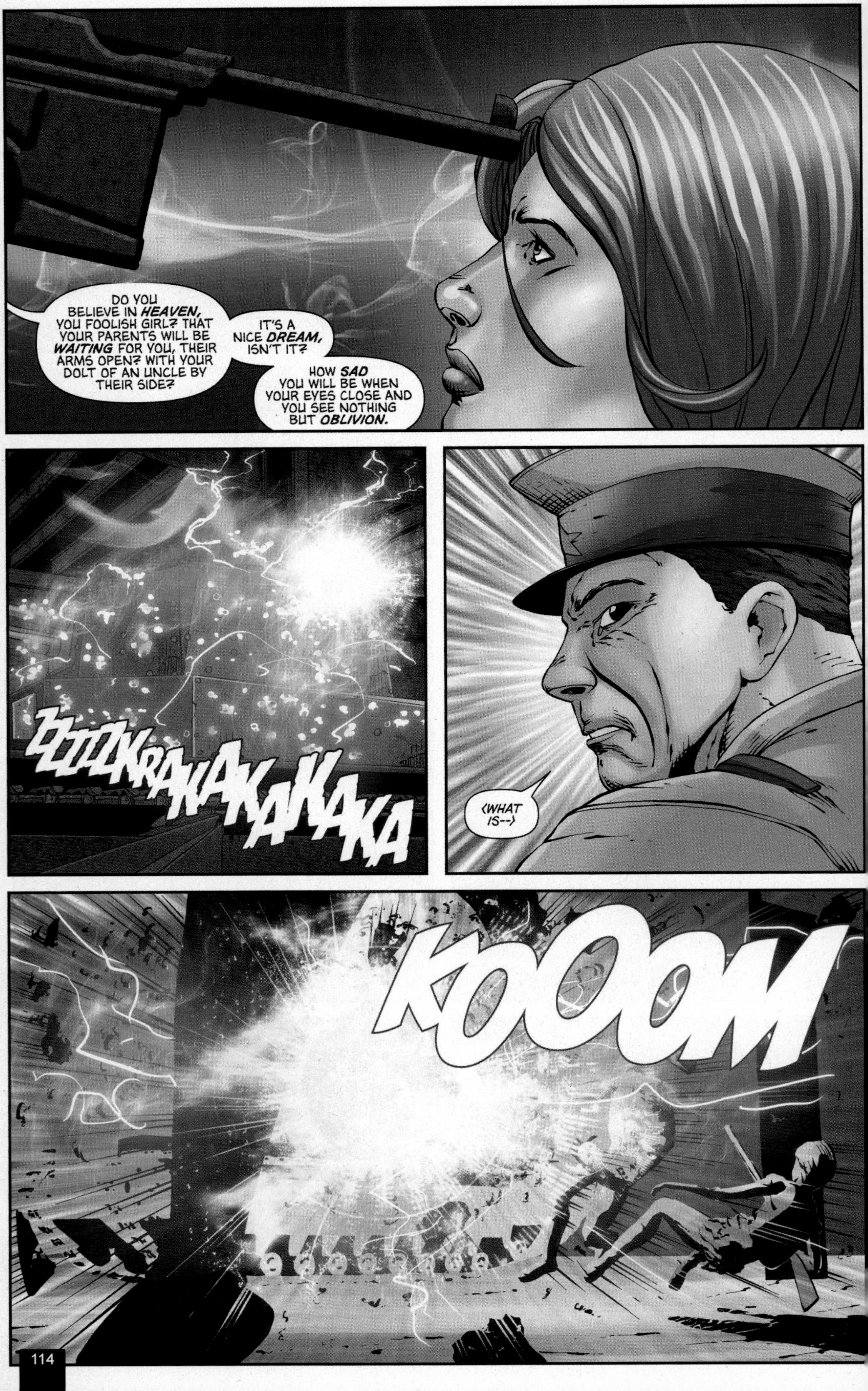
DO YOU BELIEVE IN HEAVEN, YOU FOOLISH GIRL? THAT YOUR PARENTS WILL BE WAITING FOR YOU, THEIR ARMS OPEN? WITH YOUR DOLT OF AN UNCLE BY THEIR SIDE?
IT'S A NICE DREAM, ISN'T IT?
HOW SAD YOU WILL BE WHEN YOUR EYES CLOSE AND YOU SEE NOTHING BUT OBLIVION.
ZZZZKRAKAKAKAKAKA
<WHAT IS-->
KOOOM

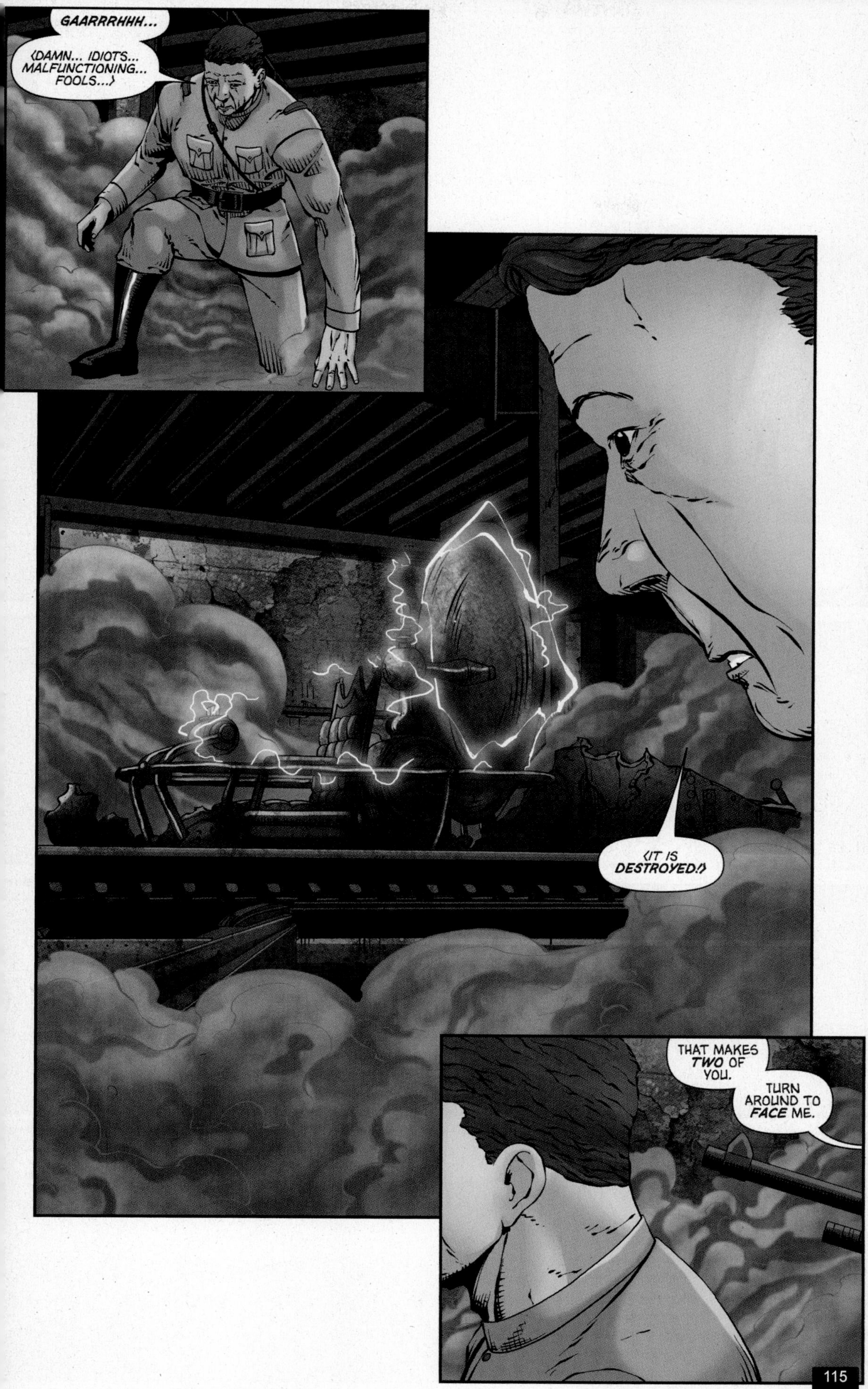
GAARRRHHH...
‹DAMN... IDIOTS... MALFUNCTIONING... FOOLS...›
‹IT IS DESTROYED!›
THAT MAKES TWO OF YOU.
TURN AROUND TO FACE ME.

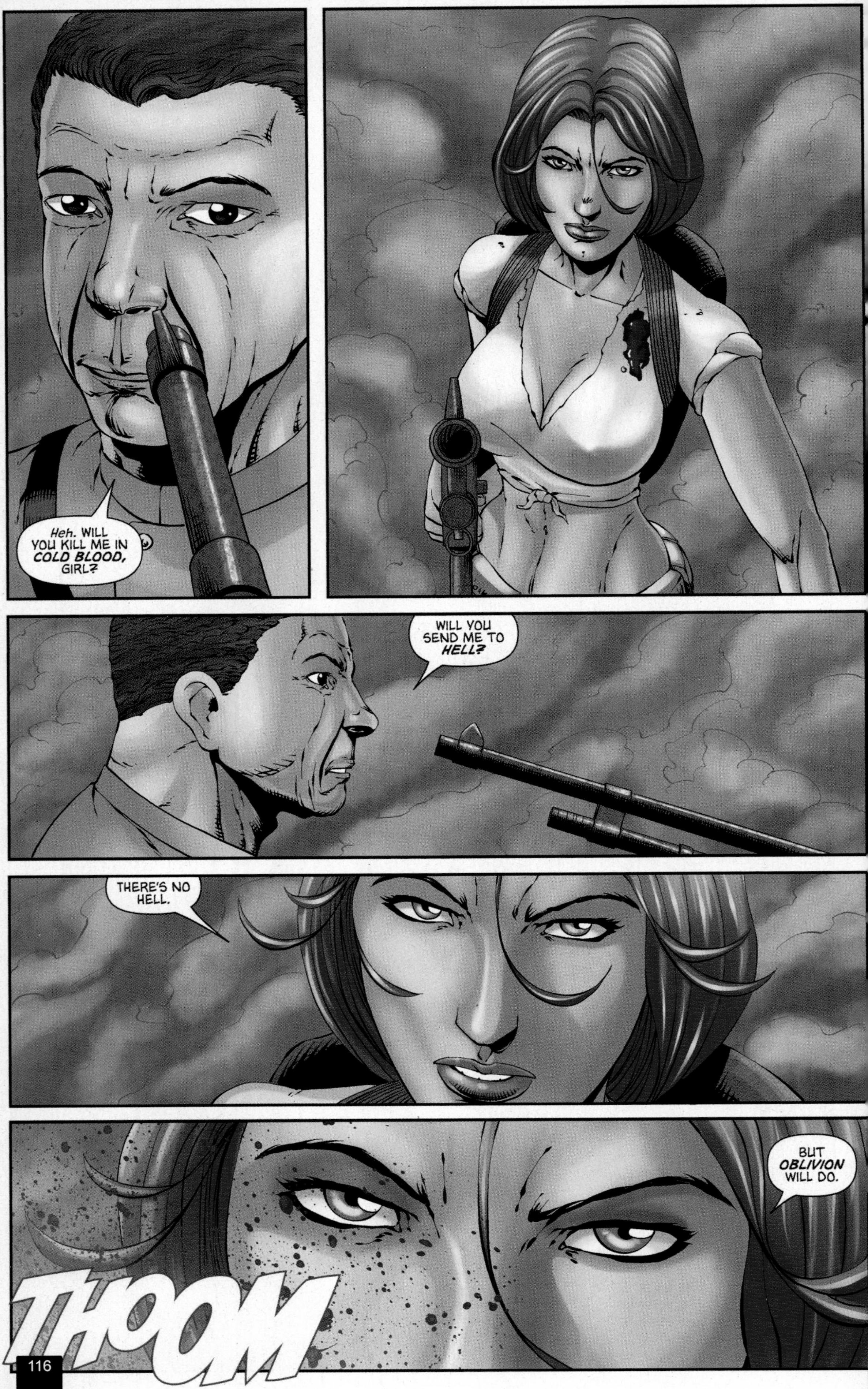
Heh. WILL YOU KILL ME IN COLD BLOOD, GIRL?
WILL YOU SEND ME TO HELL?
THERE'S NO HELL.
BUT OBLIVION WILL DO.
THOOM

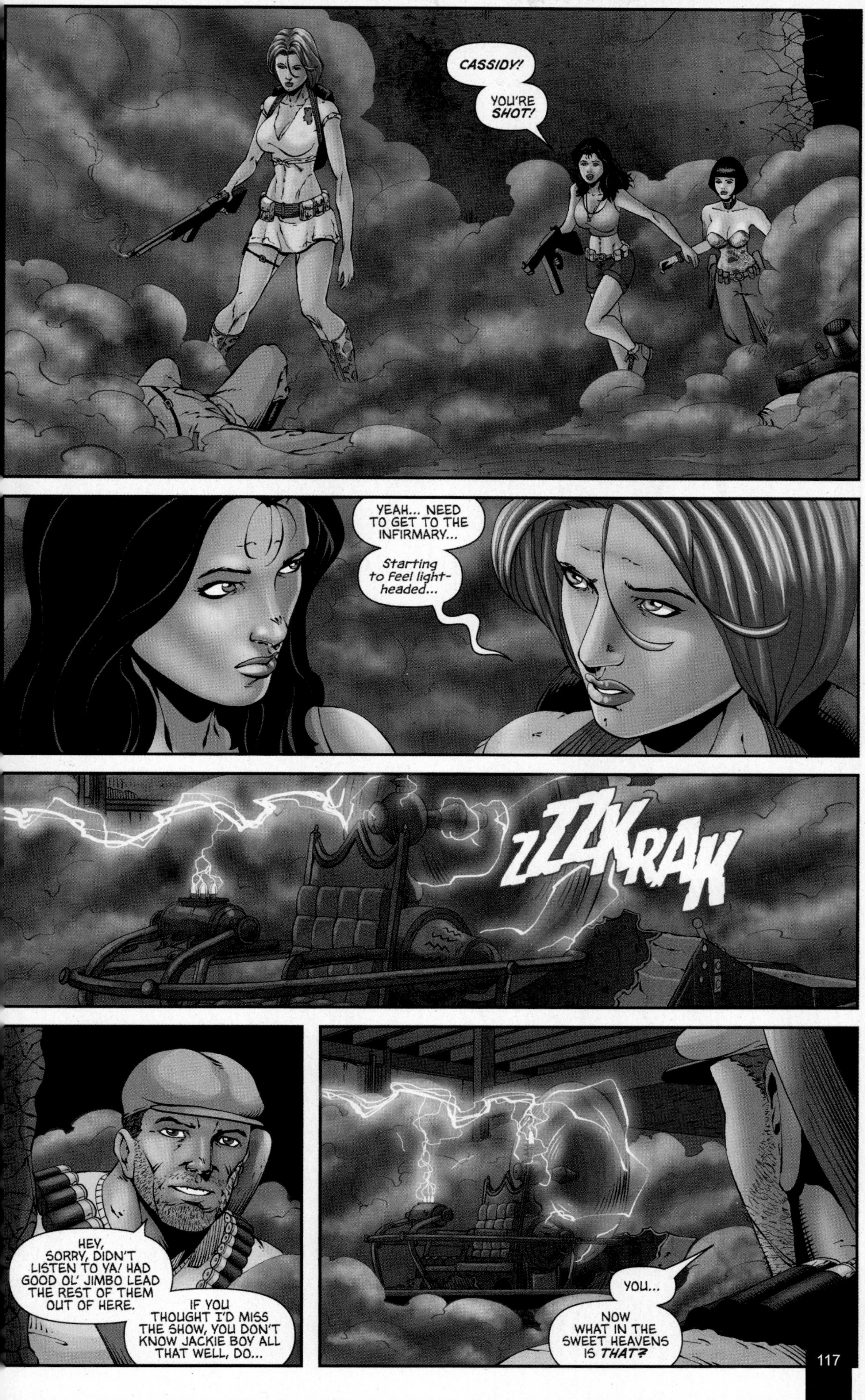
CASSIDY!
YOU'RE SHOT!
YEAH... NEED TO GET TO THE INFIRMARY...
Starting to feel light-headed...
ZZZKRAK
HEY, SORRY, DIDN'T LISTEN TO YA! HAD GOOD OL' JIMBO LEAD THE REST OF THEM OUT OF HERE.
IF YOU THOUGHT I'D MISS THE SHOW, YOU DON'T KNOW JACKIE BOY ALL THAT WELL, DO...
YOU...
NOW WHAT IN THE SWEET HEAVENS IS THAT?

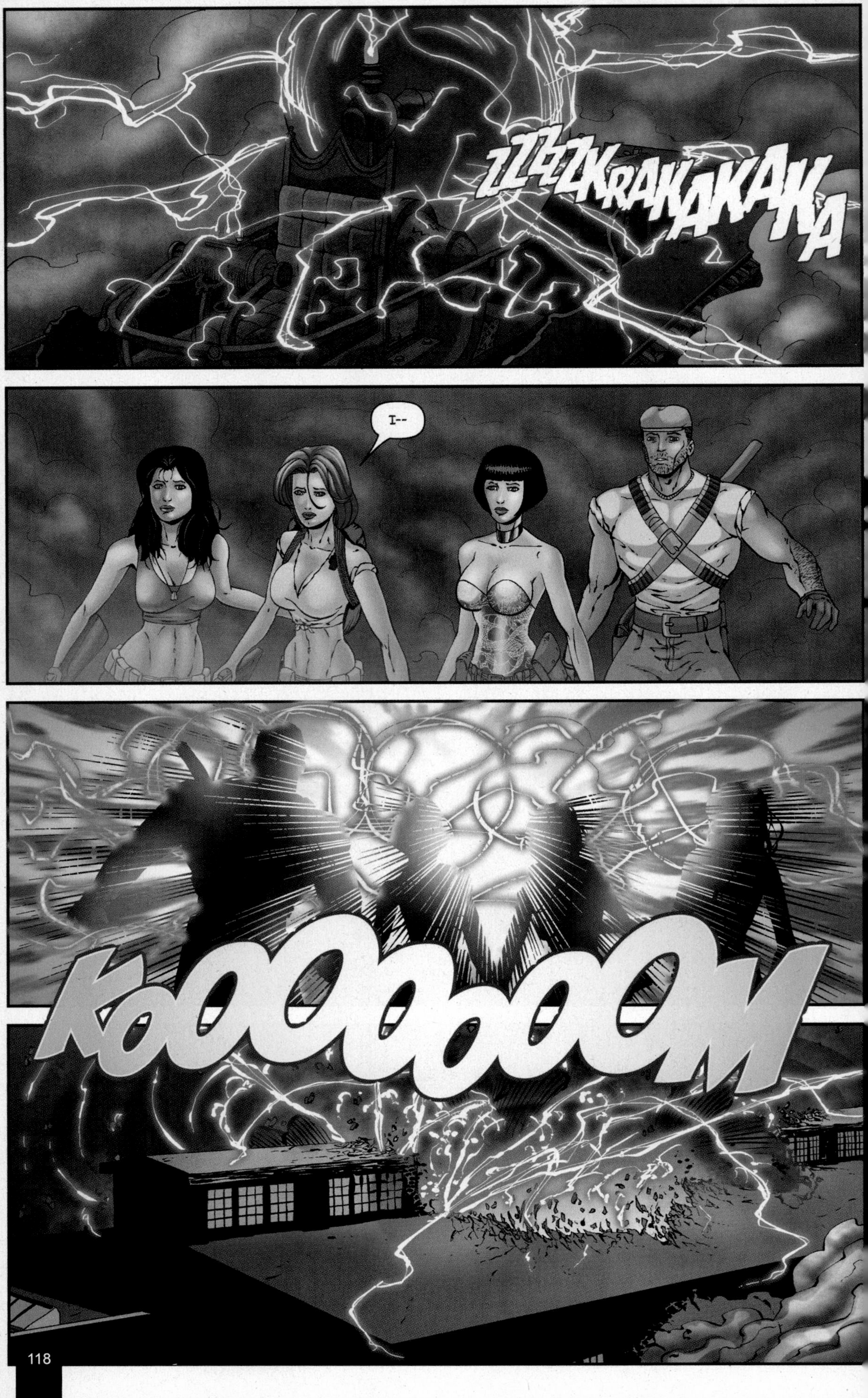
ZZZZZKRAKAKAKAKA
I--
KOOOOOOOM

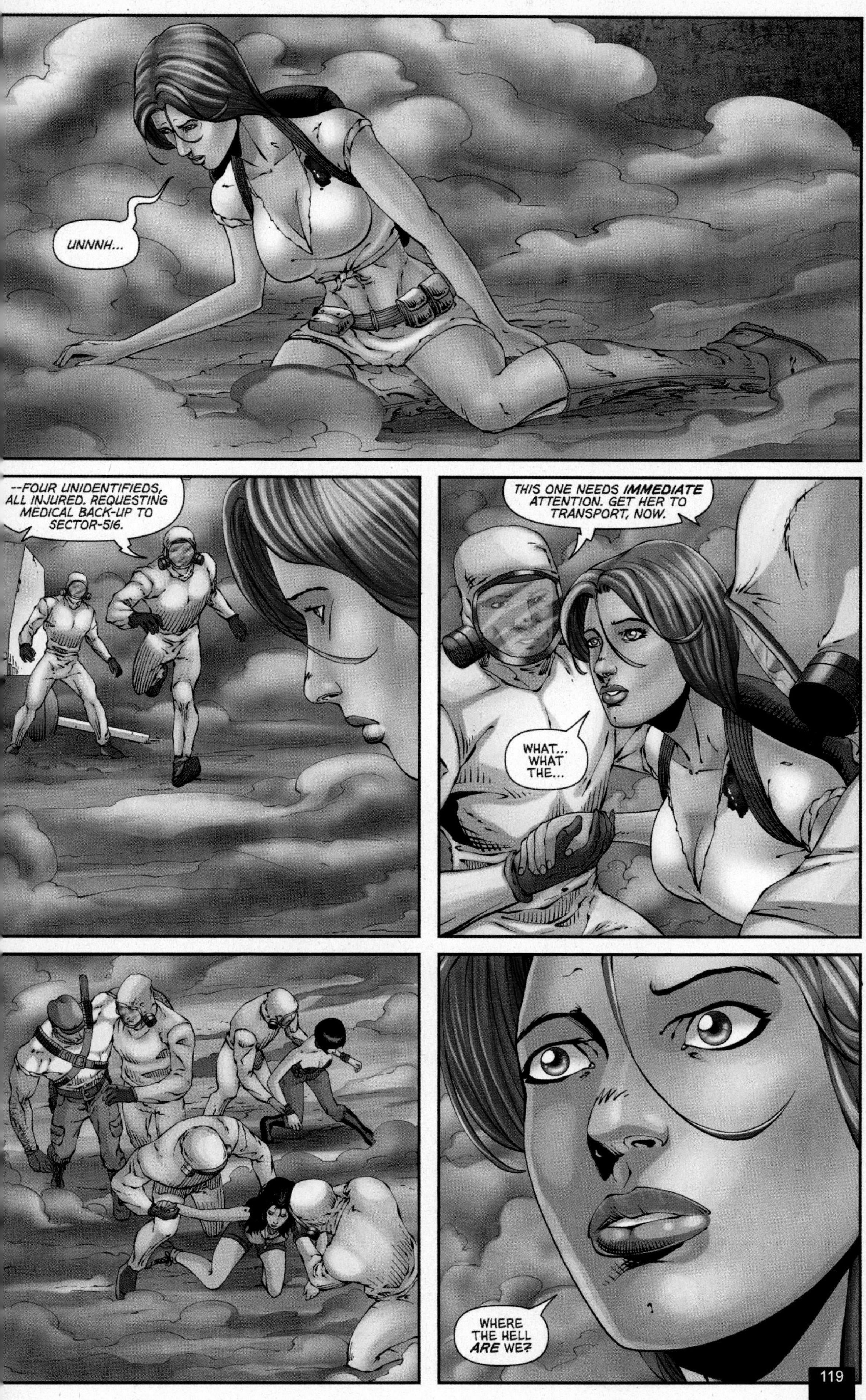
UNNNH...
--FOUR UNIDENTIFIEDS, ALL INJURED. REQUESTING MEDICAL BACK-UP TO SECTOR-516.
THIS ONE NEEDS *IMMEDIATE* ATTENTION. GET HER TO TRANSPORT, NOW.
WHAT... WHAT THE...
WHERE THE HELL *ARE* WE?

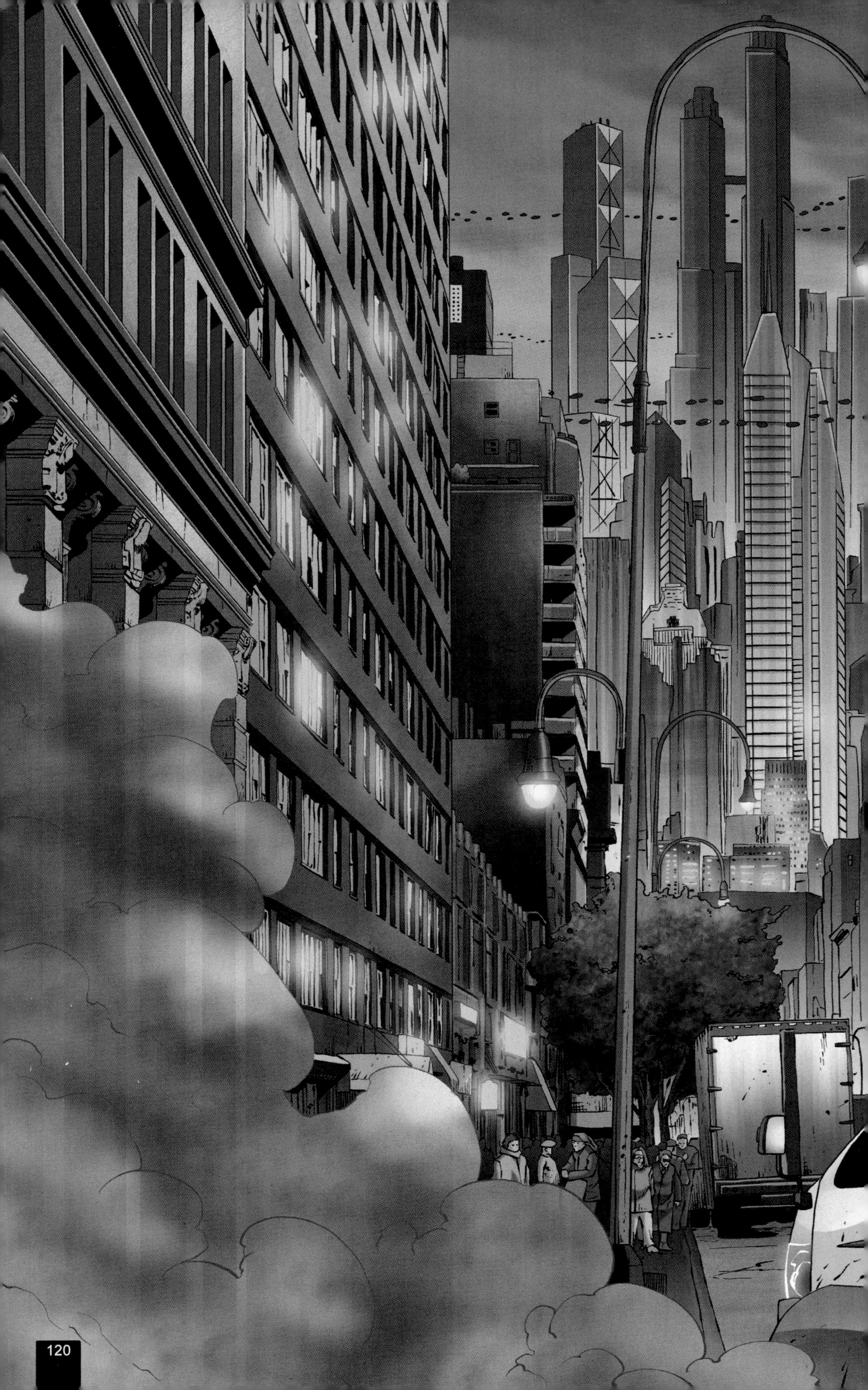

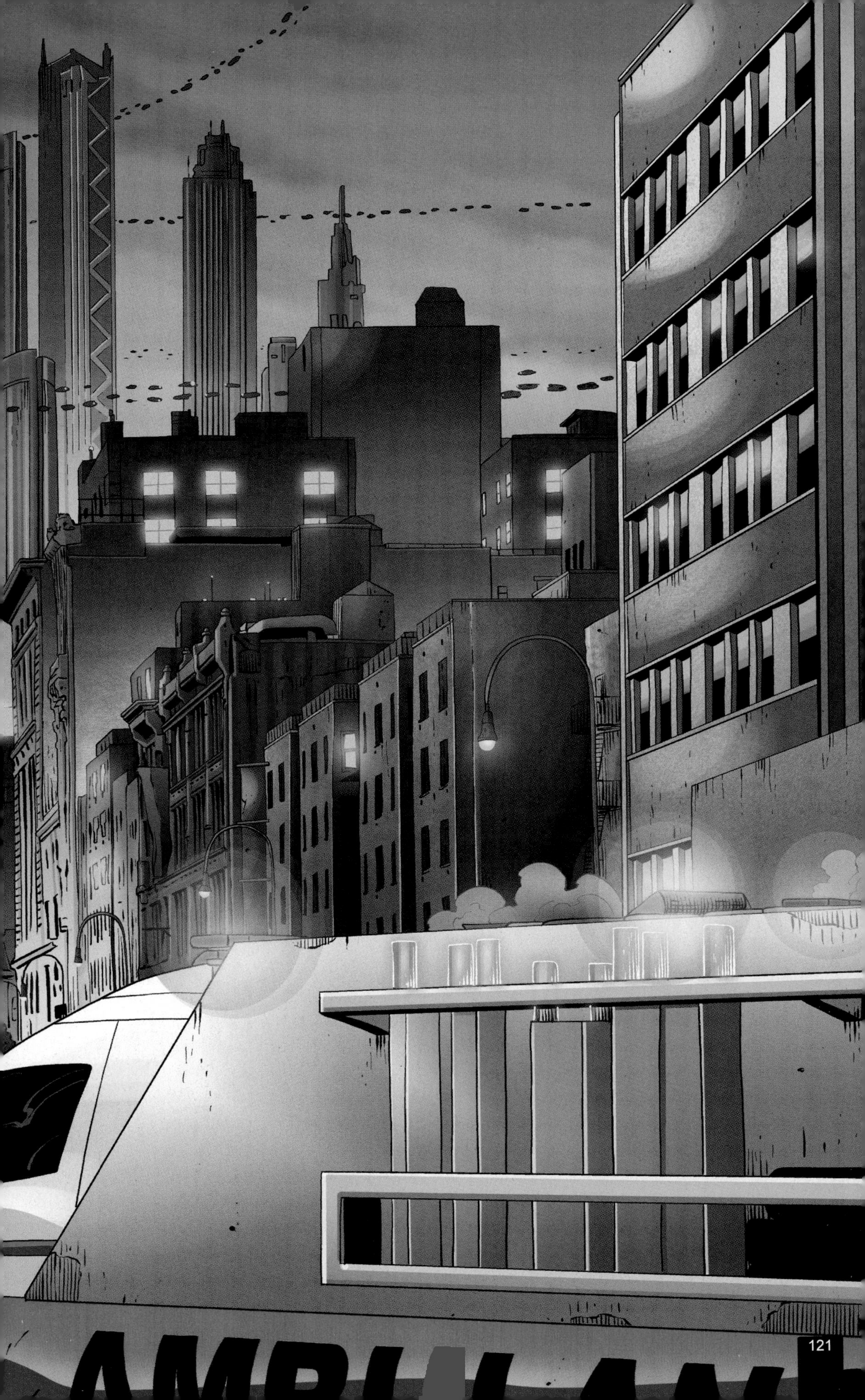

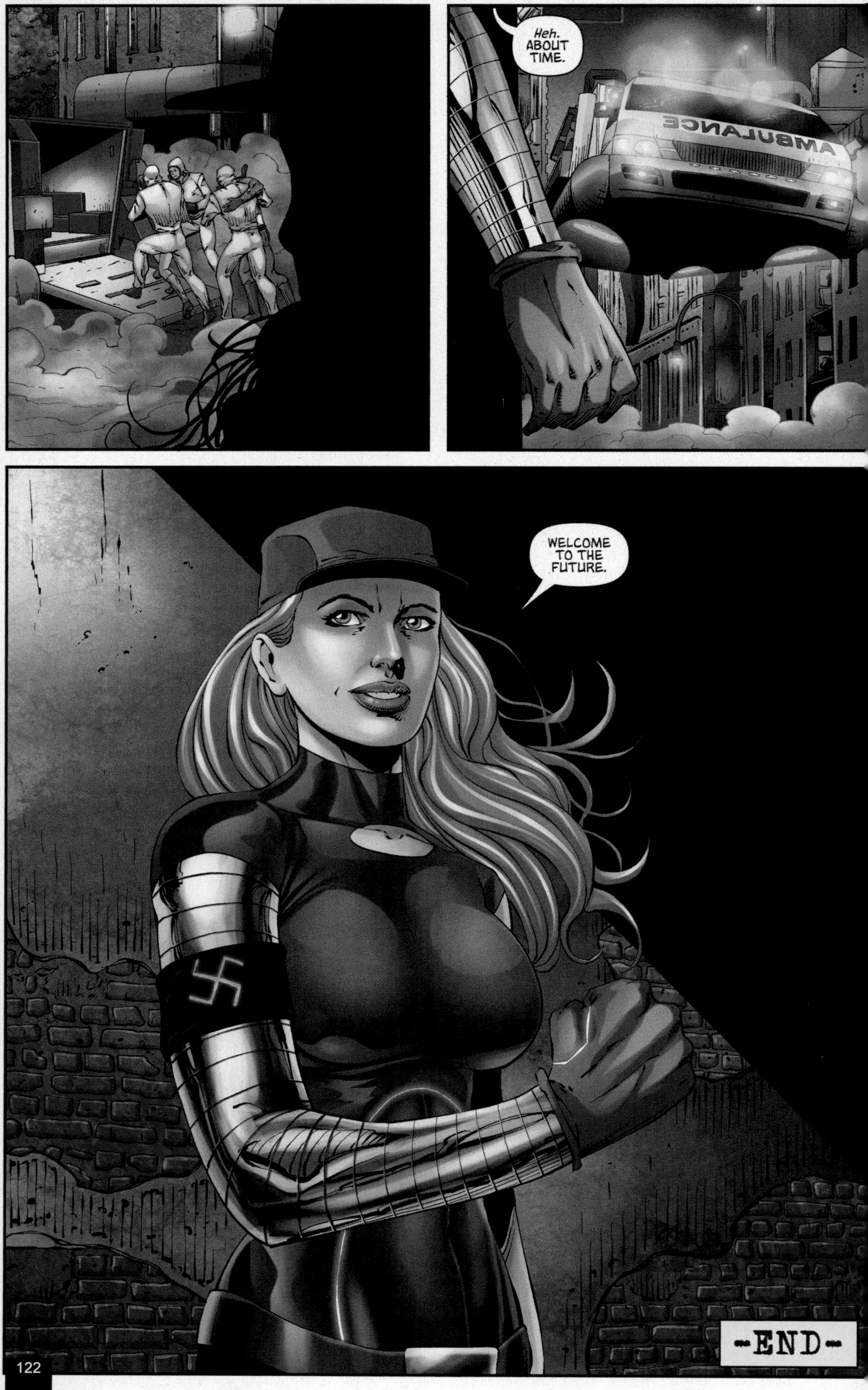
Heh. ABOUT TIME.
AMBULANCE
WELCOME TO THE FUTURE.
-END-

B.A.R Maid

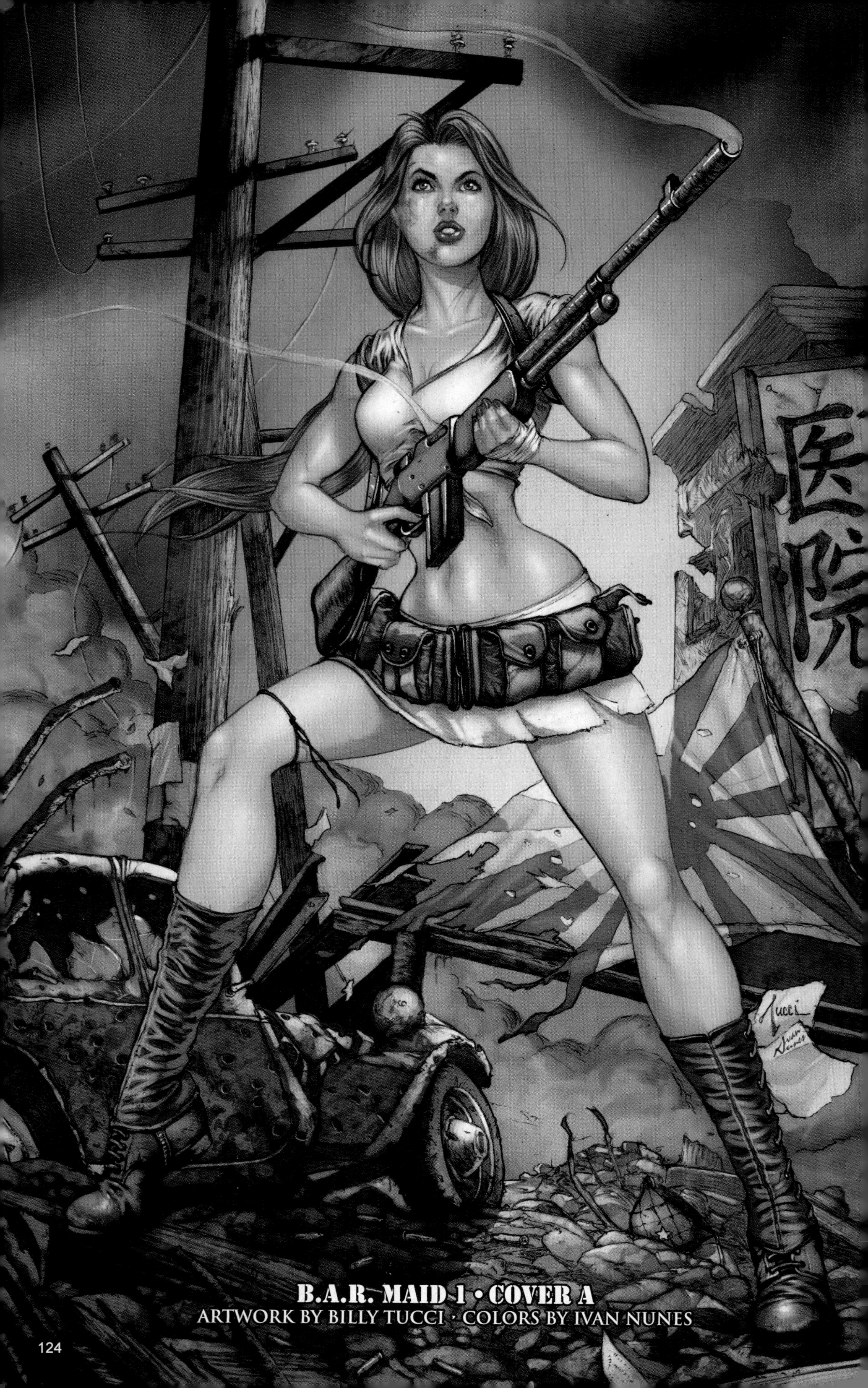
医院
Tucci

B.A.R. MAID 1 • COVER A

ARTWORK BY BILLY TUCCI · COLORS BY IVAN NUNES

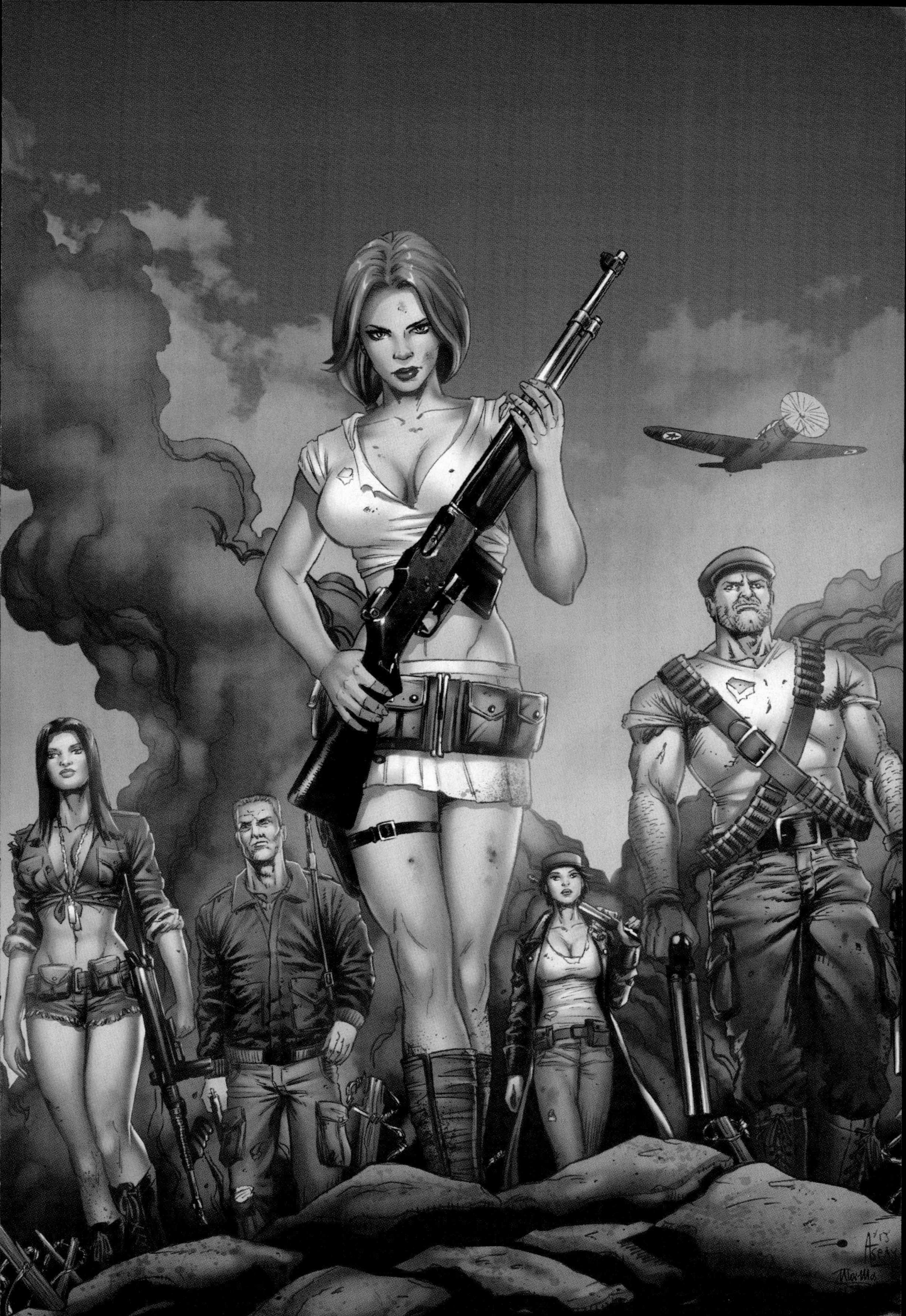

B.A.R. MAID 1 • COVER B
ARTWORK BY ANTHONY SPAY • COLORS BY ULA MOS

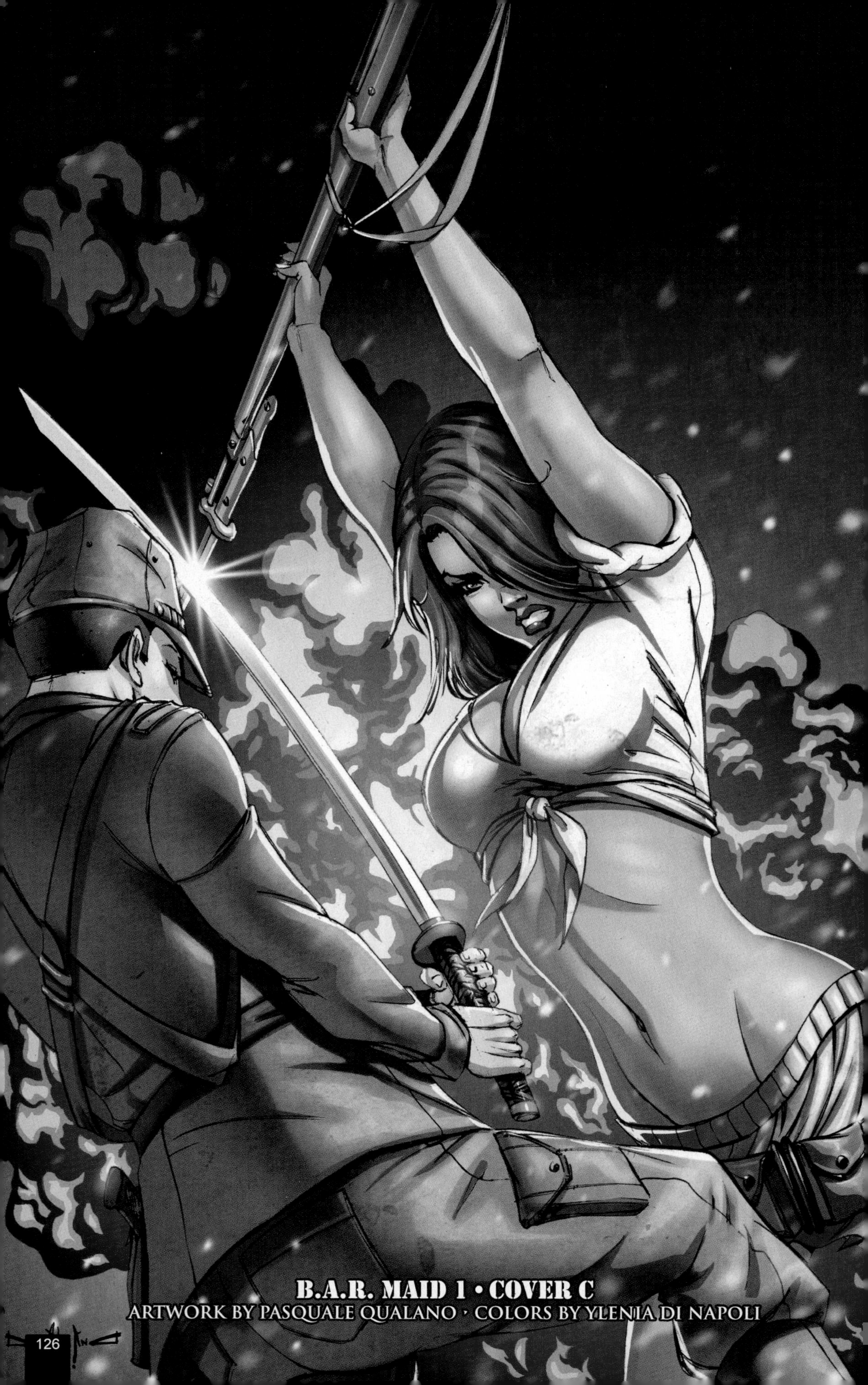

B.A.R. MAID 1 • COVER C
ARTWORK BY PASQUALE QUALANO • COLORS BY YLENIA DI NAPOLI

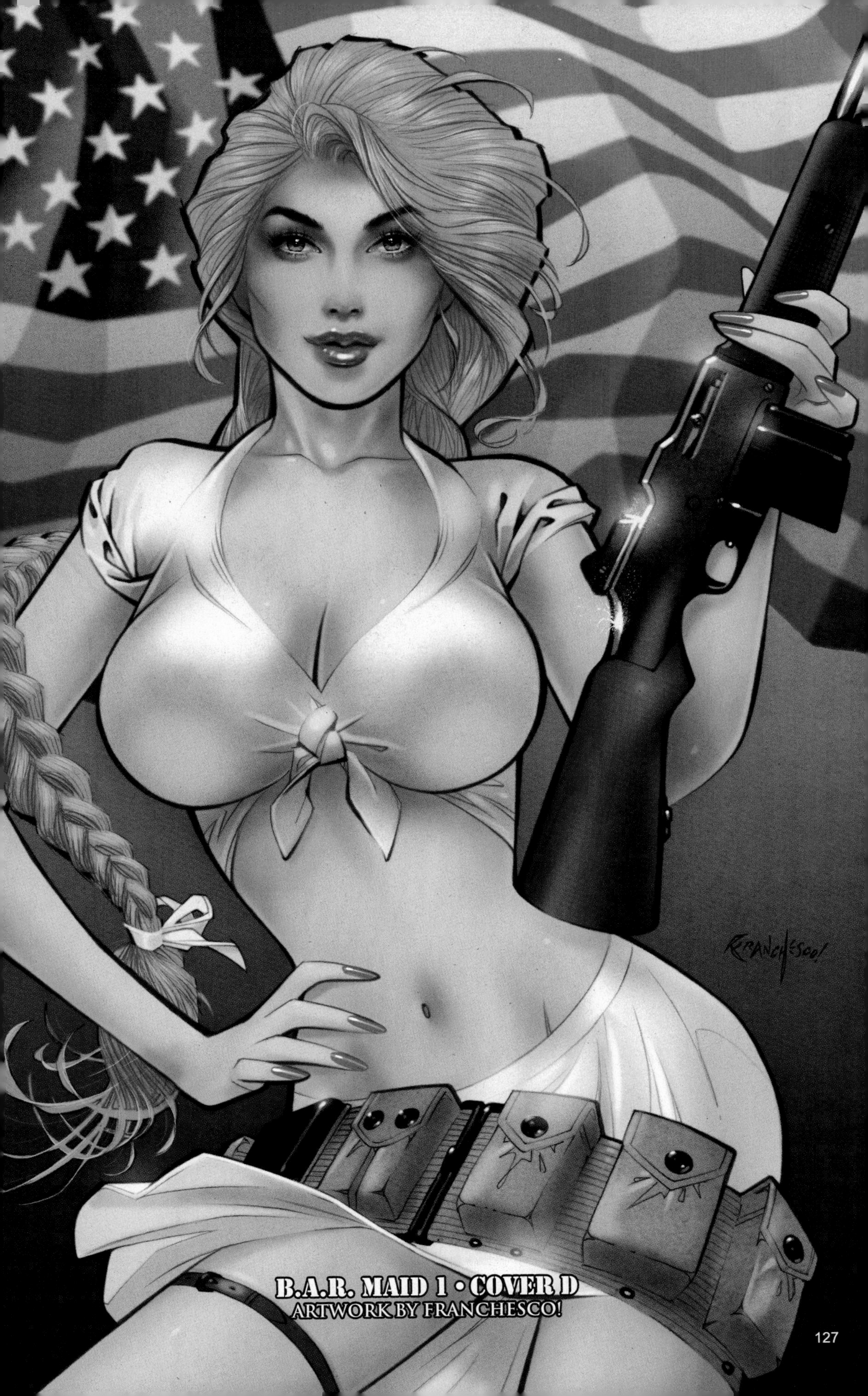

B.A.R. MAID 1 • COVER D
ARTWORK BY FRANCHESCO!

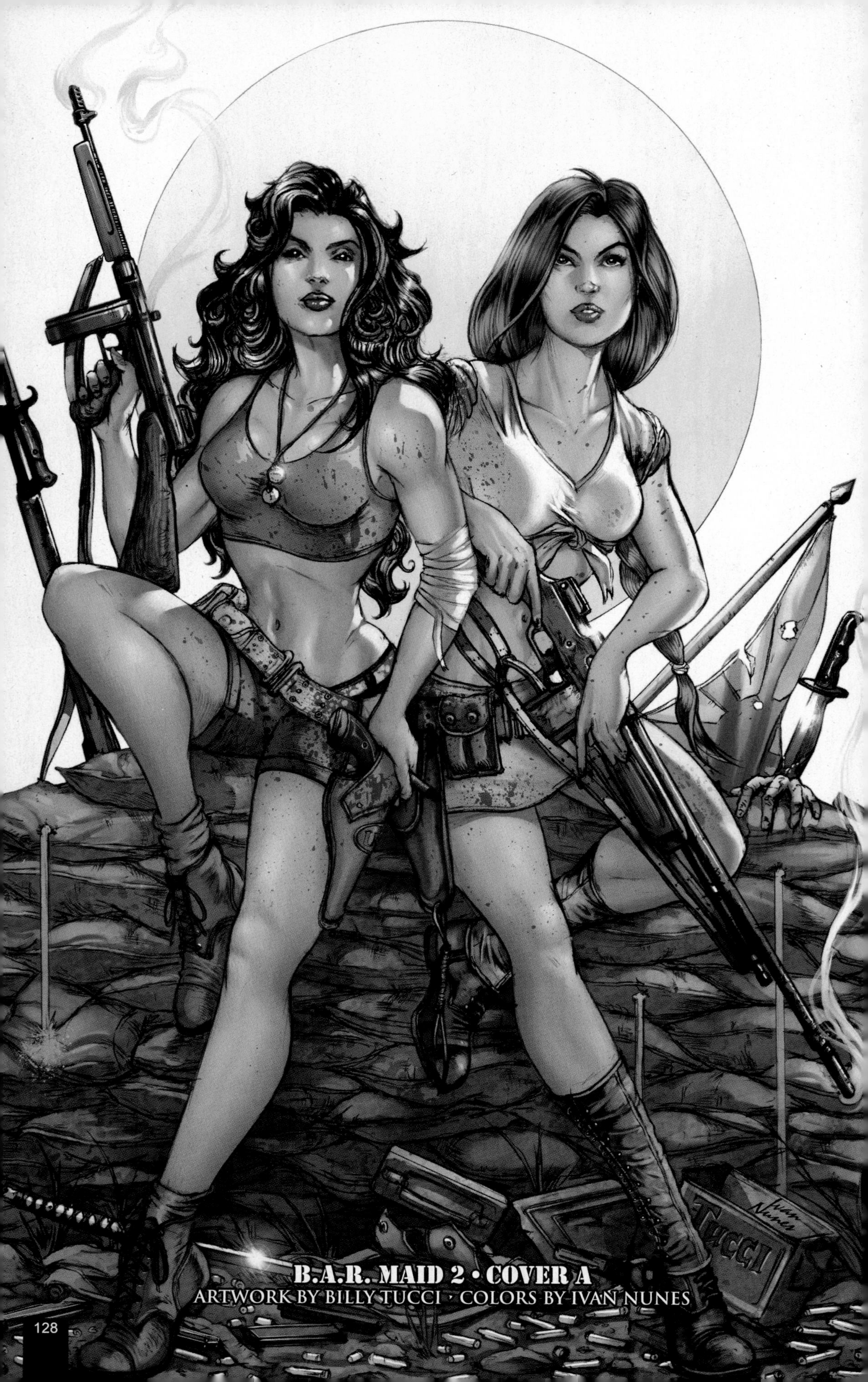
TUCCI

B.A.R. MAID 2 • COVER A
ARTWORK BY BILLY TUCCI · COLORS BY IVAN NUNES

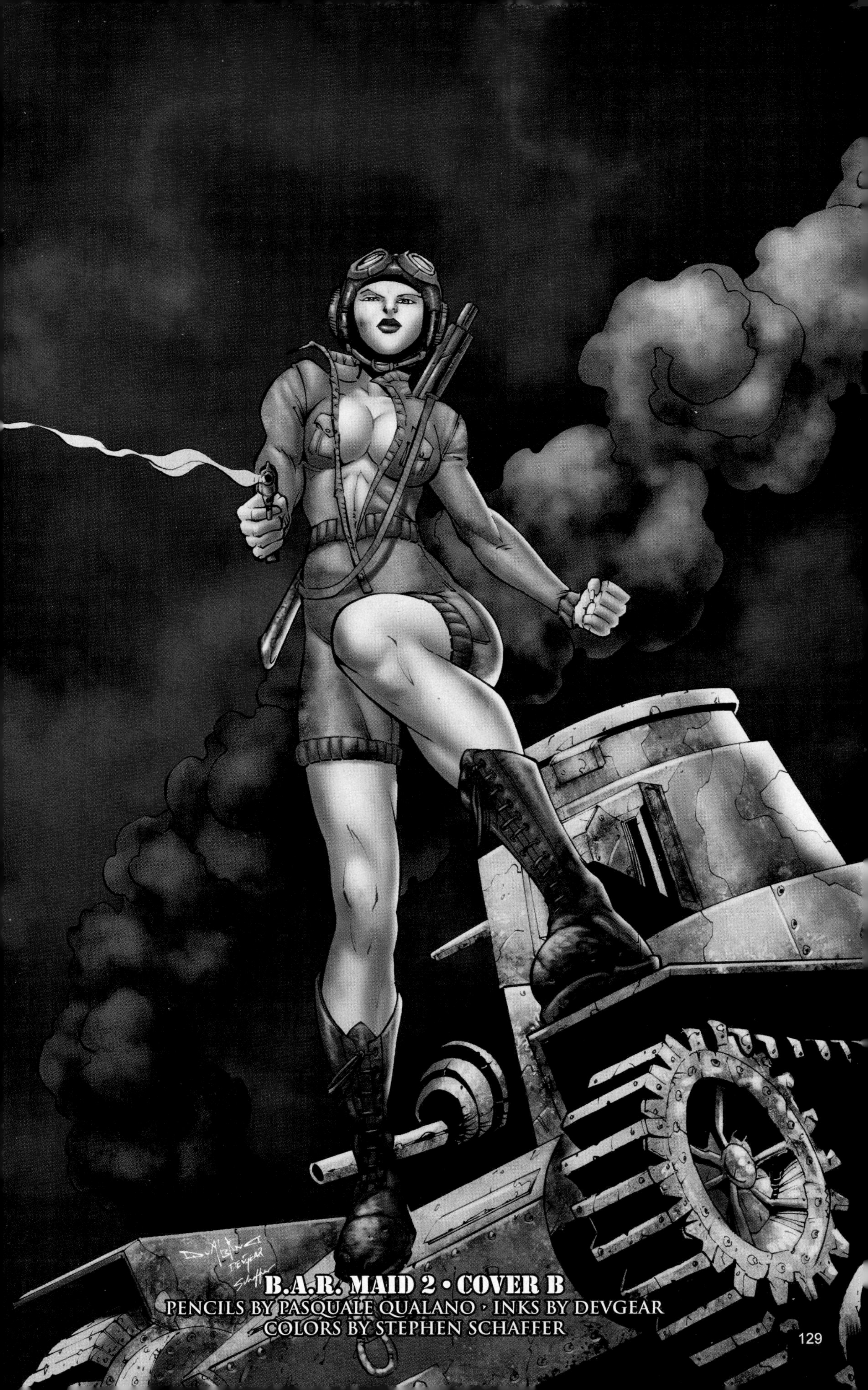

B.A.R. MAID 2 • COVER B
PENCILS BY PASQUALE QUALANO • INKS BY DEVGEAR
COLORS BY STEPHEN SCHAFFER

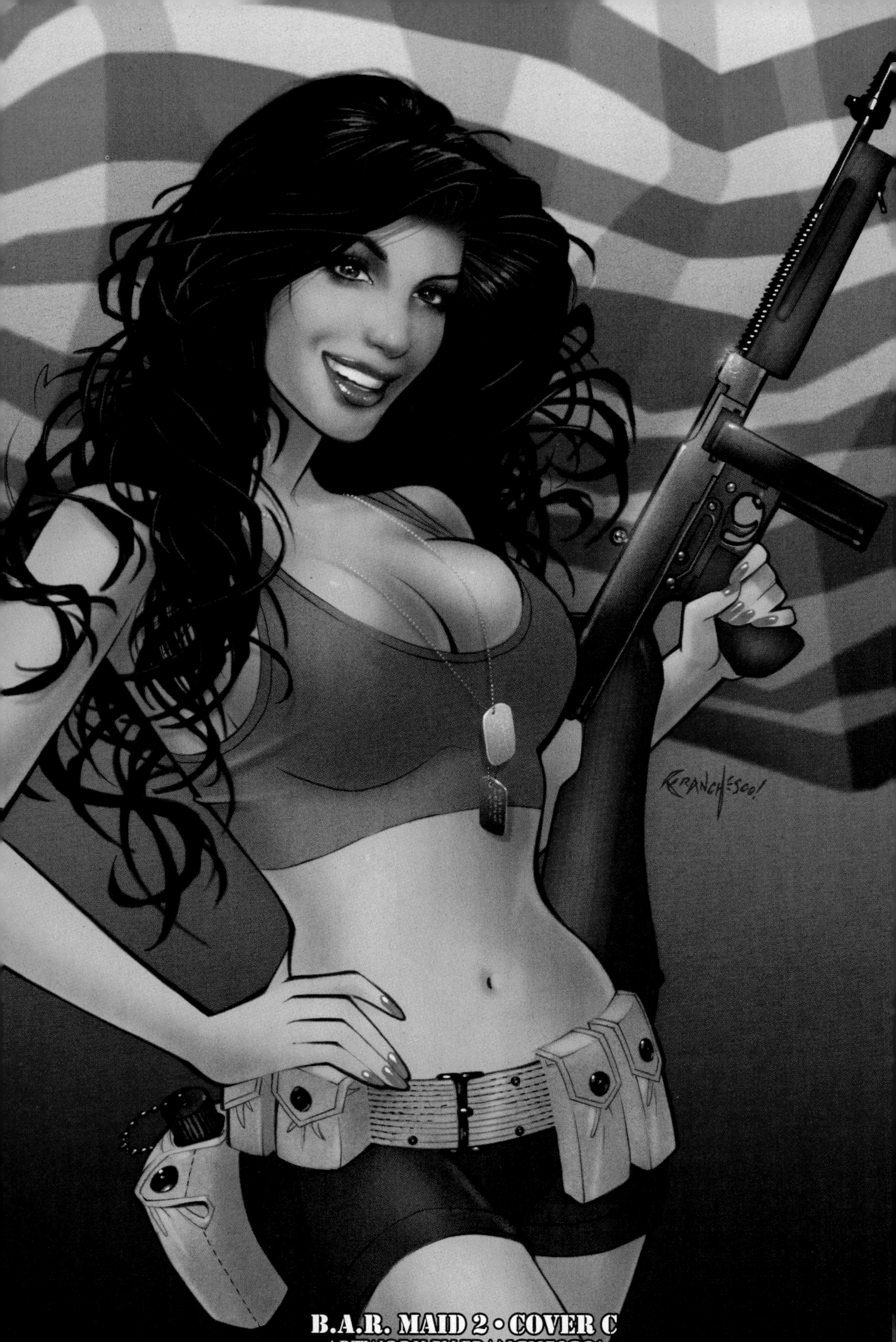
FRANCHESCO!

B.A.R. MAID 2 • COVER C
ARTWORK BY FRANCHESCO!

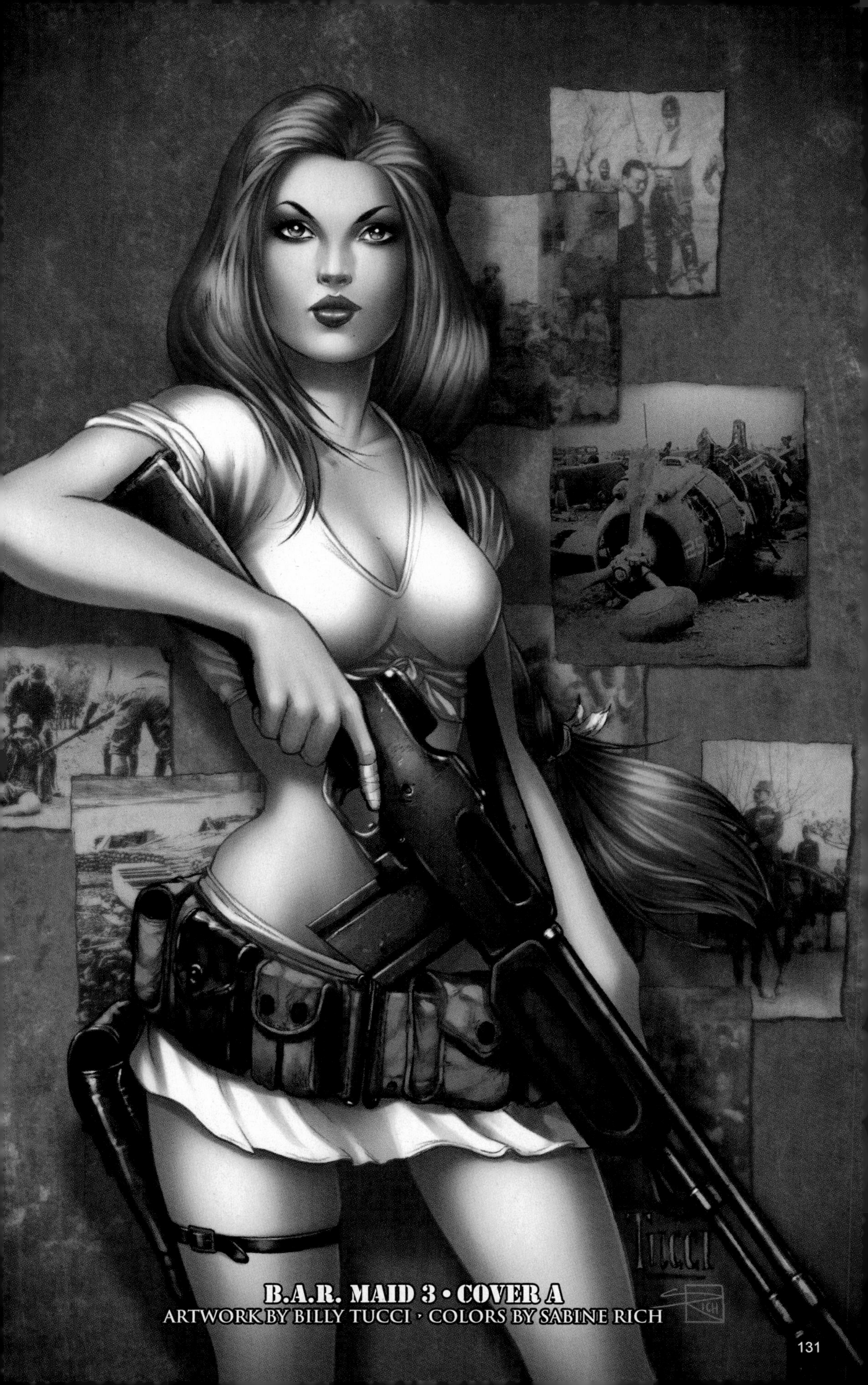

B.A.R. MAID 3 • COVER A
ARTWORK BY BILLY TUCCI • COLORS BY SABINE RICH

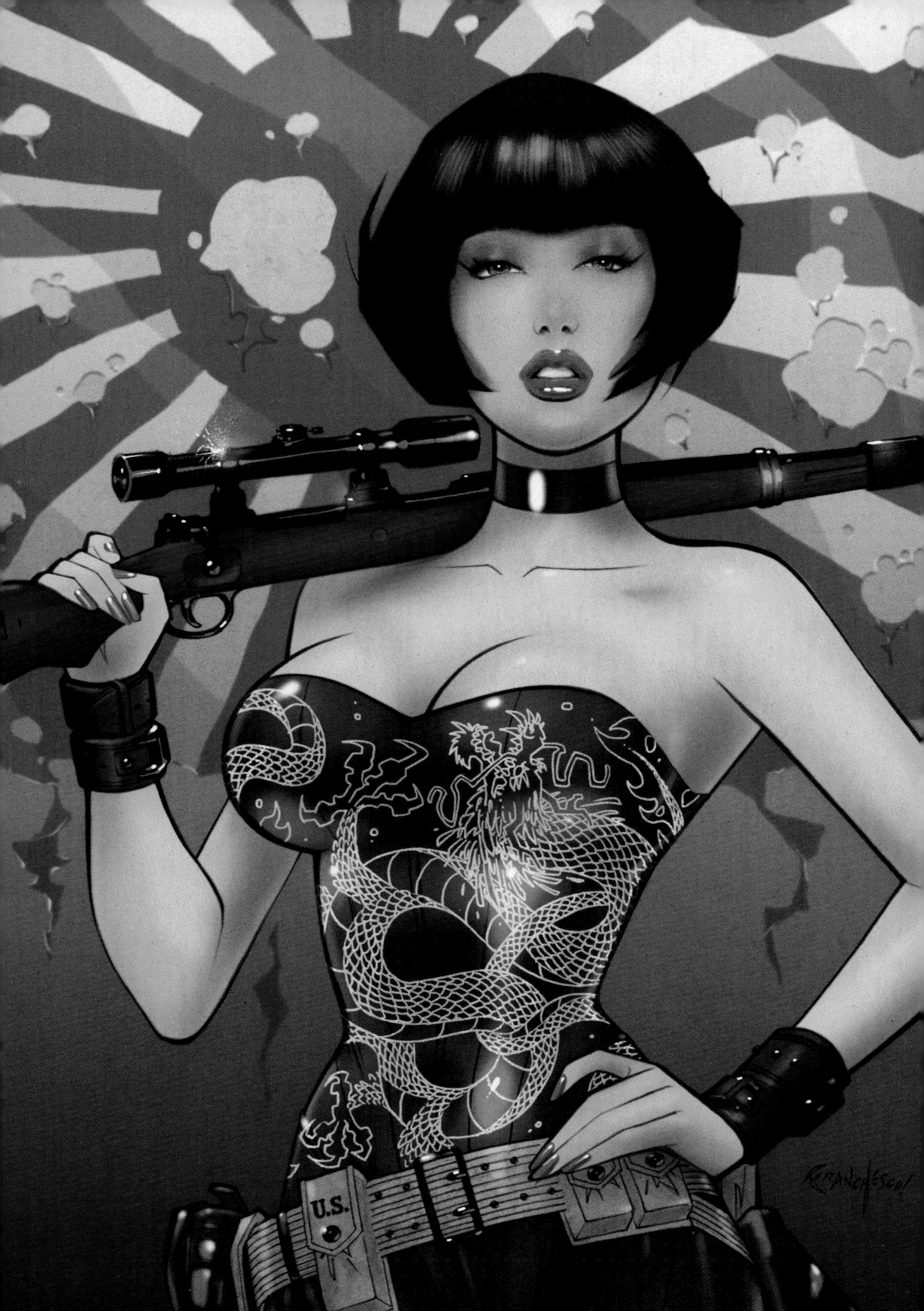
U.S.

B.A.R. MAID 3 • COVER B
ARTWORK BY FRANCHESCO!

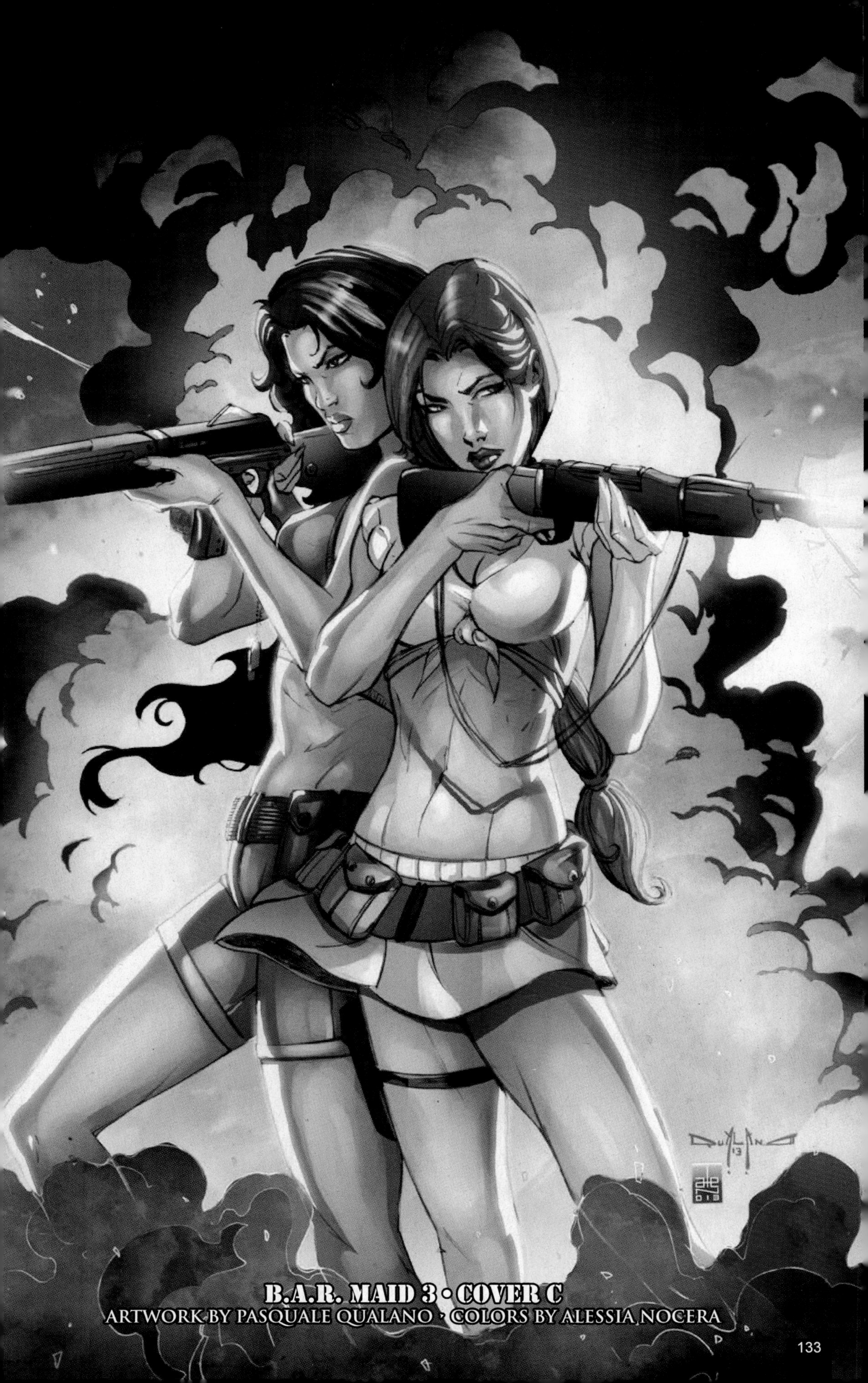

B.A.R. MAID 3 • COVER C

ARTWORK BY PASQUALE QUALANO • COLORS BY ALESSIA NOCERA

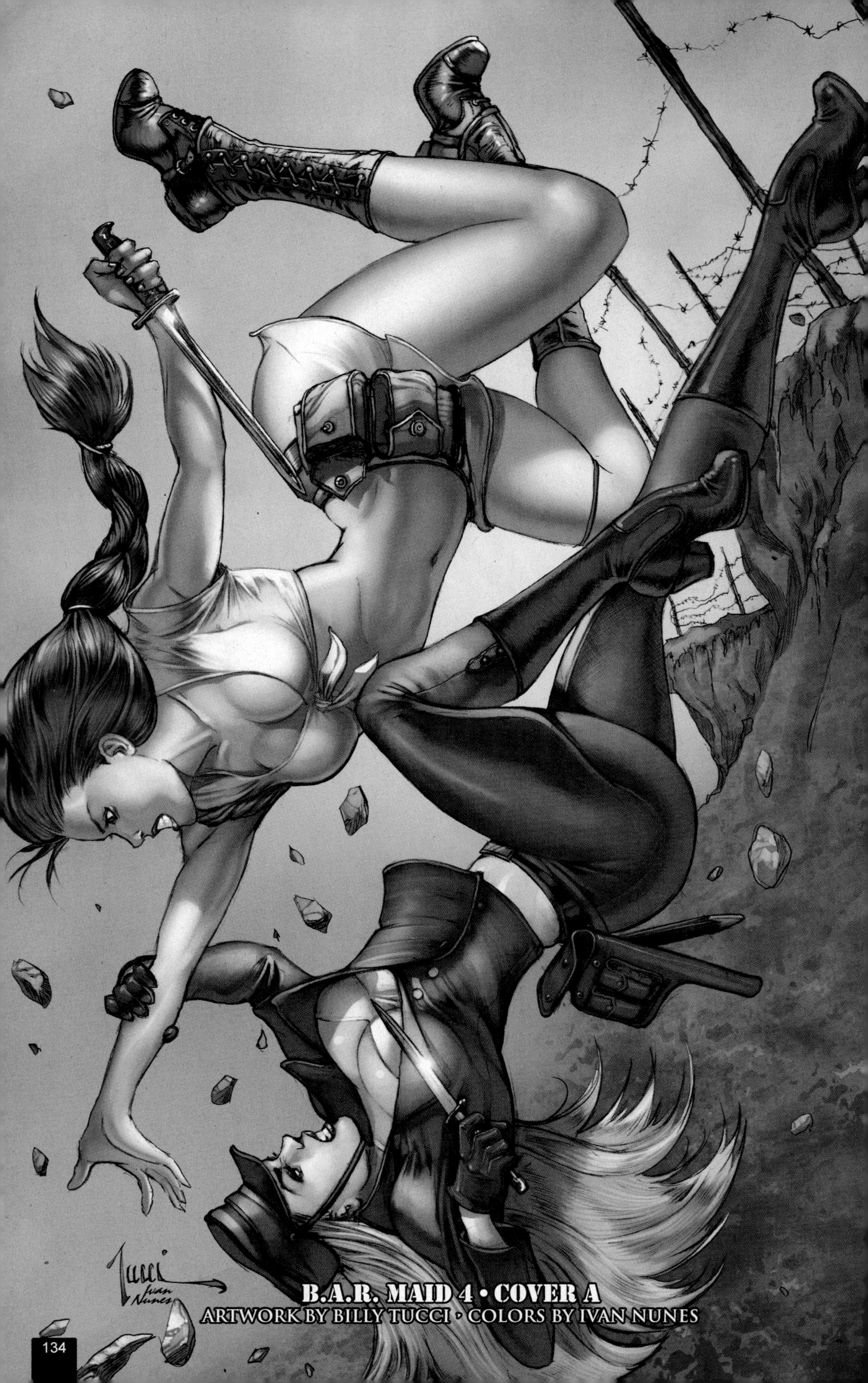

B.A.R. MAID 4 • COVER A

ARTWORK BY BILLY TUCCI › COLORS BY IVAN NUNES

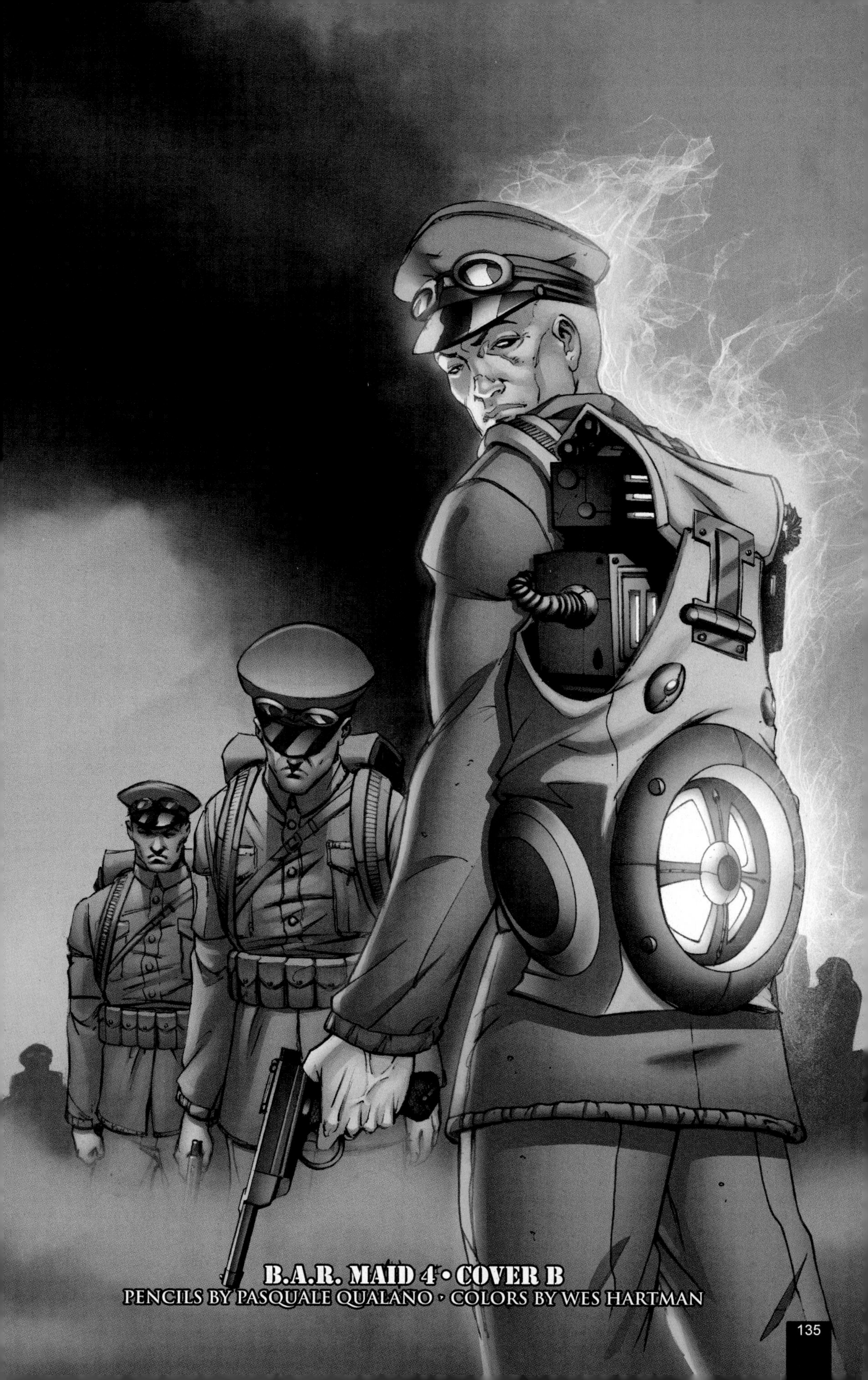

B.A.R. MAID 4 • COVER B
PENCILS BY PASQUALE QUALANO • COLORS BY WES HARTMAN

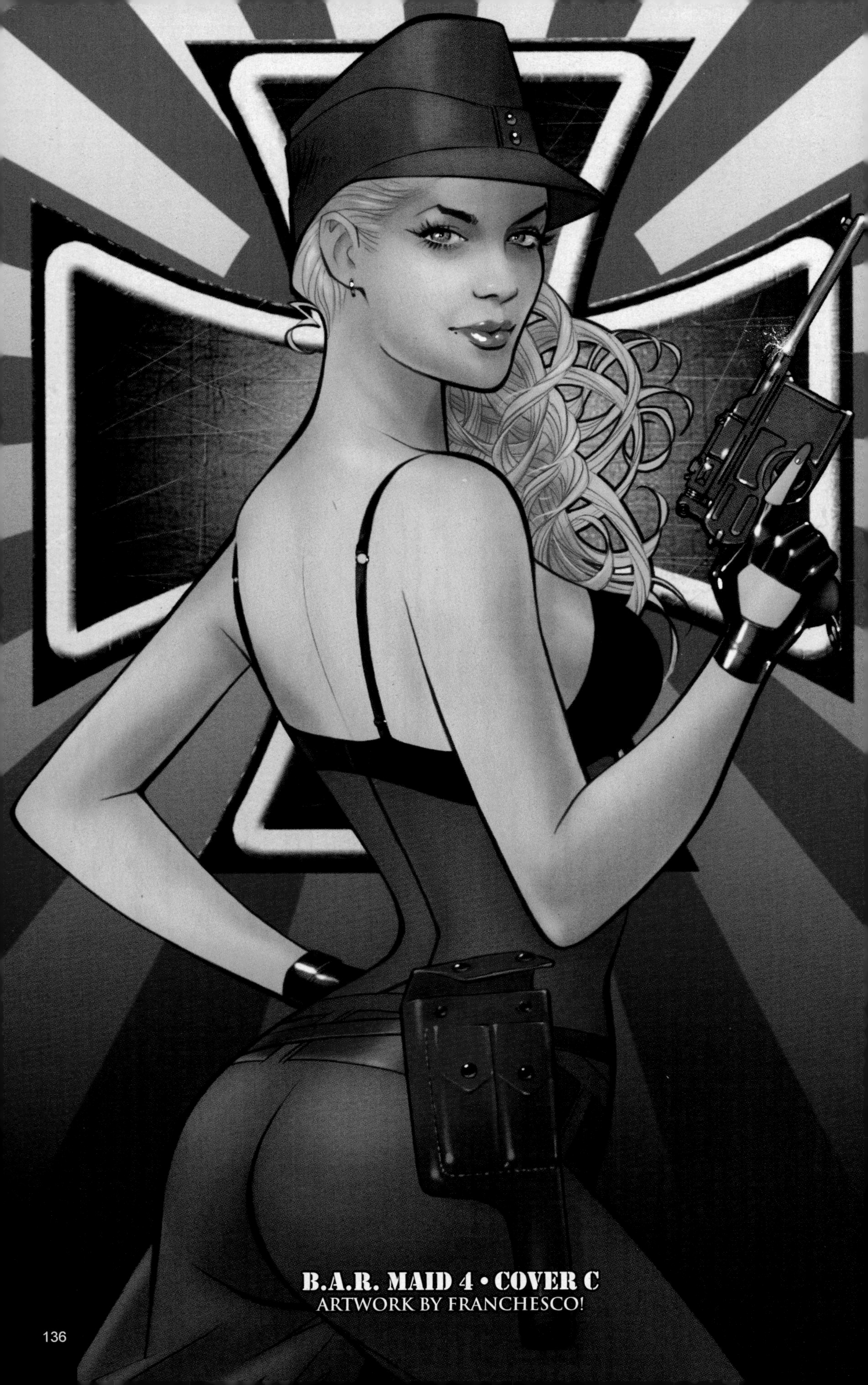

B.A.R. MAID 4 • COVER C
ARTWORK BY FRANCHESCO!

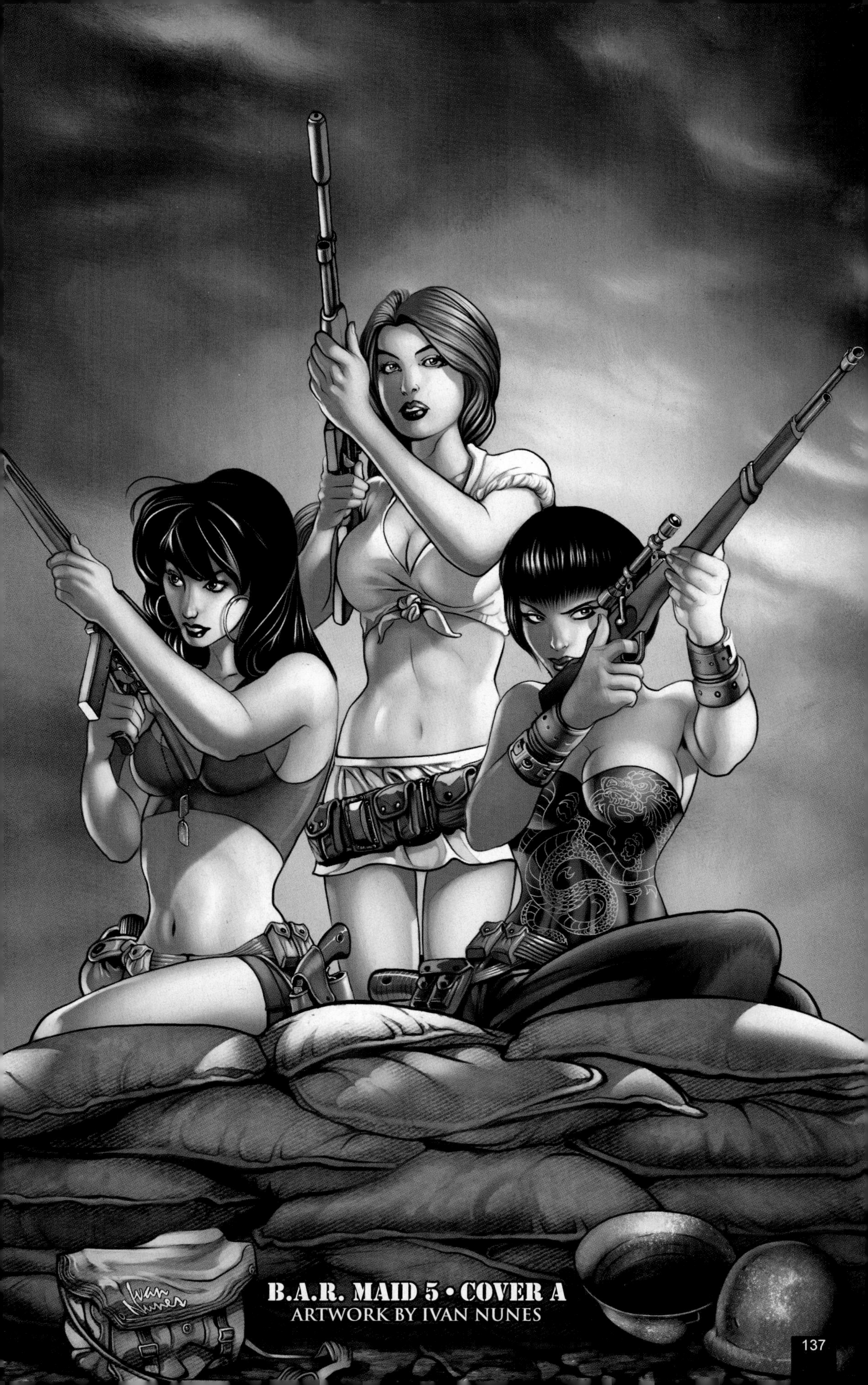
Ivan Nunes

B.A.R. MAID 5 • COVER A
ARTWORK BY IVAN NUNES

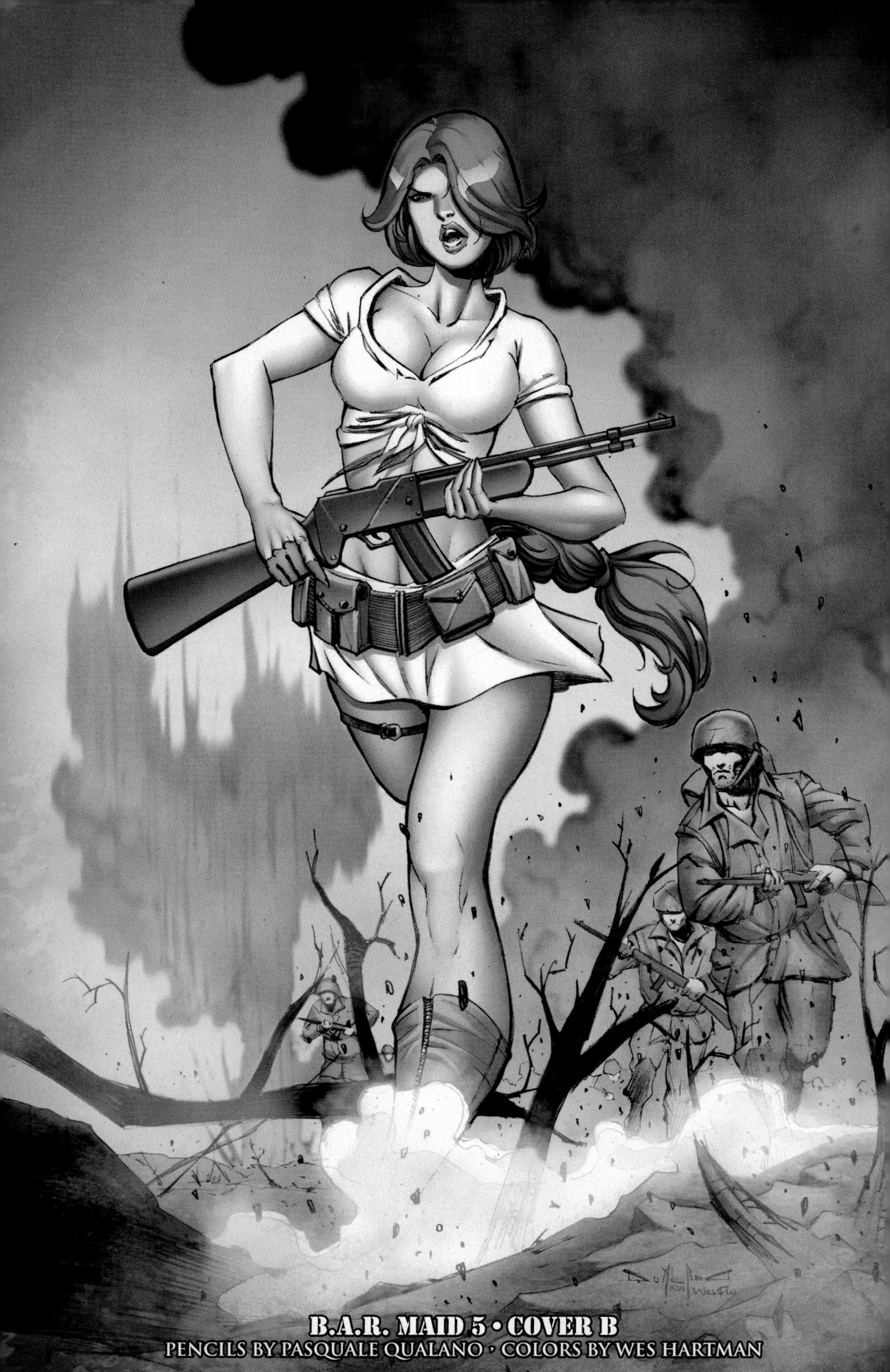

B.A.R. MAID 5 • COVER B
PENCILS BY PASQUALE QUALANO • COLORS BY WES HARTMAN

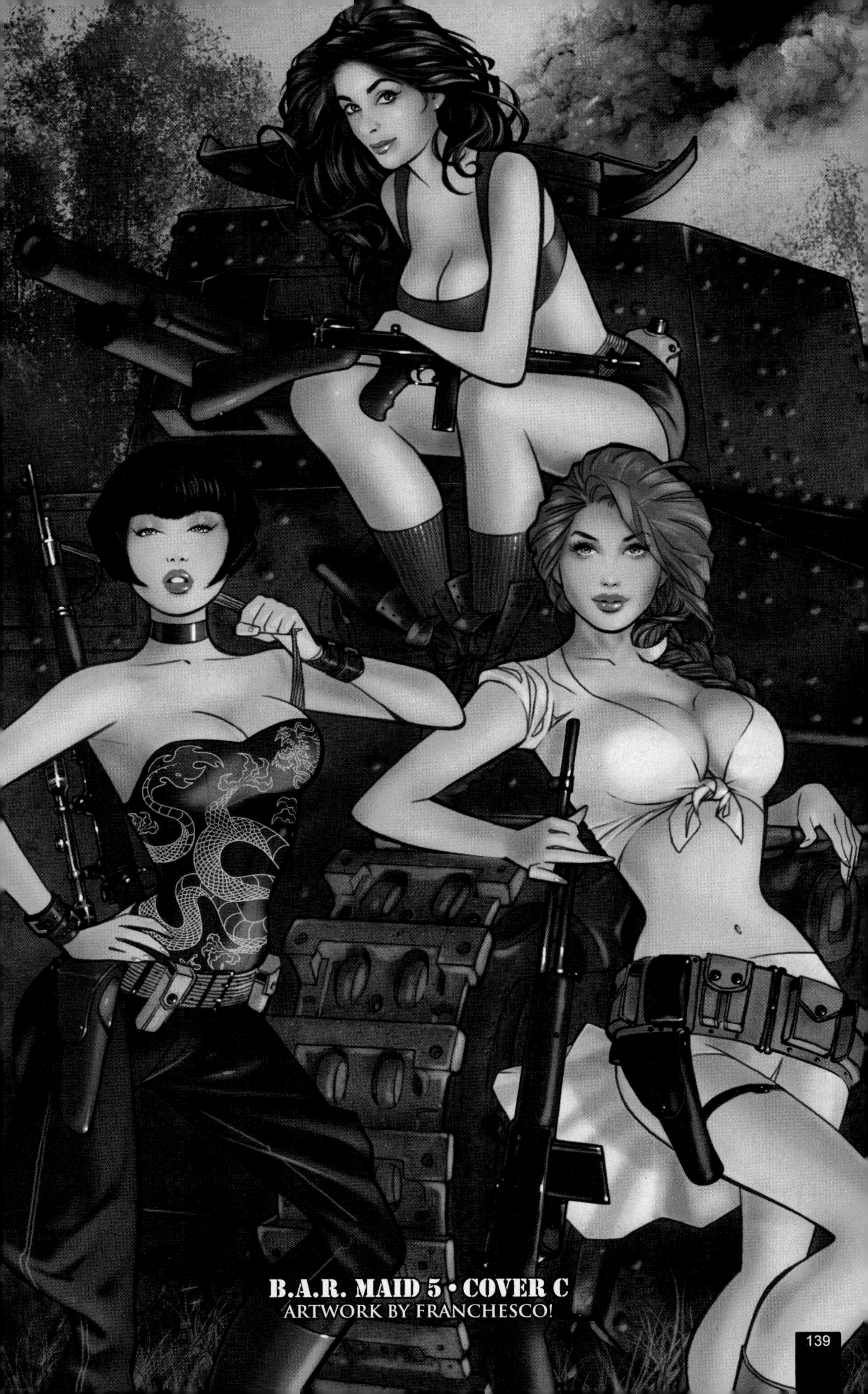

B.A.R. MAID 5 • COVER C
ARTWORK BY FRANCHESCO!

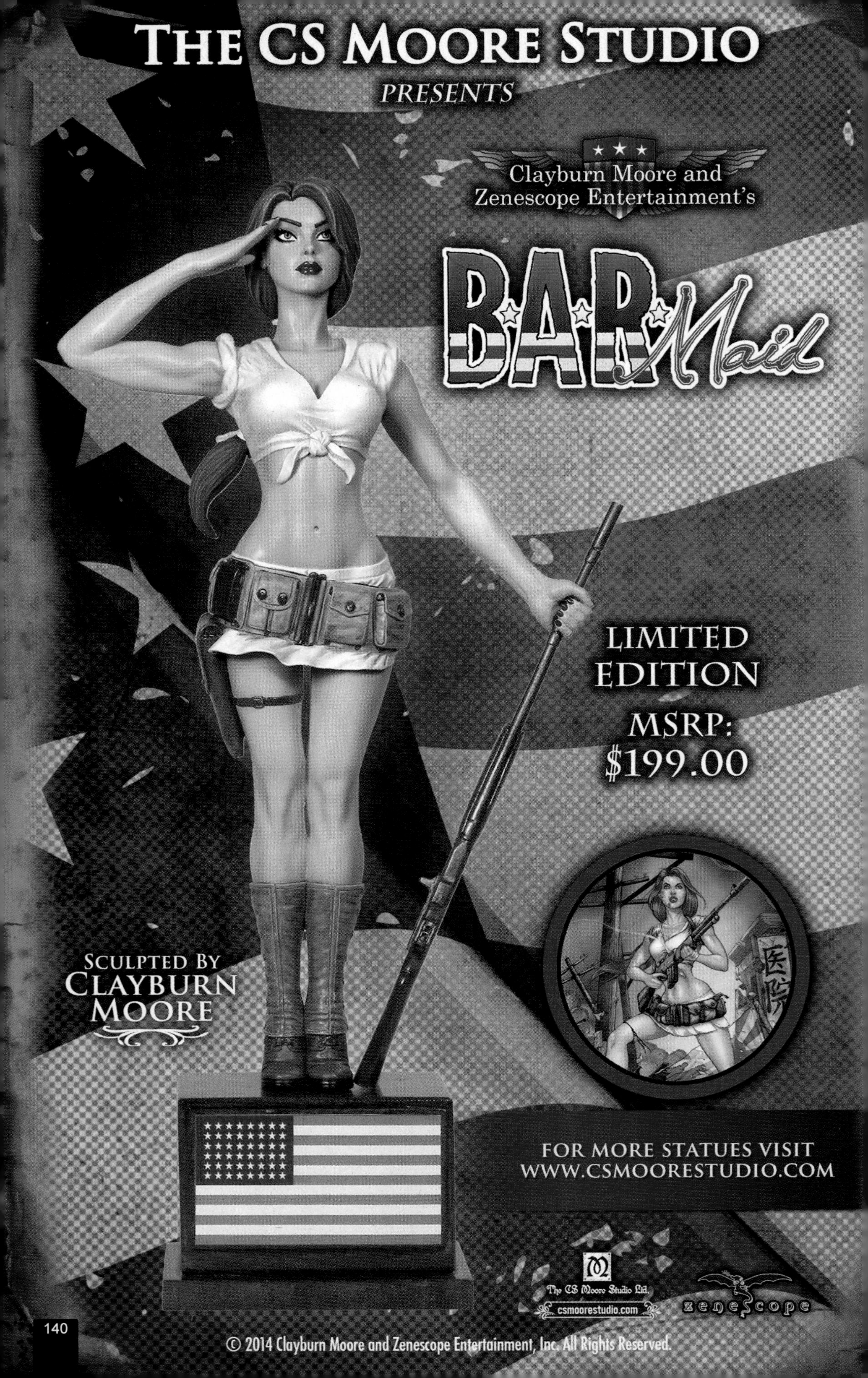
THE CS MOORE STUDIO
PRESENTS
Clayburn Moore and
Zenescope Entertainment's
B.A.R. Maid
LIMITED
EDITION
MSRP:
$199.00
SCULPTED BY
CLAYBURN
MOORE
FOR MORE STATUES VISIT
WWW.CSMOORESTUDIO.COM
The CS Moore Studio Ltd.
csmoorestudio.com
zenescope
© 2014 Clayburn Moore and Zenescope Entertainment, Inc. All Rights Reserved.

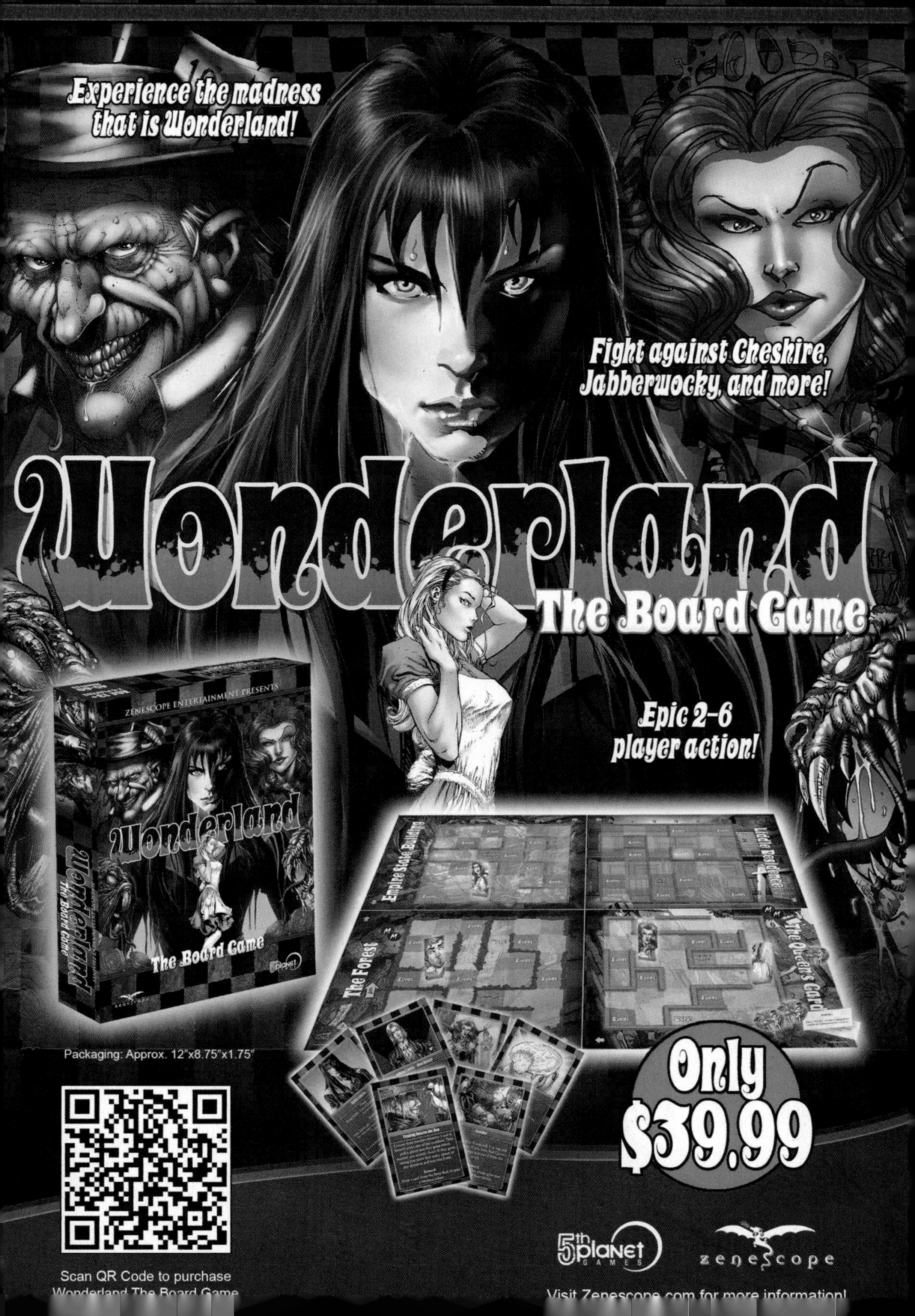
Experience the madness that is Wonderland!
Fight against Cheshire, Jabberwocky, and more!
Wonderland
The Board Game
Epic 2-6 player action!
ZENESCOPE ENTERTAINMENT PRESENTS
Packaging: Approx. 12"x8.75"x1.75"
Only $39.99
Scan QR Code to purchase Wonderland The Board Game
Visit Zenescope.com for more information!

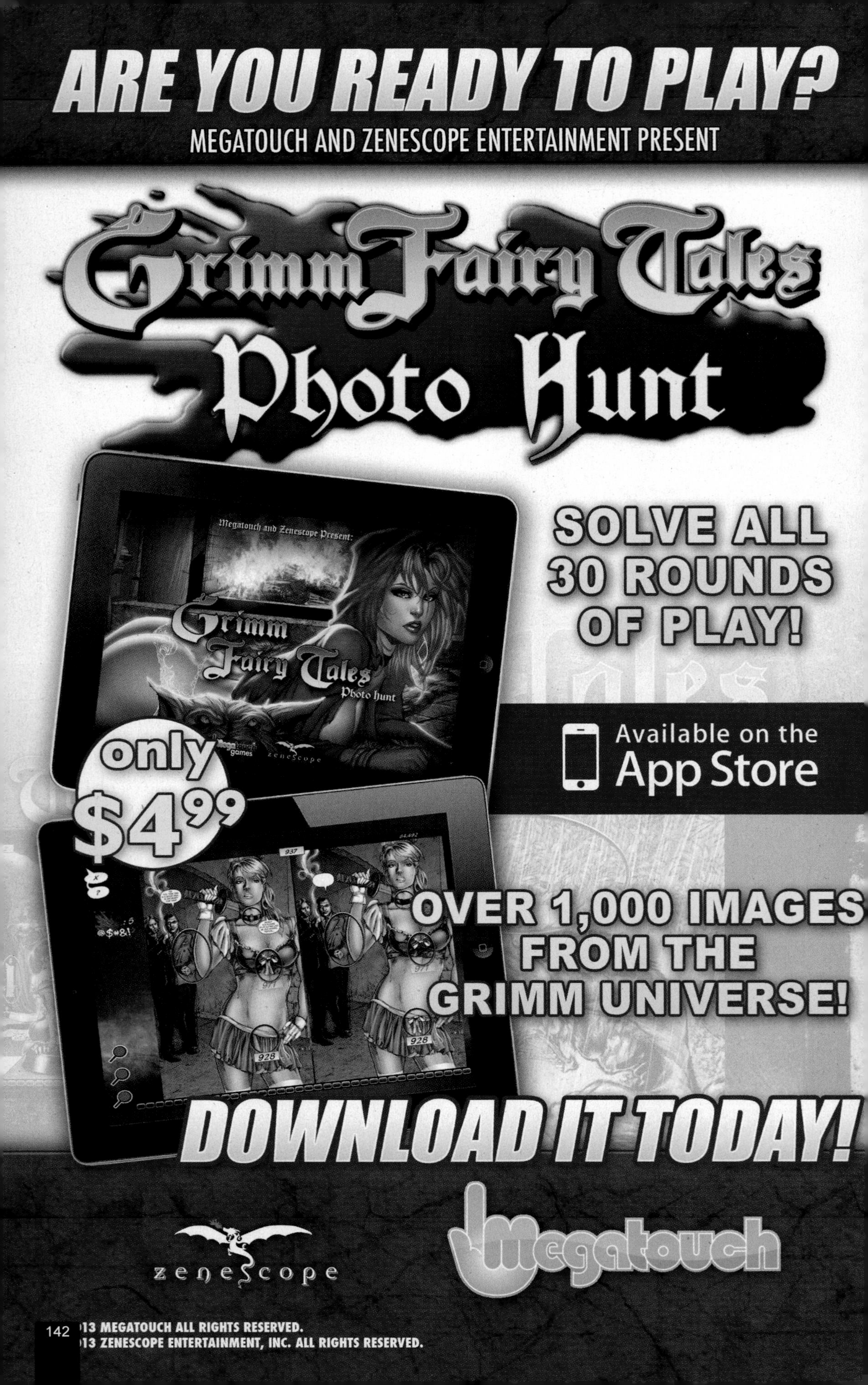
ARE YOU READY TO PLAY?
MEGATOUCH AND ZENESCOPE ENTERTAINMENT PRESENT
Grimm Fairy Tales
Photo Hunt
Megatouch and Zenescope Present:
Grimm Fairy Tales
Photo hunt
SOLVE ALL 30 ROUNDS OF PLAY!
Available on the App Store
only $4.99
OVER 1,000 IMAGES FROM THE GRIMM UNIVERSE!
DOWNLOAD IT TODAY!
zenescope
Megatouch
13 MEGATOUCH ALL RIGHTS RESERVED.
13 ZENESCOPE ENTERTAINMENT, INC. ALL RIGHTS RESERVED.

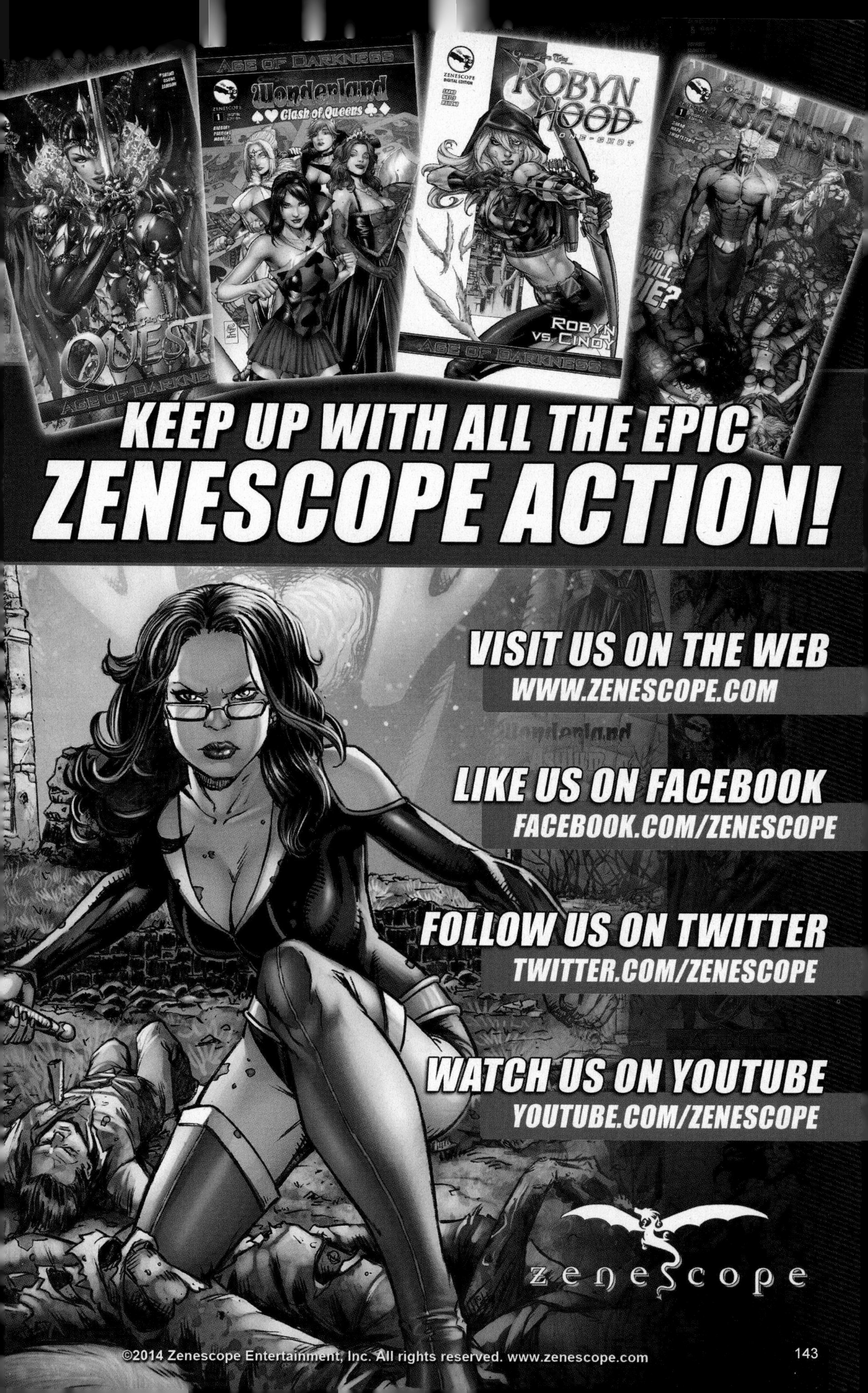
AGE OF DARKNESS
Wonderland
Clash of Queens
ROBYN HOOD
ONE-SHOT
ROBYN VS. CINDY
AGE OF DARKNESS
QUEST
KEEP UP WITH ALL THE EPIC
ZENESCOPE ACTION!
VISIT US ON THE WEB
WWW.ZENESCOPE.COM
LIKE US ON FACEBOOK
FACEBOOK.COM/ZENESCOPE
FOLLOW US ON TWITTER
TWITTER.COM/ZENESCOPE
WATCH US ON YOUTUBE
YOUTUBE.COM/ZENESCOPE
zenescope

B.A.R Maid